A2

French

Jill Duffy

Contents

Specification lists   5

AS/A2 Level French courses   12

Different types of questions in A2 examinations   14

Exam technique   15

What grade do you want?   17

Four steps to successful revision   18

Chapter 1 L'ordre public – Law and order

1.1 The legal system   19

1.2 The police   21

1.3 Patterns of crime   22

1.4 Crime and punishment   23

1.5 Grammar: Future perfect tense   25

1.6 Conditional perfect tense   26

1.7 Revision: agreement of past participle with preceding direct object   27

1.8 How to answer: Question and answer and grid completion   29

     Practice examination questions   31

Chapter 2 Questions sociales – Social issues

2.1 Living conditions   34

2.2 Social security   36

2.3 Unemployment   37

2.4 Exclusion   38

2.5 Immigration and racism   39

2.6 Equality of opportunity   41

2.7 Grammar: The passive – all tenses   44

2.8 Imperfect subjunctive   45

2.9 How to answer: Sentence completion   46

2.10 Gap-fill   46

     Practice examination questions   48

Chapter 3 Les sciences et la technologie – Science and technology

3.1 Scientific heritage of France and current research   51

3.2 Satellites and space travel   53

3.3 France and the technological revolution   54

3.4 Ethical implications of scientific and technological advances   55

3.5 Grammar: Inversion after adverbs   57

3.6 Revision: present participle, reflexive verbs, idioms and other special cases   57

3.7 How to answer: Non-verbal exercises   60

     Practice examination questions   63

Chapter 4 La politique – Politics

4.1 The political system in France	66
4.2 The voting system	68
4.3 The European Union	70
4.4 France and the rest of the world	72
4.5 Grammar: Verbs for A2	74
4.6 How to answer: Translation and transfer of meaning	77
Practice examination questions	79

Chapter 5 L'environnement – The environment

5.1 Policy and pressure groups	83
5.2 Nature and conservation	84
5.3 Pollution	85
5.4 Domestic waste and recycling	87
5.5 Energy	88
5.6 Grammar: More about verb constructions	90
5.7 How to answer: Other writing tasks	92
Sample and practice exam questions	95

Chapter 6 Questions diverses – Miscellaneous issues

6.1 Religion and belief	98
6.2 War and conflict	100
6.3 Distribution of wealth	102
6.4 Grammar: Indefinite pronouns and adverbs	104
6.5 How to answer: Questions on listening passages	106
Sample and practice exam questions	108

Chapter 7 Textes et thèmes littéraires – Literature: topics and texts

7.1 Knowledge of subject	110
7.2 Organising your essay	111
7.3 Quality of language	113
Sample questions and model answers	118

Chapter 8 Thèmes non-littéraires – Non-literary topics

8.1 AS/A2 topic areas	123
8.2 Links with other A Level subjects	124
8.3 Links with hobbies and interests	126
Sample questions and model answers	131

Chapter 9 Travail continu/études guidées – Coursework/guided studies

9.1 Pros and cons of coursework 136

9.2 Choice of topic and essay title 136

9.3 Practical points relating to coursework 138

Chapter 10 L'examen oral – The oral examination

10.1 General conversation 140

10.2 Conversation on topics 141

10.3 Conversation based on a stimulus 143

10.4 Presentation 144

10.5 Interpreting 144

10.6 Assessment of content 145

10.7 Assessment of response 145

10.8 Assessment of accuracy 148

Sample questions and model answers 150

Practice check answers 154

Practice examination answers 155

Transcript of CD 157

Index 159

Specification lists

AQA French

MODULE	SPECIFICATION TOPIC	CHAPTER REFERENCE	STUDIED IN CLASS	REVISED	PRACTICE QUESTIONS
Module 4 (M4) _Contemporary Issues_	The state and the individual	4.1, 4.2, 5.1			
	Distribution of wealth	6.3			
	Health issues	2.1, 2.2, (AS ch. 6)			
	Transport issues	5.3, (AS ch. 2)			
	Science and technology	3.3, 3.4			
	Racism	2.5			
	Crime and punishment	1.1, 1.3, 1.4			
	Future of Europe	4.3			
	Global issues	4.3, 4.4, 5.1–5.5, 6.2			
Module 5 (M5) _Cultural and social landscape in focus_	Set texts	7.1–7.3			
	Literary topics	7.1–7.3			
	Non-literary topics	7.1–7.3, 8.1–8.3			
	Coursework	7.1–7.3, 8.1–8.3, 9.1–9.3			
Module 6 (M6) _Yesterday, today and tomorrow_	(based on the same topics as Modules 4 and 5)	chs. 1–8, 10			

Examination analysis

Unit 4	**Listening, Reading and Writing** Longer texts, longer answers, transfer of meaning	2hr 30 min test	17½%
Either: Unit 5W	**Writing** Two essays in French on literary or non-literary topics	2 hr test	15%
Or: Unit 5C	**Coursework** two assignments, approx. 700 words each		
Unit 6	**Speaking** Reporting and discussion; conversation on topics	35 min test	17½%

Edexcel French

MODULE	SPECIFICATION TOPIC	CHAPTER REFERENCE	STUDIED IN CLASS	REVISED	PRACTICE QUESTIONS
Module 4 (M4) *Oral discussion of issues or Interpreting*	The Environment and citizenship	4.1, 4.2, 5.1–5.5			
	The international context all AS topic areas	4.3, 6.1–6.3 (AS chs. 1–7)			
	The working world	3.3, (AS ch. 5)			
Module 5 (M5) *Topics and texts*	Literary topics and texts	7.1–7.3			
	Non-literary topics	7.1–7.3, 8.1–8.3			
	Coursework	7.1–7.3, 8.1–8.3, 9.1–9.3			
Module 6 (M6) *Listening and Writing, Reading and Writing, Writing in registers*	Energy, pollution and the environment	5.1–5.5			
	Politics and citizenship	4.1–4.4			
	Campaigning organisations and charities	5.1			
	Customs, traditions, beliefs, religions	6.1			
	European Union	4.3			
	Worldwide problems	6.2, 6.3			
	All AS topics	(AS chs. 1–7)			

Examination analysis

Unit 4

Either:	**Paper 1**	Outline presentation and debate on issues	15 min test	15%
Or:	**Paper 2**	Interpreting	15 min test	

Unit 5

Either:	**Paper 1**	Two essays in French, at least 250 words	2 hr test	15%
Or:	**Paper 2**	Coursework: two essays, one 450–500 words, one 900–1000 words		

Unit 6

Unit 6	**L and W:** questions in French, summary in English	45 min test	20%
	R and W: questions in French and translation into French (80 words)	45 min test	
	Writing in registers: **either** creative writing **or** discursive essay **or** task-based assignment	1hr 15 min test	

OCR French

MODULE	SPECIFICATION TOPIC	CHAPTER REFERENCE	STUDIED IN CLASS	REVISED	PRACTICE QUESTIONS
Module 4 (M4) *Speaking and Reading*	Social issues	2.1–2.6			
	The Environment	5.1–5.5			
	Education	(AS ch. 5)			
	Law and order	1.1–1.4			
	Politics	4.1–4.4			
	Technological and scientific advantages	3.1–3.4			
	AS topic areas	(AS chs.1–7)			
Module 5 (M5) *Reading, Listening and Writing*	Topics as in module 4 with the addition of Human interest news items	chs.1–6, (AS chs.1–7)			
Module 6 (M6) *Culture and society*	Set texts	7.1–7.3			
	Literary topics	7.1–7.3			
	Non-literary topics	7.1–7.3, 8.1–8.3			
	Coursework	7.1–7.3, 8.1–8.3, 9.1–9.3			

Examination analysis

Unit 4	Discussion of stimulus, general conversation, discussion of issues	15 min test	15%
Unit 5	Q/A in French, range of other verbal and non-verbal questions, transfer of meaning into French	2hr 45 min test	20%
Unit 6 **Either:** **Or:**	Two essays in French of 300–500 words each Coursework: one essay of 1200–1400 words **or** two essays of 600–700 words	2 hr test	15%

WJEC French

MODULE	SPECIFICATION TOPIC	CHAPTER REFERENCE	STUDIED IN CLASS	REVISED	PRACTICE QUESTIONS
Module 4 (M4) *Oral (for greater detail see Module 6)*	Contemporary France and other French-speaking countries	chs. 1–6			
	The Media	(AS ch.1)			
	Environmental issues	5.1–5.5			
Module 5 (M5) *Cultural studies option*	Set texts	7.1–7.3			
	or Independent studies	7.1–7.3, 8.1–8.3, 9.1–9.3			
	or Guided studies	7.1–7.3, 8.1–8.3, 9.1–9.3			
Module 6 (M6) *Listening, reading and responding*	Current affairs	chs. 1–6, (AS chs. 1–7)			
	European Union	4.3			
	World of work	(AS ch. 5)			
	Employment/unemployment	2.2–2.4, (AS ch. 5)			
	Immigration	2.5			
	The media	(AS ch.1)			
	Energy	5.5			
	Conservation	5.2			
	Pollution	5.3			
	All AS topics	(AS chs. 1–7)			

Examination analysis

Unit 4	Discussion based on stimulus, oral exposé and discussion		15–20 min test	15%
Unit 5				
Either:	**Literary studies** Two essays in French, 250 words each			20%
Or:	**Independent studies** One assignment 1500 words			
Or:	**Guided studies** One assignment 1500 words			
Unit 6	Passages for reading and listening comprehension: Short essay or article in French; short translation into French.		3 hr test	15%

CCEA French

MODULE	SPECIFICATION TOPIC	CHAPTER REFERENCE	STUDIED IN CLASS	REVISED	PRACTICE QUESTIONS
Module 4 (M4) *Exchanging ideas and opinions (for greater detail see Module 5)*	Everyday life	(AS chs. 1, 2, 4, 5, 6)			
	Personal and social relationships	2.6, (AS ch. 3)			
	The world around us	2.1, 5.1–5.5			
	World of work	(AS ch. 5)			
	Social and political issues	2.1 – 2.6, 4.1–4.4			
	International and global issues	4.3, 4.4, 6.1, 6.2			
	All AS topics	(AS chs. 1–7)			
Module 5 (M5) *Extended information handling*	The Media	(AS ch. 1)			
	Gender issues	2.6			
	Rural and urban concerns	2.1			
	Transport issues	5.3, (AS ch. 2)			
	Industrial, commercial and professional life	(AS ch. 5)			
	Prejudice and racism	2.5			
	Unemployment	2.3			
	Disability issues	2.6			
	Third world	4.4, 6.3			
	Violence and conflict	6.2			
	Democracy and human rights	4.4, 6.1, 6.2			
Module 6 (M6) *Literature/ Society*	Set texts	7.1–7.3			
	Topics on Society	7.1–7.3, 8.1–8.3			

Examination analysis

Unit 4	Discussion of stimulus, presentation of topic, general conversation, conversation on issues	15 min test	17½%
Unit 5	Q/A in French, summary in French, translation from English to French	2 hr 30 min test	17½%
Unit 6	Two essays in French of 250 words each	2 hr test	15%

Grammar

A2 GRAMMAR (COMMON TO ALL SPECIFICATIONS)	CHAPTER REFERENCE	STUDIED IN CLASS	REVISED
Future perfect tense	1.5		
Conditional perfect tense	1.6		
Passive: all tenses	2.7		
Imperfect subjunctive	2.8		
Inversion after adverbs	3.5		
You will find additional information about the following points, which were covered in the AS study guide:			
Reflexive verbs	3.6		
Agreement with preceding direct object	1.7		
Idioms and other special cases	3.6		
Impersonal verbs	5.6		
Constructions with some verbs	5.6		
Present participle	3.6		
Miscellaneous points	6.4		
Also a list of more unusual verbs in all tenses:			
Verbs for A2	4.5		

AS GRAMMAR (COMMON TO ALL SPECIFICATIONS)	CHAPTER REFERENCE (AS STUDY GUIDE)	STUDIED IN CLASS	REVISED
Nouns			
• Gender	1		
• Singular/plural	1		
Articles			
• Definite, indefinite, partitive	1		
Adjectives			
• Agreement	2		
• Position	2		
• Comparative and superlative	2		
• Demonstrative (*ce, cet, cette, ces*)	2		
• Possessive (*mon, ma, mes* etc.)	2		
• Interrogative (*quel?*)	2		
Adverbs			
• Formation	7		
• Comparative and superlative	7		
• Interrogative and other adverbs	7		
Pronouns			
• Personal	3		
• Reflexive	3		
• Place (*y, en*)	3		

AS GRAMMAR (COMMON TO ALL SPECIFICATIONS)	CHAPTER REFERENCE	STUDIED IN CLASS	REVISED
• Emphatic (*moi, toi*, etc.)	3		
• Relative (*qui, que, dont* etc.)	4		
• Demonstrative (*celui*)	4		
• Possessive (*le mien* etc.)	4		
• Interrogative	4		
Verbs			
• Regular and irregular forms inc. reflexive	1, 2, 3		
• Modes of address (*tu, vous*)	5, 6		
• Impersonal forms	1, 2, 3		
• Followed by an infinitive	5		
• Dependent infinitives (*faire réparer* etc)	5		
• Perfect infinitive	5		
• Negative forms	1, 3, 6		
• Question forms	1, 3		
• Tenses:			
present	1		
perfect (inc. agreement of past participle)	3		
imperfect	2		
future	2		
conditional	2		
future perfect (R)	7		
conditional perfect (R)	7		
pluperfect	4		
past historic (R)	7		
• passive: present tense	4		
• other tenses(R)	4		
• Imperative (command)	1, 6		
• Present participle	5		
• Subjunctive:			
present	6		
perfect	6		
• Direct and indirect speech	4		
• Prepositions	7		
• Conjunctions	6		
• Number, quantity and time	7		

Note: (R) indicates that the construction should be recognised but not used at AS Level. You will need to be able to use all constructions at A2 Level (except the Past Historic).

AS/A2 Level French courses

The French specifications for courses beginning in September 2000 are all new. They are divided into six units or modules, three of which are set at Advanced Subsidiary (AS) Level, and three at Advanced (A2) Level. AS may be a qualification in itself, or the first half of the full A2 qualification; the standard of the AS examination is that expected of students who are halfway through a full Advanced Level course. There is a core linguistic content common to all awarding bodies, and a series of topics to be studied.

How will you be tested?

Assessment units

For AS French, you will be tested by three assessment units. For the full A Level in French, you will take a further three units. AS French forms 50% of the assessment weighting for the full A Level.

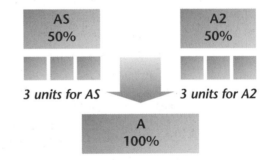

ach unit can normally be taken in either January or June though some awarding odies may not offer the oral test in January. Alternatively, you can study the whole ourse before taking any of the unit tests. There is a lot of flexibility about when xams can be taken and the diagram below shows just some of the ways that the ssessment units may be taken for AS and A Level French.

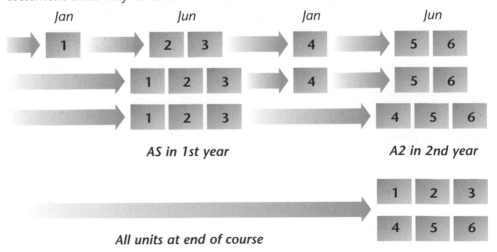

If you are disappointed with a module result, you can resit it. From 2004 there is no limit to the number of times you can retake a module. The highest mark counts.

Coursework

All awarding bodies (except CCEA) accept coursework as an alternative to the written Literature/Topics paper at A2 Level only. There are strict regulations which must be followed; separate booklets explaining these rules should be available in your centre. For general advice on Coursework, refer to chapter 9 of this guide; you will find information on writing essays as well as specific points relating to literary topics in chapter 7, and advice on how you could link your Coursework topic (non-literary) to your other A Level subjects or to your own interests in chapter 8.

Synoptic assessment

Individual modules or units can no longer be treated as completely separate items in the new examinations: you cannot forget about the content of a module as you finish the paper, as some of the information you have learnt may be required later in the course. There is nothing new here for students of Modern Foreign Languages: papers have always been inter-related because they are based on skills more than knowledge. You cannot write an essay in French on any topic unless you know the grammar and structures to use; you cannot conduct a conversation in French unless you understand the language when it is spoken by a French national.

The four skills (Reading, Listening, Speaking and Writing) that formed the basis of your GCSE assessment are all part of your AS and A2 courses, with the addition of 'Knowledge and understanding of aspects of French society', which covers the factual element of the course.

Synoptic assessment – the testing of knowledge and skills learnt throughout the two years – has to form 20% of the A2 course. To comply with the regulations, the awarding bodies state that this is covered in part of the mixed-skill module (Listening, Reading and Writing) and in the oral examination; but in fact the whole of the examination could be said to fulfil the requirements.

Edexcel, WJEC and NICCEA Specifications also state that topics studied at AS Level may also be tested at A2.

Key skills

Modern Language specifications offer considerable opportunities for developing the following key skills:

- Communication: oral and written work
- Information technology: coursework – word processing and DTP, research via the Internet
- Working with others: oral pair and group work
- Improving learning and performance: research for topics and coursework.

Different types of questions in A2 examinations

Listening and Reading

Passages for comprehension are likely to be longer than at AS Level. You will find non-verbal and verbal question types, but the trend is towards longer answers in French. Some awarding bodies also include Q/A in English on one of the passages. To test your understanding you may have to translate or to convey the meaning of part of a passage from or into French.

Writing

You may have to write a short essay or response in French as part of a comprehension (mixed-skill) paper, but Writing is also tested at this level by means of the topic essay or coursework. Length varies according to the awarding body, but as a general rule you have to write at least 250 words for the topic essay. Coursework length could be from 500–700 words for a short essay, or 1200–1500 words for a long essay, so you need to check the regulations for your own examination.

There is detailed advice in this A2 guide ('How to answer' sections) to help you with all question types; refer to the individual chapters as shown in the list below. Whenever possible the practice questions in each chapter use the test-types for which advice has just been given, but this is not always appropriate and in that case there is a page reference to lead you to the right section.

'How to answer' sections

	CHAPTER REFERENCE
Q/A	1
Grid-completion	1
Sentence-completion	2
Gap-fill	2
Non-verbal exercises	3
Translation	4
Transfer of meaning	4
Other writing tasks	5
Questions on Listening passages	6

Advice on writing topic essays is given in chapters 7 and 8, and on Coursework in chapter 9.

Speaking

Chapter 10 (The oral examination) deals with all elements of the Speaking test.

Exam technique

Some awarding bodies state that all topics studied for AS automatically form part of the A Level final assessment, in addition to the new topics covered in A2. Even if this is not the case for your exam, you will find that much of the vocabulary overlaps from AS to A2 as well as from one topic to another. For example:

- Environmental pollution (A2 ch. 5) is partly caused by exhaust emissions, so it's helpful to revise the vocabulary from the Transport section (AS ch. 2).
- Unemployment (A2 ch. 2) may be high among those who have few qualifications, so you may need the vocabulary from Education, training and work (AS ch. 5).
- The crime rate (A2 ch. 1) may be higher among young people, so information and word lists from the chapter on Young people and family relationships (AS ch. 3) are useful.
- Living conditions (A2 ch. 2) may affect diet and health (AS ch. 6).

You will meet many more 'crossover' examples as you continue with your course.

Language

There was a great deal of new grammar to learn for AS Level. The list is much shorter for A2 – you have already learnt most of what you need to know. The important thing is not to forget it – as you know very well, you may need any of the French grammar you have ever learnt in order to write or speak French, and it's a fact that many A Level students remember the complicated items such as the subjunctive and the conditional perfect tense, but forget to make adjectives agree with the nouns they describe.

So – don't sell or give away your AS Study Guide: you'll need it!

What are examiners looking for?

Each paper, for every awarding body, has its own marking grid. This doesn't just mean a mark scheme, listing the correct and acceptable answers; it also involves descriptions of what a candidate has to do to gain a particular mark in those parts of the paper which don't have a 'mark per question' scheme.

Examples include:

Writing

Grammatical accuracy: **5/5 Very Good**. High and consistent level of accuracy.

Speaking

Fluency: **8/10 Good**. Generally fluent with occasional hesitation to find the right word.

Transfer of meaning

Content: **4/15 Poor**. Much misunderstanding and/or missed detail.

In general terms, the skills (these are also known as Assessment Objectives) you have to use to the best of your ability in the study of French are:

- understand and respond, in speech and writing, to spoken language
- understand and respond, in speech and writing, to written language

- show knowledge of, and apply accurately, the grammar and syntax prescribed in the specification (syntax means the way in which phrases and sentences are constructed)
- demonstrate knowledge and understanding of aspects of the chosen society.

Some dos and don'ts

Do:

- keep a file of articles relating to French and French-speaking countries that appear in the British media, and refer to them when you are revising each topic
- listen to French radio whenever you can – it doesn't matter what the programme is; all listening practice is good
- set aside a time with other members of your French group when you all agree to speak French, as part of a normal conversation. The oral exam will be less of a strain if speaking French is a natural part of your everyday life.

Don't:

- try to get away with reading a set text in the English version; it won't give you the flavour of the original, and it may not even be the same
- ignore basic grammar because you think you know it; it needs to be revised just as much as the new constructions you have just learnt
- assume that something you know about a topic is what is actually being stated in the comprehension passage. Understanding of the situation being described is a great help but is not a substitute for reading or listening carefully.

French examinations rely for much of their material on newspaper, magazine and radio articles concerned with current affairs. Inevitably, therefore, the dates quoted may have passed by the time you are working on the passages and (particularly in the case of politics) names may have changed. This does not affect the content of the articles for comprehension purposes.

Every effort has been made to ensure that the information in the chapters is up to date, but if you wish to use it in written or oral presentations you are advised to check the latest situation via the media or the Internet.

What grade do you want?

The short answer to this question is that you want – and you should aim for – the best grade you are capable of achieving. 'I only need a C' shouldn't make you lazy; it can lead to disappointment if you get your C but could actually have achieved an A. Talk to your teachers or lecturers about what grade they think you are capable of; if you don't like what they say, it's up to you to prove them wrong. Be realistic about your abilities; but there's no harm in having ambition. Your standard should improve steadily throughout your course; and it will improve if you revise each topic and each grammar point thoroughly.

The best way of consolidating the grammar you have just learnt is to put it into practice straight away. Look for opportunities to use it in written and spoken French (unless it's something like the Past Historic which is not used in speech) so that it becomes a natural part of the French you use.

Individual papers in the new specifications are in theory targeted as follows:

Grade a	80%
Grade b	70%
Grade c	60%
Grade d	50%
Grade e	40%

These percentages cannot be absolutely guaranteed from year to year, particularly in mixed-skill comprehension papers; sometimes a paper can turn out to be harder in one session than in another, and allowance is usually made for this.

Most candidates have particular strengths and weaknesses, and it is the overall number of marks (linked with the percentage 'weighting' of each unit) that count towards your final grade, not the notional a–e grade that you may be awarded on each module. A good performance in the oral may compensate for a weaker topic essay; excellent comprehension skills make up for a mediocre French accent. Ideally, you should:

• consolidate your strong points
• work hard to improve your weak points.

The most useful attributes of all when you are actually answering the questions in your exam (this applies particularly to comprehension papers) are common sense and alertness. Don't give up too soon; but be ready to move on when you know you have done all you can with a particular question. Above all, enjoy the course; if you do that, you may even find that you enjoy the examination!

Four steps to successful revision

Step 1: Understand

- Study the topic to be learned slowly. Make sure you understand the logic or important concepts.
- Mark up the text if necessary – underline, highlight and make notes.
- Re-read each paragraph slowly.

GO TO STEP 2

Step 2: Summarise

- Now make your own revision note summary:
  What is the main idea, theme or concept to be learned?
  What are the main points? How does the logic develop?
  Ask questions: Why? How? What next?
- Use bullet points, mind maps, patterned notes.
- Link ideas with mnemonics, mind maps, crazy stories.
- Note the title and date of the revision notes.
  (French: Law and order, 3rd March).
- Organise your notes carefully and keep them in a file.

This is now in short-term memory. You will forget 80% of it if you do not go to Step 3. GO TO STEP 3, but first take a 10 minute break.

Step 3: Memorise

- Take 25 minute learning 'bites' with 5 minute breaks.
- After each 5 minute break test yourself:
  Cover the original revision note summary
  Write down the main points
  Speak out loud (record on tape)
  Tell someone else
  Repeat many times.

The material is well on its way to long-term memory. You will forget 40% if you do not do step 4. GO TO STEP 4

Step 4: Track/Review

- Create a Revision Diary (one A4 page per day).
- Make a revision plan for the topic, e.g. 1 day later, 1 week later, 1 month later.
- Record your revision in your Revision Diary, e.g.
  French: Law and order, 3rd March 25 minutes
  French: Law and order, 5th March 15 minutes
  French: Law and order, 3rd April 15 minutes
  ... and then at monthly intervals.

Chapter 1

L'ordre public

The following topics are covered in this chapter:

- The legal system in France
- The police
- Patterns of crime
- Crime and punishment

- Grammar: Future perfect; Conditional perfect tenses
- How to answer: Q/A and grid-completion

Law and order

After studying this chapter you should be able to:

- understand how the French legal system works and what crimes are prevalent in France
- identify the vocabulary you will need to understand this topic
- use the future perfect and conditional perfect tenses
- improve your skill in answering questions and completing grids in French

LEARNING SUMMARY

1.1 The legal system

AQA	M4, M6
EDEXCEL	M4, M6
OCR	M4, M5
NICCEA	M4, M5

The laws relating to inheritance have caused particular problems to the agricultural industry.

The structure of the legal system in France has in essence changed little in the last 200 years. The **Code Napoléon** or *Code civil* was established in the early nineteenth century and is still the basis of French law. Other codes include the *code de procédure civil*, the *code de commerce*, the *code d'instruction criminelle* and the *code pénal*. Some changes took place in 1958 (when De Gaulle's Fifth Republic came to power) and further amendments were made in 1981 under François Mitterrand. The penal code was reformed in 1992.

Laws are passed by parliament and implemented by the courts. The two 'arms' of the legal system, i.e. civil and criminal law, are closely linked. In theory, justice is free and accessible to all; in practice, legal costs may be high except for those who qualify for legal aid (*aide judiciaire*).

As a member of the European Union, France may apply to the **European Court of Justice** for a decision if a question on European law arises in a French court; in that case the French process must be halted until the European ruling has been given.

Court structure

- **Tribunal de police** – police court
- **Tribunal d'instance** – magistrate's court (for civil cases)

  These deal with minor matters (*contraventions*). The *tribunal de police* has limited sentencing powers.

- **Tribunal de grande instance**

  This consists of the *tribunal civil* or the *tribunal correctionnel* and deals with more serious offences (*délits*). Its sentencing powers extend to longer terms of imprisonment and larger fines.

- **Cour d'assises**

  This is equivalent to the Crown Court in England. Cases are tried by three *magistrats* and a jury of nine. Each *département* has one *cour d'assises*. It can impose custodial sentences up to and including life imprisonment.

- **Cour d'appel** – the court of appeal

- **Cour de cassation**

  This is the final arbiter of legal matters within France (other than questions that are referred to the European Court of Justice).

  Employment-related disputes are settled by the *conseil des prud'hommes* (industrial tribunal). There are separate courts and personnel to deal with offences committed by children and young people under the age of 18 (*mineurs*).

Vocabulary for the legal system

la procédure judiciaire	legal system	**déposer plainte**	to lodge a complaint
la cour	court	**porter plainte**	to lodge a complaint
l'audience (f)	hearing	**juger**	to try
l'affaire (f)	case	**comparaître**	to appear in court
le procès	trial, case	**plaider**	to plead
le pouvoir	power	**prouver**	to prove
la loi	law	**gagner**	to win
le droit	law, right	**perdre**	to lose
le décret	decree	**témoigner**	to give evidence
le règlement	rule	**acquitter**	to acquit
le parquet	public prosecutor's department	**décharger**	to acquit
la défense	defence	**infliger (une peine)**	to impose a penalty
l'accusation (f)	prosecution	**faire appel**	to appeal
les poursuites (f)	prosecution	**se prononcer**	to reach a verdict
la plainte	complaint	**déposer en faveur (de)**	to come out in favour
l'inculpation (f)	charge	**déposer contre**	to come out against
la déposition	sworn statement	**reconnaître coupable**	to convict
le témoin	witness	**déclarer non coupable**	to acquit
le témoignage	evidence	**mettre en examen**	to accuse, charge
la preuve	proof, evidence	**poursuivre**	to prosecute
le jugement	judgement, verdict	**judiciaire**	judicial, legal
le verdict	verdict	**juridique**	legal
la condamnation	sentence	**légal**	legal
la peine	sentence	**illégal**	illegal
l'appel (m)	appeal	**condamné**	convicted
le prisonnier	prisoner	**acquitté**	acquitted
le notaire	solicitor	**déchargé**	acquitted
faire un procès à	to take proceedings against	**coupable**	guilty
intenter un procès à	to start proceedings against	**non coupable**	not guilty
engager un procès contre	to take action against	**huis clos**	behind closed doors (hearing)

Several of the words below have precise meanings in this context.

- *audience*: not 'audience'.
- *loi/droit*: *la loi* is a particular law; use *le droit* for 'the Law' in a more general sense (*faire son droit* = to study law).
- *accusation/poursuites*: *accusation* is the Prosecution as opposed to the Defence; *poursuites* is an accusation made against a criminal by the police.
- *témoignage/preuve*: *témoignage* is the statement made by a witness; *preuve* is proof or evidence that supports a case.
- *condamnation/peine*: *condamnation* is the sentencing of a convicted criminal; *peine* is the sentence he is given. *La sentence* may also be used.
- *notaire*: usually refers to the person who draws up wills, etc.
- *juger*: in the sense of 'trial', not 'attempt'.
- *judiciaire/juridique*: use *judiciaire* for the process of law; *juridique* is used in phrases such as *études juridiques*.
- *légal/illégal*: remember that the masculine plural is *légaux/illégaux*.

KEY POINT

> The Ministre de la Justice also has the title of *Garde des Sceaux* (keeper of the seals).

Reports of court proceedings may refer to certain institutions and personnel.

These could include:

la magistrature assise/du siège – the Bench, the judges

la magistrature debout/du parquet – State prosecutors

le magistrat – judge, magistrate (a general term)

le juge – judge

le magistrat du parquet – public prosecutor

le procureur (de la République) – public prosecutor

l'avocat de la défense – lawyer for the defence, defence counsel

l'avocat – lawyer, barrister

le juge d'instruction – examining magistrate, who is responsible for investigating the case against an accused person

le juge d'instance – magistrate

le jury – jury. Its foreman is *le président*

les jurés – members of the jury (*le juré* = juryman, *la femme juré* = jurywoman)

le défendeur, la défenderesse – defendant

le prévenu/la prévenue – defendant

l'accusé(e) – defendant, the accused

l'inculpé(e) – the accused

l'huissier – usher, bailiff

le greffier – clerk of the court

1.2 The police

AQA	M4, M6
EDEXCEL	M4, M6
OCR	M4, M5
NICCEA	M4, M5

Policing in France is the responsibility of two separate organisations: the *Police Nationale* and the *Gendarmerie Nationale*.

- The *Police Nationale* acts under the aegis of the *Ministère de l'Intérieur*. Its main tasks are to **maintain law and order in the streets** and to bring criminals to justice (the *police judiciaire*), but it is also responsible for **ensuring public safety at sporting events and other gatherings**, and carrying out enquiries into accidents. One of its branches is the **CRS** (*Compagnies Républicaines de Sécurité*), often thought of as the 'riot police' but whose role is also to **police motorways** and to **direct proceedings in the event of disasters** and mountain and sea rescue. Other branches include the *Renseignements généraux*, the *Direction de la surveillance du territoire* (DST) which is responsible for intelligence matters, and the *Police de l'air et des frontières*.

> Young men in France could choose to do their National Service (now being phased out) in the police service.

- The *Gendarmerie Nationale* is responsible to the *Ministère de la Défense* and counts as one of the armed forces. It tends to operate in country regions and in small towns, whereas the **Police Nationale** takes responsibility for urban areas.

Vocabulary for the police

les forces (f) de l'ordre	forces of law and order	**le fourgon**	police van
le maintien de l'ordre	upholding the law	**les menottes** (f)	handcuffs
la police	police, policing	**l'empreinte digitale**	fingerprint
le commissariat	police station	**le portrait-robot**	photofit
le poste de police	police station	**l'indice** (m)	clue
la gendarmerie	police station	**la balance** (slang)	informer, 'grass'
le préfet de police	senior police officer in Paris	**le taux d'élucidation**	clear-up rate
le commissaire	senior police officer	**l'enquête** (f)	enquiry, investigation
l'officier de (la) paix	police inspector	**patrouiller**	to patrol
le gardien de la paix	police constable	**contrôler**	to check
l'agent	policeman	**fouiller**	to search
la femme agent	policewoman	**perquisitionner**	to search
le policier	policeman	**élucider**	to clear up, solve

Vocabulary for the police (continued)

la femme policier	policewoman	dresser une contravention	to 'book', fine
le motard	motorcycle policeman	mener une enquête	to carry out an enquiry
le casier judiciaire	police record	dénoncer	to denounce, inform
le constat	report of accident	arrêter	to arrest
la carte d'identité	identity card	appréhender	to arrest
la pièce officielle	official document	interpeller	to question
l'arrestation (f)	arrest	placer en garde à vue	to hold in custody
l'interpellation (f)	questioning	mettre en garde à vue	to hold in custody
la fouille	search	relâcher	to release
la perquisition	search	libérer	to set free
le dossier	file	détenir	to detain, hold
la brigade	squad, brigade	soupçonner	to suspect
la police de proximité	community policing	admettre	to admit
les flics	'the cops'	avouer	to confess
le soupçon	suspicion	antiterroriste	anti-terrorist
		inculpé de	charged with

- *agent/policier*: note the feminine versions of these words.
- *pièce officielle*: any official document that proves one's identity.
- *fouille/perquisition*: use *fouille* for people or vehicles, *perquisition* for premises.
- *balance*: this topic lends itself to slang, but you would not be expected to recognise the word without some additional help.

KEY POINT

1.3 Patterns of crime

AQA	M4, M6
EDEXCEL	M4, M6
OCR	M4, M5
NICCEA	M4, M5

Despite the high incidence of theft, the French have been slow to accept the need for alarm systems.

Examiner's tip

This is not specifically a French issue, but a reflection of a current worldwide problem.

Keeping up to date with media reports in English will give you the vocabulary needed to help your comprehension of listening and reading passages.

Over 60% of all crimes in France involve theft. About half of these are linked to vehicles, generally cars or *deux roues*; burglary comes next, and there are relatively few cases of armed robbery, though inevitably these have a higher profile in the media. Crimes against the individual are on the increase: these include murder and attempted murder, the taking of hostages, rape, domestic violence and criminal damage. In recent years there have been many high-profile cases involving large-scale fraud. The clear-up rate for such financial crimes is very high, whereas the success rate for solving cases of burglary is low. Driving under the influence of alcohol is a factor in almost half the number of road deaths recorded each year. Nevertheless, the number of deaths in road accidents has decreased considerably in the last 30 years. **The incidence of juvenile and youth crime is on the increase**, possibly due to the level of alcohol and substance abuse. (See also AS Study Guide Chapter 3.)

Drug-related offences are on the increase, often (but not exclusively) among young people. Such crimes include not only those committed while under the influence of drugs but also theft and violence committed in order to obtain money to buy drugs.

Vocabulary for patterns of crime (see also the main text of 1.4)

la criminalité	crime, criminality	le chantage	blackmail
la sécurité	security	l'escroquerie (f)	swindle
l'insécurité (f)	lack of security	la fraude	fraud
la délinquance (juvénile)	(juvenile) delinquency	le détournement de fonds	embezzlement
la tentative	attempt		
le règlement de comptes	settling of scores	la pagaille	chaos, shambles
le viol	rape	le coupable	guilty person
l'agression (f)	attack, mugging	le filou	crook (slang)
coups et blessures	aggravated assault	la manifestation	demonstration
coups de pied	kicking	les émeutes (f)	rioting
coups de poing	punching	la bagarre	fighting, scuffling

Vocabulary for patterns of crime (continued)

le crime passionnel	crime of passion	le meurtrier	murderer
la violence	violence	l'escroc (m)	swindler, crook
le meurtre	murder	le criminel	criminal
l'homicide involontaire	manslaughter	tirer sur	to shoot at
le blanchiment	laundering (money)	agresser	to attack, mug
le vol	theft	blesser	to wound, injure
le vol à main armée	armed robbery	violer	to rape
le vol à l'étalage	shop-lifting	faire du chantage	to blackmail
le cambriolage	burglary	voler	to steal
l'enlèvement (m)	kidnapping	prendre des mesures	to take steps
le vandalisme	vandalism	venger	to avenge
l'attaque (f)	attack	abattre	to shoot down
le racket	extortion	frapper	to hit
le pitbull	pitbull terrier	incendier	to set fire to
la victime	victim	briser	to break
la vengeance	vengeance	casser	to break
la cible	target	attaquer	to attack
le décès	death	saigner	to bleed
la mort	death	vivre	to live
l'arme (f)	weapon	mourir	to die
le voyou	hooligan	tuer	to kill
le coup de feu	gunshot	voler en éclats	to splinter
le trafic des stupéfiants	drug trafficking	détruire	to destroy
la bande	gang	fuir	to flee
l'assassinat (m)	murder	s'enfuir	to flee, escape
l'attentat (m)	attempt at murder	se sauver	to run away
le sang	blood	suspect	suspicious
la soirée arrosée	evening spent drinking	mortel, mortelle	fatal
la fugue	flight	apeuré	frightened
la fuite	flight, escape	impliqué	involved

- *la sécurité/l'insécurité*: it can be difficult to tell the difference between these two words in a listening passage. However, they may mean the same thing, depending on the context; if someone is worried about security he/she is actually worried about the lack of it.
- *viol/vol*: these look and sound similar; distinguish carefully between them.
- *agression*: note the spelling; only one *g*.
- *crime passionnel*: a possible plea in mitigation in the French courts.
- pitbull terriers are being used by street gangs in France as a weapon.
- *victime*: one of the nouns that is always feminine.
- *détruire* (like *conduire*), *mourir*, *fuir* and *vivre* are all very irregular.
- *manifestation*, often shortened to *manif*: street demos have long been an accepted method of protest in France; marchers in recent years have included health workers protesting against delays in hospital treatment, *salariés* protesting at the proposed closure of their place of work or at their pay and conditions, and lorry drivers and agricultural workers complaining about the importing of goods and produce from abroad. Demonstrations are not, of course, crimes in themselves, but they can lead to instances of public disorder and violence and as such may be used as the subject of comprehension passages.

1.4 Crime and punishment

AQA	M4, M6
EDEXCEL	M4, M6
OCR	M4, M5
NICCEA	M4, M5

The general term for an offence is *infraction*.

The judicial system distinguishes between different categories of crime:

- *contravention*, which is a minor offence
- *délit*, a more serious crime such as burglary or fraud. The phrase *flagrant délit* applies when the criminal is caught in the act of perpetrating the offence

- *crime*, which is a serious offence such as murder, armed robbery or grievous bodily harm.

A suspect may be arrested and questioned; the police have powers of detention (*garde à vue*) for up to 24 hours, but this may be extended under certain circumstances. For serious offences *détention provisoire* (remand) for a period of up to four months, may be imposed.

The punishment meted out by the courts may vary, though there are upper and lower limits for any given misdemeanour. A minor offence is often dealt with by means of a fine (*amende forfaitaire*). Probation is a possibility, and **pilot schemes involving electronic tagging** by means of a *bracelet électronique* have been introduced. For many offences the usual punishment is imprisonment.

A convicted criminal may be released early (*libération anticipée*) or on parole (*libération conditionnelle*). Life imprisonment has a maximum sentence of 30 years. **The decision to abolish capital punishment was made in 1981**; the method used in France was the guillotine.

> The French for a sash window is *fenêtre à guillotine*, which conjures up a graphic picture of possible injury if the catch doesn't work properly...

Vocabulary for crime and punishment

la punition	punishment	la réclusion à perpétuité	life imprisonment
la sanction	punishment	la peine capitale	capital punishment
le malfaiteur	wrongdoer	la peine de mort	death penalty
la faute	fault	commettre	to commit
l'amende (f)	fine	punir	to punish
le forfait	crime	sanctionner	to punish
le contrôle judiciaire	probation	condamner	to sentence
l'emprisonnement (m)	imprisonment	détenir	to detain
la prison	prison	incarcérer	to imprison
le détenu	prisoner	être en taule (slang)	to be in the nick
la cellule	cell	sous peine de	on pain of
le maton/la matonne	prison officer (slang)	incompressible	to be served in full
la remise de peine	reduction of sentence	avec sursis	suspended (sentence)
le châtiment corporel	corporal punishment	impuni	unpunished

Examiner's tip

Comprehension passages on this topic are likely to involve items about specific crimes as well as articles on the general theme of law and order. In either case, understanding of statistics may be required, so revise numbers carefully.

- *amende*: sounds exactly like *amande* ('almond') but there should be no risk of confusion here.
- *prison*: there has been considerable public disquiet recently about conditions, particularly overcrowding, in prisons.
- *châtiment corporel/peine capitale*: don't confuse capital and corporal punishment when you are talking or writing about possible sanctions for criminals. If you appear to be suggesting the death penalty for crimes such as vandalism and theft the examiner will be fairly certain that you have chosen the wrong word.
- *commettre*: this is a compound of *mettre* so the past participle is *commis*.
- *sous peine de*: i.e. if you do this you will suffer. Example: *sous peine de poursuites* – 'will be prosecuted'.
- *incompressible*: the sentence may not be compressed into a shorter time.

KEY POINT

Progress check

When you have learnt the vocabulary for this section, write down the following key words, then check them with the lists.

Give the French for: court, charge, complaint, prisoner, not guilty, lawyer, defendant, policewoman, police record, clue, to check, to search (person), to question, to suspect, kicking, shoplifting, demonstration, fatal, capital punishment, to commit.

Give the English for: l'audience, les poursuites, le témoignage, décharger, l'appel, huis clos, intenter un procès à, la déposition, le procureur, le commissaire, le portrait robot, mettre en garde à vue, dénoncer, l'insécurité, le viol, les émeutes, le chantage, inculpé de, la sanction, l'amende.

Grammar

Neither of the tenses in this section should be entirely new to you; they had to be recognised, but not used, at AS Level.

1.5 Future perfect tense – 'will have (done)'

Formation

This tense uses the future of the auxiliary verb *avoir* or *être*, plus the past participle (*jugé, puni, perdu, commis*, etc.). **If a verb takes *avoir* to form its perfect tense, it does so in the future perfect too.** Agreements are the same as for the perfect tense.

Avoir verbs

The past participle does not change its spelling (but see note on pp. 27–28).

-er verbs	-ir verbs	-re verbs
j'aurai dénoncé	j'aurai puni	j'aurai perdu
tu auras dénoncé	tu auras puni	tu auras perdu
il/elle/on aura dénoncé	il/elle/on aura puni	il/elle/on aura perdu
nous aurons dénoncé	nous aurons puni	nous aurons perdu
vous aurez dénoncé	vous aurez puni	vous aurez perdu
ils/elles auront dénoncé	ils/elles auront puni	ils/elles auront perdu

Examples of irregular verbs: j'aurai commis (*commettre*), tu auras fait (*faire*), il aura détenu (*détenir*), nous aurons reconnu (*reconnaître*), vous aurez écrit (*écrire*), ils auront suivi (*suivre*).

Être verbs

The past participle agrees with the subject.

The pattern below is made up of nine different verbs; remember that there are only thirteen basic verbs that take *être*, although many of them have compounds (*devenir, repartir*, etc.). Where an alternative is given, the second spelling is for the feminine form. For *vous*, singular and plural forms are given.

je serai allé/allée	(aller)
tu seras retourné/retournée	(retourner)
il sera monté	(monter)
elle sera descendue	(descendre)
on sera sorti /sortis (when on is used to mean 'we')	(sortir)
nous serons partis/parties	(partir)
vous serez venu/venue/venus/venues	(venir)
ils seront morts	(mourir)
elles seront nées	(naître)

Reflexive verbs

The following pattern applies to all normal reflexive verbs, i.e. those in which the reflexive pronoun is the direct object meaning 'myself', 'yourself', etc. (For other verbs used reflexively, see p. 58).

je me serai débrouillé/débrouillée
tu te seras couché/couchée
il se sera ennuyé
elle se sera intéressée
nous nous serons entraînés/entraînées
vous vous serez spécialisé/spécialisée/spécialisés/spécialisées
ils se seront récupérés
elles se seront installées

Remember that not all reflexive verbs are –*er* verbs; past participles should be revised, e.g. *je me serai détendu/détendue* (from *se détendre*), *elles se seront assises* (from *s'asseoir*).

Uses of the future perfect tense

The future perfect tense is found **more often in French than in English**. It is used

- with its basic meaning of 'will have (done)':

  Le policier aura arrêté le voleur avant l'arrivée de ses collègues –
  'The policeman will have arrested the thief before his colleagues arrive'

- with the meaning of 'have/has done' when the future is implied:

  the main verb is likely to be in the future tense, and the clause requiring the future perfect will probably be introduced by *quand*, *lorsque* ('when'), *dès que* or *aussitôt que* ('as soon as')

  Dès que le juge sera arrivé le procès commencera –
  'As soon as the judge has arrived the trial will begin'

- occasionally with the meaning of 'must have' or 'has probably' (some parts of the UK have a similar idiom in English):
  Il a l'air triste; il aura perdu le procès –
  'He looks sad; he must have lost the case'

1.6 Conditional perfect tense – 'would have (done)'

Key points from AS

- Formation of conditional tense
  AS Study Guide p. 47

Formation

The conditional tense of the auxiliary verb *avoir* or *être* is used, plus the past participle. As with the pluperfect and future perfect tenses, **verbs taking** *être* **in the perfect tense also do so in the conditional perfect**. Again, all agreements are the same as for the perfect tense.

Avoir **verbs**

-er verbs	-ir verbs	-re verbs
j'aurais gagné	j'aurais fini	j'aurais attendu
tu aurais gagné	tu aurais fini	tu aurais attendu
il/elle/on aurait gagné	il/elle/on aurait fini	il/elle/on aurait attendu
nous aurions gagné	nous aurions fini	nous aurions attendu
vous auriez gagné	vous auriez fini	vous auriez attendu
ils/elles auraient gagné	ils/elles auraient fini	ils/elles auraient attendu

Examples of irregular verbs:
j'aurais admis (*admettre*), tu aurais été (*être*), il aurait fallu (*falloir*), nous aurions atteint (*atteindre*), vous auriez cru (*croire*), elles auraient eu (*avoir*).

Être verbs

je serais rentré/rentrée	(rentrer)
tu serais tombé/tombée	(tomber)
il serait né	(naître)
elle serait partie	(partir)
nous serions arrivés/arrivées	(arriver)
vous seriez mort/morte/morts/mortes	(mourir)
ils seraient devenus	(devenir)
elles seraient restées	(rester)

Reflexive verbs

je me serais levé/levée
tu te serais relaxé/relaxée
il se serait écrasé
elle se serait nourrie
nous nous serions divertis/diverties
vous vous seriez consacré/consacrée/consacrés/consacrées
ils se seraient déplacés
elles se seraient amusées

Examiner's tip

If you can use the conditional perfect with confidence (especially when writing about or discussing your chosen topic) you will impress the examiner immensely.

It is very useful when you are expressing your own opinions; literary texts lend themselves particularly well to this sort of language, and it should be possible to prepare a few appropriate phrases.

Uses of the conditional perfect tense

- with its basic meaning of 'would have (done)':

  Je ne l'aurais jamais cru – 'I would never have believed it'.

- in the main clause of conditional sentences when the verb in the *si* clause is in the pluperfect tense ('had … would have'):

  S'il n'avait pas été sur les lieux il n'aurait pas été arrêté –
  If he hadn't been on the spot he wouldn't have been arrested'.

- when the facts being given are unsupported by proof; it is often used in this way in media reports. The conditional tense may be used in the same way (see AS Study Guide p. 47). It is best translated as 'apparently', 'appear to have' or 'alleged to have':

  Les criminels se seraient enfuis en voiture –
  'the criminals apparently escaped by car'.

  L'attaque aurait été le résultat d'un règlement de comptes –
  The attack appears to have been the result of a settling of scores'.

- The conditional perfect of *devoir* means 'should have' or 'ought to have':

  Vous auriez dû avouer que vous aviez volé l'argent –
  'You should have confessed that you had stolen the money'.

1.7 Revision: agreement of the past participle with a preceding direct object (pdo)

As the future perfect and conditional perfect are both compound tenses, like the perfect and pluperfect, they are likely to need a pdo agreement occasionally.

> The direct object of a verb is the person or thing that is having the action of the verb done to it (*il appréhende le malfaiteur*).

You may remember that although the past participle of verbs which use *avoir* to form their past participle does not normally agree, there are certain circumstances in which it may do so. These are:

- if the verb has a direct object
- if that direct object is placed before the verb.

If these conditions apply, the past participle **agrees with the direct object**.

A reminder of the three types of sentence in which this agreement may occur:

- With the relative pronoun *que*:

  La preuve qu'il aurait montrée aurait été irréfutable –
  'The evidence he would have shown would have been/was apparently irrefutable'.

  Here, *que* stands for *la preuve*, which is the direct object, so *montrée* agrees with *la preuve*, which is feminine singular.

- With the direct object pronoun *la (l')* or *les*:

  Le voleur a pris les CD-ROM. Il les aurait cachés dans sa voiture –
  'The thief took the CD-ROMs. He is alleged to have hidden them in his car'.

  Here, *les* stands for the CD-ROMs, which are plural; the direct object pronoun is placed before the verb (see AS Study Guide pp. 65–66) so *cachés* agrees with *les*.

- With questions starting with *combien* or *quel*:

  Combien d'agressions auront-ils commises dans les années à venir? –
  'How many muggings will they have carried out in the years to come?'

  Here, *agressions* is the direct object of *commettre* and is placed before the verb, so *commises* agrees with *agressions* (feminine plural).

Although you learnt this for AS Level, you may not have needed to use it. However, it will improve the standard of your written French if you are able to do so now.

Monter, descendre, rentrer, sortir

These four verbs, which normally take *être*, may occasionally have a different meaning and in this case **use *avoir* instead to form their compound tenses**. All agreements are then the same as for *avoir* verbs.

> monter – to bring/take up
> descendre – to bring/take down
> rentrer – to bring in
> sortir – to bring out, put out

Elle aura monté ses valises – 'She will have taken her cases up'.

Si nous avions su que tu allais amener des amis, nous aurions descendu plus de chaises – 'If we had known that you were going to bring some friends, we would have brought down more chairs'.

Progress check

Future perfect and conditional perfect tenses

Translate the following sentences into French (answers on p. 154):

1 When the senior police officer has arrived we shall be able to continue the enquiry.

2 They're late; there must have been an accident.

3 At five o'clock this evening we will have finished questioning the suspects.

4 Would you have believed me if I had told you earlier?

5 Why would he have done such a thing?

6 They have apparently been taken in for questioning.

Progress check

Translate into English:

7 Dès que vous aurez donné votre témoignage vous devrez quitter la cour.

8 Les victimes seront arrivées à l'hôpital dans vingt minutes.

9 Elle est morte: elle se sera suicidée.

10 Je n'aurais pas pensé qu'elle veuille le faire.

11 Si tu avais été plus courageux tu m'aurais accompagné.

12 Le taux de violence serait monté à un niveau inacceptable.

Pdo agreement

Translate into French:

1 Photofit pictures? No, he hasn't looked at them yet.

2 The complaints they made have already been investigated.

3 Which faces did you recognise?

How to answer

1.8 Question and answer, grid-completion

In all comprehension exercises at this level in which you have to write a complete answer in French or English there are four things to do:

- read the instructions (the 'rubric') carefully
- show that you have understood the passage on which the questions are set
- show that you have understood the question
- make your answer clear.

Instructions

Reading the instructions is essential for any type of question; if you don't follow them you may lose all the marks, and will certainly lose some of them. Check:

- whether you have a choice (almost certainly not, in an exercise of this sort, but it's not impossible)
- whether you have to answer in complete sentences or if brief notes will do; the form of the questions should help you here as well
- whether you have to answer in French or English; take particular care if the paper requires a mixture of both languages
- how many marks are allocated to each part of the question. A one-word answer won't be sufficient if four marks are allocated; on the other hand you can't be sure that there will be four separate points to find, as some might be complex and worth more than one mark.

It's very likely that the answers will be in the right order in the passage, though there could be general 'summing-up' points to be made at the end. Some papers tell you where to look, in the case of a longer text. If so, you must keep to the section indicated; an answer taken from a different part of the passage may be wrong.

Understanding the passage

The first and most important thing to do when dealing with a comprehension passage is to **read it, or listen to it, right to the end.** You'll probably find that some of it is repeated in different words later in the extract. If you have learnt the vocabulary for the topic carefully, it will give you a 'gist' understanding, which in turn will help you to find the precise details you need.

Then, **look or listen for 'trigger' words in the text**: words that are linked with the questions so that you know where to find the answer. These could be the same words, but they are more likely to be either:

- synonyms – e.g. *arrêter* in the question, *appréhender* in the passage
- a different part of speech – *décès* in the question, *décédé* in the passage.

The best way to show that you have understood the passage is to answer the questions succinctly, **using your own words.** If you 'lift' words from the original there is a danger that you will write too much and thus indicate to the examiner that you haven't really understood at all but you know the answer is here and you would like him/her to pick out the relevant details and ignore the rest, please …

Even if your answer is correct you may lose marks because all you have shown is that you know where the answer is and can copy it out; it doesn't necessarily follow that you have understood it.

Understanding the question

Reading the questions themselves is just as important as reading the passage. Answer all sections: this is easy to do when it's subdivided into parts (a), (b) and (c), but less so when it asks '*Où et quand?*' or adds '*…et pourquoi?*' Don't be afraid to **underline or highlight the important words**; as long as your answer is clear, examiners don't mind if you have marked the paper or written notes.

Don't just seize on one word and assume you know what you are being asked to do: a question in a recent paper asked '*Quelle est l'opinion des écologistes sur les centrales à gaz, et pourquoi cela semble-t-il surprenant?*' Many candidates answered the question as though it had stopped at '*et pourquoi*', which was not the same.

Making your answer clear

You can do this in several ways:

- keep it separate from any notes you have made.
- if you have to change it, cross out the original answer neatly and if necessary draw an arrow to the new answer, labelling it with the number and section of the question.
- never leave alternatives; it's up to you, not the examiner, to make the decision.
- for answers written in French, write accurately; use the grammar and structures you have learnt, and don't make basic errors.
- for answers written in English, make sure that what you have written makes sense and is spelt correctly.
- write legibly and in ink. If the examiner genuinely cannot read what you have written, he/she cannot give you any marks.

Practice examination questions

Examiner's tip

Papers are set a long time in advance of the actual examination, so look back over the items you have collected since the beginning of your course just in case they form the subject of comprehension passages.

You will find help on how to deal with gap-fill exercises on pp. 46–47.

The first listening passage refers to a case that was widely reported in France at the time. There are two points to note here. Firstly, if you had made a note of some of the details (if you were reading French newspapers or listening to French radio or keeping a file of references to France that appeared in the British press) you would already know a great deal about the incident. Secondly, a passage of this nature will not be composed only of 'crime' words; there will be vocabulary from other topic areas too.

Q 1

1 Écoutez le passage sur la disparition d'Yves Godard, puis remplissez les blancs dans le résumé ci-dessous avec un mot ou une courte expression qui montre que vous avez bien compris le sens.

Yves Godard, médecin du Calvados, est (1) _disparu_ d'avoir tué sa femme avant de (2) _____ à bord d'un bateau avec ses enfants. Cette possibilité naît du fait qu'on a analysé des traces de (3) _____ trouvées à sa maison et dans le (4) _voiture_ qu'il avait (5) _____ dans un parking à Saint-Malo. Personne ne sait où (6) _____ le docteur Godard et ses enfants à présent.

Selon le maire de Tilly-sur-Seulles il y a une grande possibilité que les enfants (7) _____ encore. En revanche il craint que la femme du médecin ne (8) _____ ; c'est l' (9) _____ de la maison familiale aussi bien que celui de la voiture qui le (10) _____ .

De plus, ça fait presque une (11) _____ qu'on ne voit pas Mme Godard; le maire ne croit pas qu'elle (12) _____ à bord du bateau parce qu'on sait qu'elle le (13) _____ .

Il y a quand même beaucoup de questions à (14) _____ : quel a été le dernier (15) _____ où l'on a vu Mme Godard, et qu'est-ce que le docteur Godard a fait depuis qu'il a (16) _____ Saint-Malo. En ce moment on est en train d' (17) _____ les communications de son téléphone portable, et de découvrir s'il a retiré (18) _____ de ses comptes bancaires.

L'enquête ne va pas être (19) _____ et pour l'instant on n'a aucune idée où se trouve le (20) _____ , qui a été loué à Saint-Malo.

Q 2

2 The next passage is a straightforward question and answer exercise in English.

If you are not sure what point in the passage the question is referring to, listen for 'trigger words' that will guide you to the right section.

(a) Why did the inhabitants of Givors and Grigny protest yesterday? (2)

(b) What was the mayor's purpose in meeting the *préfet*? (2)

(c) Describe the incidents that had taken place the previous weekend. (5)

(d) When had Givors signed the 'local security contract'? (1)

(e) According to the person being interviewed, what had upset the inhabitants, and why? (3)

(f) What does he think should happen? (2)

(g) In what way have the lives of people from the town been affected, and why? (3)

3 Reading

PATRICK HENRY

En 1977, Robert Badinter sauvait la tête du meurtrier d'enfant, Patrick Henry, et en faisait un symbole de l'abolition de la peine de mort. Aujourd'hui, le prisonnier demande sa libération conditionelle. A la garde des Sceaux de trancher.

Échappera-t-il à la prison à vie?

Il n'est pas le premier condamné à perpétuité – ni le premier meurtrier d'enfant – à demander une libération conditionnelle. S'il l'obtient, il ne sera pas le premier non plus. Et pourtant, une émotion viscérale surgit à l'idée d'une éventuelle libération de Patrick Henry. Il faut dire que les circonstances de son crime sont particulièrement horribles. Nous sommes en 1976. Le 30 janvier, un petit garçon de 7 ans est enlevé à la sortie de l'école. Pendant quinze jours, le ravisseur, qui a demandé une rançon de 1 million de francs, promène la police. Au début du mois de février, un jeune homme de 22 ans, Patrick Henry, est interpellé. Faute de preuves, il est relâché et, devant les écrans de télévision, hurle que le kidnappeur mérite la mort. Très vite, il sera à nouveau arrêté et le corps de Philippe Bertrand, retrouvé, enroulé dans une couverture : il a été étranglé tout de suite après son enlèvement. Un an après, c'est le procès. Robert Badinter défend celui que toute la France appelle «le monstre» et pour lequel la guillotine est réclamée à cor et à cri.

L'avocat sauve l'assassin de la peine capitale. Aujourd'hui, Patrick Henry demande sa libération conditionnelle. Son dossier a recueilli un avis favorable de la commission consultative des libérations conditionnelles ainsi que de nombreux experts psychiatres. En effet, l'homme a changé: parcours sans tache en prison, licence de mathématiques, diplôme d'informaticien, promesse d'embauche, etc. A présent, c'est à la garde des Sceaux, Elisabeth Guigou, de décider. Elle doit le faire dans les prochaines semaines mais elle a déclaré que c'était une des décisions les plus difficiles de sa carrière.

The first of the reading questions is a true/false/not given exercise. Read the sentences very carefully – every word – and don't be misled by a word that looks as though it makes the answer easy. For hints on how to answer this type of question, see pp. 60–61.

Lisez le passage au sujet de Patrick Henry, puis décidez si les phrases ci-dessous sont VRAIES (V) ou FAUSSES (F) ou si les renseignements NE SONT PAS DONNÉS (?).

	V	F	?
(a) Plusieurs meurtriers ont obtenu la libération conditionnelle.	…	…	…
(b) Patrick Henry est déjà en prison depuis plus de vingt ans.	…	…	…
(c) Le coupable est allé à pied chercher la rançon.	…	…	…
(d) Il a prouvé que l'évidence était fausse.	…	…	…
(e) Il a essayé de tromper les téléspectateurs.	…	…	…
(f) Il avait caché le petit garçon pendant quelques jours avant de le tuer.	…	…	…
(g) Patrick Henry a été jugé tout de suite.	…	…	…
(h) L'opinion publique voulait qu'il soit mis à mort.	…	…	…
(i) Pendant les années qu'il a passées en prison il n'a eu rien à faire.	…	…	…
(j) La décision qui sera prise par Elisabeth Guigou ne sera pas difficile.	…	…	…

4 Reading

For the next question you have to tick the appropriate boxes to show where the information is given. Make sure you don't exceed the maximum number of ticks permitted or you will lose marks.

Nice

Il suffit de pénétrer dans la maison d'arrêt de Nice pour se rendre compte de son délabrement. Les toits tombent en ruine, les murs sont décrépits et les fils électriques pendent du plafond. La demeure est vieille, plus d'un siècle. La prison de Nice connaît également les effets de la surpopulation carcérale, avec près de 600 détenus (dont 80% en préventive ou en attente de transfert) par an... pour 334 places.

Comme dans tout le parc pénitentiaire, les cellules n'excèdent pas 9m² et comptent au moins deux détenus.

Les 40 femmes incarcérées sont un peu privilégiées : des cellules plus grandes, et surtout un accès permanent à l'eau chaude, à l'inverse des quartiers des hommes. En journée, certains peuvent quitter leur cagibi pour travailler dans les ateliers de confection de santons ou de conditionnement de parfums, et toucher un salaire pour « cantiner ».

Luynes

La maison d'arrêt d'Aix-Luynes est peinte en vert. Un vert qui pourrait être synonyme d'espoir. C'est un petit village de 700 pensionnaires, dont une cinquantaine de mineurs délinquants. Vols, trafics de drogue, agressions en tout genre, meurtres parfois... Pour ces petits hommes, la vie est un dérapage incontrôlé, avec un passé déjà lourd de conséquences. Ils sont arrivés là un jour, sans comprendre vraiment pourquoi. Nombre d'entre eux sont issus des quartiers « chauds » de Marseille, où la délinquance est quotidienne et la vie pas facile à vivre.

Chez les mineurs, pas de matons ni de tortionnaires. Rien que des grands frères et des grandes sœurs (ils sont onze) chargés de leur inculquer quelques principes, le temps d'une détention. Pas facile, car l'on ne peut rattraper en quelques mois ce qui n'a pas été fait dès la naissance. Se lever à 7 heures, aller à l'école de la prison, faire du sport, apprendre un métier, être propre, retrouver un rythme de vie normal. Voilà tout ce que le personnel peut imposer.

Dans les cellules (9m² pour un détenu, 12m² pour deux), chacun recrée son univers, affiches et musique à l'appui.

On parle foot, rap, belles voitures, mais pas de la prison. Certains la vivent comme une punition, d'autres la subissent comme une injustice, mais tous sont incertains quant à leur avenir.

Avignon

La maison d'arrêt d'Avignon aurait pu conserver le nom de « maison des Insensés», donné par la Confrérie des Pénitents noirs en 1691, alors qu'ils y recueillaient malades et orphelins. Bâtie au sud du rocher des Doms et à proximité du palais des Papes, la prison se fait discrète, juste signalée par quelques barbelés. Intra–muros, l'atmosphère est étouffante.

Une odeur d'égouts vous poursuit jusque dans les cuisines. Dans les cellules, la crasse grimpe du sol au plafond. Quelques rats se baladent de temps à autre le long des coursives. La maison d'arrêt est vieille et construite sur une « sorgue », une rivière souterraine. Côté ambiance, ce n'est pas mieux. L'agressivité est aussi présente que la saleté. Les trois cellules du fameux « mitard » sont occupées, pour agressions de surveillants. *« Ils sont un peu agités en ce moment »*, explique M. Alves, directeur de l'établissement. Deux à six détenus peuvent être enfermés dans une même cellule, de 9 à 25m².

Lisez les descriptions des trois prisons et cochez (✓) les cases ci-dessous pour indiquer si les renseignements sont mentionnés ou non pour chaque prison. Attention! Ne cochez pas plus de onze cases.

	Nice	Luynes	Avignon
(a) Ambiance sale ou délabrée			
(b) Dimensions des cellules			
(c) Nombre de prisonniers			
(d) Crimes pour lesquels les détenus ont été condamnés			
(e) Conditions moins strictes pour certains détenus			
(f) Tâches précises entreprises par les détenus			

Chapter 2
Questions sociales

The following topics are covered in this chapter:

- Living conditions
- Social security
- Unemployment
- Exclusion

- Immigration and racism
- Equality of opportunity
- Grammar: The passive; Imperfect subjunctive
- How to answer: Sentence-completion; Gap-fill

Social issues

The topics in this chapter are all very much interconnected: poor living conditions may trigger help from social security, people may be *exclus* because they have a different way of life, immigrants may be the target of racism, unemployment may be more widespread among disadvantaged groups. The vocabulary is divided into sections as usual, but you should be aware that it will overlap.

After studying this topic you should be able to:

- answer questions relating to a range of social issues
- identify the vocabulary to help you to understand, speak and write about these issues
- use all tenses of the passive and recognise the imperfect subjunctive
- answer sentence-completion and gap-fill exercises with confidence

LEARNING SUMMARY

2.1 Living conditions

AQA	M4, M6
EDEXCEL	M4, M6
OCR	M4, M5
NICCEA	M4, M5

At the end of the 20th century, France was second (behind Canada) in a table based on the economy. The **rise in the standard of living** means that many more people are now buying their own property than used to be the case, and that many now live in houses in the suburbs rather than in town-centre flats. Living conditions are very much better than they were even in the 1960s; home improvement schemes have brought many of the older buildings up to the same standard as those constructed more recently, and the amount of living space has also increased.

The urban/rural divide is less marked than it used to be; many town-centre dwellings, which once consisted of *immeubles* in narrow cobbled streets, have been converted or even demolished to make way for **pedestrianisation schemes**, and new blocks of flats have been built in the suburbs to take their place. Further out there are developments of *maisons individuelles* which are duplicated in the villages. The *exode rural* (the movement of people away from the country towards the towns) has gained pace as the percentage of workers employed in agriculture has decreased; this is one reason for the **frequent protests by agricultural workers** who feel that their livelihood is at risk because of lower prices elsewhere. There was a conscious attempt in the second half of the 20th century to 'decentralise' and 'regionalise' – to transfer power to the regions – and this had a knock-on effect in increasing the desirability of living and working in towns other than Paris.

> There are relatively few major cities in France. You should certainly recognise and be able to spell the most important of them.

About 50% of the French population lives in just 10% of the land; it follows that there are large areas of the country that are very sparsely populated, generally in mountain and forest areas.

Examiner's tip

Streets in France are often named after a famous person or event from French history or the arts: Place Charles de Gaulle, Rue de la République, Avenue Victor Hugo, etc. If you have to write a letter as part of your examination it may help to create an authentic-looking address.

For local government administration purposes, the unit is the **commune**; each has a mayor and a town council. There are 38,000 of them in France; they may be very small in terms of population, and may consist of several small villages. The word **agglomération** is applied to an urban area, which may be several *communes* grouped together.

Many of the **Habitations à loyer modéré** (HLM – see p. 36) were built in the 1950s and 1960s and seemed at the time like an ideal solution to the problem of *taudis* (hovels) and *bidonvilles* (shanty-towns) in which the poorest people lived; with the coming of greater unemployment in the 1970s, unrest began to grow and some housing estates developed into 'no-go areas'. Some of these have become a focus for violence, but in others there has been a call for a new understanding between different social and ethnic groups.

Houses in country areas often have their own regional characteristics; the half-timbered farms in Normandy are an example of this.

It has recently become a more popular practice to buy a *résidence secondaire*, a second home generally situated in the country or on the coast. These are particularly useful for families during the long four-week break in July or August and in the frequent long weekends which can accompany, and sometimes link, the many *fêtes* and *jours fériés* (see AS Study Guide pp. 37–38).

This is not an entirely new phenomenon; if you have read *Le Blé en herbe* you will remember that the *Ombres* were thinking of buying the house in Brittany where they spent the summer.

Vocabulary for living conditions

la campagne	country	le paysan	small farmer, country dweller
la commune	town, village	le citadin	town dweller
l'agglomération (f)	town, built-up area	le banlieusard	commuter
la (grande) ville	city	le/la propriétaire	owner
la ville dortoir	dormitory town	le voisin	neighbour
le faubourg	outskirts	le campagnard	countryman
la banlieue	suburbs	l'agriculteur (m)	farmer
le quartier	district	l'éleveur (m)	breeder
la région	area	le/la locataire	tenant
le voisinage	neighbourhood	l'habitant (m)	inhabitant
la location	renting, hiring	vivre	to live
la cité	housing estate, city	habiter	to live, live in
l'appartement (m)	flat, apartment	demeurer	to live
la maison jumelle	semi-detached house	louer	to rent
la maison individuelle	detached house	faire la navette	to commute
le pavillon	detached house	quitter	to leave
l'immeuble (m)	block of flats	posséder	to own
le bâtiment	building	urbain	urban
la propriété	property	rural	rural
le domicile	address, place of residence	agricole	agricultural
le logement	accommodation	piéton, -ne (adj.)	pedestrian
le cadre	surroundings, background	défavorisé	neglected, run-down
le niveau	level, standard	immobilier	property
le niveau de vie	standard of living	zone de non-droit	no-go area
la norme	standard	zone périurbaine	outlying area
le loyer	rent	l'aménagement (m) du territoire	national and regional development

- *(grande) ville/cité*: it's best to use *grande ville* for 'city'; *cité* can be used, but more often means 'housing estate'.
- *banlieue*: sometimes has a derogatory sense as city suburbs may be a focus for violence.
- *quartier/région*: a clear distinction should be made between these two words: use *quartier* for an area within a town. *Région* is much bigger.
- *appartement*: spell this word carefully.
- *loyer/louer*: don't confuse these two; *loyer* is a noun, *louer* a verb.
- *paysan*: originally 'peasant', but this tends to have a derogatory sense in English.
- *vivre*: a general word for 'to live'. The verb is very irregular.
- *demeurer*: has the same meaning as *habiter* (i.e. to live in a place). It can also mean 'to remain' (like *rester*) in which case it takes *être* in compound tenses.
- *quitter*: must have a direct object: *Les gens quittent la campagne*.
- *posséder*: belongs to the *espérer* group of verbs.
- *immobilier*: as in *le marché immobilier* – 'the property market'. Don't confuse with *immobile* ('motionless').

KEY POINT

2.2 Social security

AQA	M4, M6
EDEXCEL	M4, M6
OCR	M4, M5
WJEC	M4, M6
NICCEA	M4, M5

The benefit system in France raises its money partly from contributions made by employers and employees, who pay a certain proportion of their wages bill and salary respectively into the scheme. The number of allowances available to families and individuals in need is large; they cover the basics such as **housing, health, pay, unemployment and retirement**. The total proportion of the government budget set aside for social security is over a third of the PIB (*produit intérieur brut* – the gross domestic product, i.e. the annual total of goods produced and services provided entirely within a country). This places France towards the top of the EU list.

Certain groups are entitled to extra benefits; these include *familles nombreuses*, large families (three or more children) which were encouraged in order to increase a declining population. They are also able to obtain a card which gives them access to reduced-fare travel on public transport.

Housing (see also Living conditions, above)

Habitations à loyer modéré (HLM) are the equivalent of council housing in the UK; their rents are usually less than half the full market value. *Immeubles à loyer moyen* (ILM) are similar, but a little more expensive.

Health

The aim is to allow everyone equal access to healthcare. This aim has not yet been fully realised; there are differences depending on such factors as where people live or their standard of living and education, but these differences are less marked in healthcare than in other spheres. A **policy of preventive medicine** has reduced the number of infant deaths and has extended life expectancy.

Costs linked with serious illness and surgery are covered, but some contribution has normally to be made by the patient in the event of relatively minor problems, although it is of course possible to take out insurance to cover these. Those who cannot afford to pay are exempt from charges.

Pensions

These are financed by contributions made by employer and employee during the course of the working life. As in the UK, there is currently some concern about the total cost of pensions as life expectancy increases and early retirement becomes more prevalent. Those who have not been able to contribute towards a pension are nevertheless entitled to an allowance (the *minimum vieillesse*).

Vocabulary for social security
(see also Unemployment and Equal opportunity sections)

l'aide sociale	social security	la pauvreté	poverty
le besoin	need	la précarité	lack of (job) security
la santé	health	la cible	target
l'hôpital (m)	hospital	le trou	hole, shortfall
les services médicaux	healthcare	la vie active	working life
la cotisation	contribution	dépendre de	to rely on
la prestation	benefit (money)	disposer de	to have available
l'allocation (f)	allowance	verser	to pay out
les fonds (m)	funds	recevoir l'aide sociale	to be on benefits
l'aide-ménagère	home help	toucher une pension	to receive a pension
la pension	pension	avoir droit à	to be eligible for
la retraite	retirement	être en droit de (+ inf.)	to be entitled to
la caisse	office	viser	to target, aim at
le salaire	pay	cotiser	to contribute
l'assurance (f)	insurance	disponible	available
l'espérance (f) de vie	life expectancy	précaire	precarious, insecure
la dispense	exemption	répandu	prevalent, widespread

KEY POINT

- *allocation*: take care not to confuse this with *la location*; both could make sense in the context. Decide whether the passage is talking about money or housing.
- *caisse*: you know this already as 'till' or 'chest'. In this context it means the place from which the money is administered.
- *disposer de*: a *faux ami*; it doesn't mean 'to dispose of'.
- *verser*: can also mean 'to pour'.
- *avoir droit à/être en droit de*: the meanings are interchangeable, but note the difference in construction.

2.3 Unemployment

AQA	M4, M6
EDEXCEL	M4, M6
OCR	M4, M5
WJEC	M4, M6
NICCEA	M4, M5

For up to date unemployment figures you should check the French media or the Internet.

Examiner's tip

Passages for listening comprehension set on this topic often concentrate on the unemployment figures which are released regularly. Revision of numbers and associated terms (*au moins, moins de, baisse, augmentation, croissance, pourcentage,* etc.) is vital.

The unemployment rate is likely to be **higher for women than for men**; the rate is also higher for the under 25s. Those who are less well qualified are also at greater risk of being out of work.

Between 1964 and the end of the 1990s the rate of unemployment increased tenfold; such figures are a cause for concern to the government, and various plans have been considered and implemented to encourage firms to take on more employees.

These plans have included relieving them of some of the financial contributions they were required to make towards social security allowances.

Schemes in which young people work on projects designed to help the community have also been funded, and other measures have included:

- persuading people to work part-time
- increasing the number of paid training courses for the long-term unemployed
- lowering the retirement age for some professions
- encouraging early retirement in some spheres.

The RMI (*revenu minimum d'insertion*) is an allowance made by the state to people over 25 who do not qualify for unemployment benefit; in some ways an equivalent to Income Support, it is intended to help with the costs of re-training for work.

The introduction of the 35 hour working week has reduced unemployment; 500,000 jobs have been created since January 2000.

Vocabulary for unemployment

le chômage	unemployment	baisser	to drop
le taux de chômage	rate of unemployment	diminuer	to lessen
le chômeur	unemployed person	reculer	to retreat
le demandeur d'emploi	job-seeker	augmenter	to increase
l'emploi (m)	employment, job	s'accroître	to grow
les effectifs (m)	workers, staff	(s') améliorer	to improve
le personnel	staff	faire un stage	to go on a course
les chiffres (m)	figures, statistics	au chômage	unemployed
le licenciement	redundancy	de longue durée	long-term
le chômage partiel	short-time working	de courte durée	short-term
la baisse	drop, fall	élevé	high
la diminution	fall	bas, basse	low
l'augmentation (f)	increase	moins de	less than
le recul	retreat	plus de	more than
le déclin	fall	au moins	at least
la prévision	forecast	environ	about (with figures)
embaucher	to take on (staff)	vers	about (with figures)
créer (des emplois)	to create (jobs)	à peu près	approximately
chômer	to be out of work	presque	almost, nearly
toucher le chômage	to get unemployment benefit	en hausse	going up
licencier	to make redundant	en baisse	going down
supprimer	to get rid of (jobs)	croissant	growing
renvoyer	to sack	de plus en plus	more and more
financer	to finance	de moins en moins	less and less
s'inscrire	to register	à la recherche de	looking for
		intérimaire	temporary (worker)

KEY POINT

- *s'inscrire*: its endings are like those of *écrire*.
- *(s') améliorer*: the reflexive form is used when there is no object, e.g. *la situation s'améliore*.
- *s'accroître*: a compound of *croître* (see verb list pp. 74–76).
- *croissant*: the present participle of *croître*. The shape of the croissant that you eat for breakfast is the crescent, or 'growing' moon.
- *au moins/moins de*: you must get these right. A mixture of the two ('*au moins de*') means nothing.

2.4 Exclusion

AQA	M4, M6
EDEXCEL	M4, M6
OCR	M4, M5
WJEC	M4, M6
NICCEA	M4, M5

In the educational sense *exclusion* means suspension or expulsion.

Exclusion is a general term; it may refer to any category of 'social outcast' (or to anyone who feels him/herself to be outcast) but is most often taken to mean the homeless. The SDF (*sans domicile fixe*) may be living on the streets for various reasons: poverty, unemployment or lack of official papers (illegal immigrants).

Many organisations are working to relieve the problems faced by the SDF. These include:

- *SAMU social* (*SAMU* stands for *Service d'assistance médicale d'urgence*; the *SAMU social* is concerned particularly with the homeless). Its mission is '*aller à la rencontre de ceux qui ne demandent plus rien*'. The services offered by the *Samu social* in Paris include a free emergency telephone number, a hospice and a centre where spectacles can be obtained free. 24-hour nursing care is available, there is a day-time reception centre and night-time mobile teams. Its *Observatoire* amasses and collates information about the current situation.

- *Restos (Restaurants) du Coeur*, which provide hot food and drinks in the streets during the winter. In the worst of the winter many métro stations are opened at night to give shelter to the homeless.

- *ATD Quart Monde*, which is an international organisation fighting poverty and social exclusion.
- *SOS Amitié*, an organisation similar to the Samaritans.

The French government is trying to help by **providing job-creation schemes**; one of these involves making gardens and then growing vegetables for sale to the public. There is, however, a problem associated with projects such as this, which provide work for the unemployed; the very fact of having a job may deprive the person of benefits he or she was receiving for being out of work. If the job is poorly paid it may not help the financial situation in the long run.

L'Itinérant is a magazine similar to the Big Issue, which highlights the plight of the homeless and other *marginalisés*.

Vocabulary for *Exclusion*

l'exclusion (f)	rejection	**marginaliser**	to edge out
l'indifférence (f)	indifference	**fournir**	to provide
les démunis	the destitute	**survivre**	to survive
les exclus	social outcasts	**mendier**	to beg
les SDF	the homeless	**maltraiter**	to mistreat
les sans-abri	the homeless	**mépriser**	to despise, scorn
le toit	roof	**se méfier de**	to distrust
l'abri (m)	shelter	**réinsérer**	to rehabilitate
la faim	hunger	**marginalisé**	rejected
le froid	cold	**exclu**	excluded, outcast
le bénévole	volunteer	**inutile**	useless
le mendiant	beggar	**insalubre**	unhealthy, squalid
les soins (m)	care	**en marge de**	on the fringe of
l'hygiène (f)	hygiene	**à la dérive**	adrift
le clochard	tramp	**sans papiers**	without official papers
le vagabond	tramp	**provisoire**	temporary
le trottoir	pavement	**dépourvu de**	deprived of
le carton	cardboard	**ne pas prêter attention à**	to ignore
le cercle vicieux	vicious circle	**faire semblant de ne pas voir**	to ignore

- *faim*: sounds exactly like *fin*, so don't confuse *la faim dans le monde* with *la fin du monde*…
- *fournir*: the construction is not the same as in English; *fournir quelque chose à quelqu'un* (to provide something to someone).
- *survivre*: a compound of *vivre*, so the past participle is *survécu*.

KEY POINT

2.5 Immigration and racism

AQA	M4, M6
EDEXCEL	M4, M6
OCR	M4, M5
WJEC	M4, M6
NICCEA	M4, M5

The economic growth in the post-war years meant that there were too few French workers for the jobs available, and a **conscious decision was made to encourage immigration**. Between the two world wars Italians and Poles had made up a large proportion of immigrants, together with people of other nationalities such as Armenians, Spanish and Portuguese. Since the Second World War the profile of the immigrant population has changed, so that now the **Maghreb** (North Africa) and other African countries provide a large proportion of the foreigners who come to live and work in France. These latter often have the advantage of speaking French, either as their first language or as their country's official language.

At first the French workers were only too pleased to allow the immigrant population to take on the jobs that no-one else wanted; these were often the dirty and poorly-paid tasks. But the economic growth could not be maintained for ever;

when the inevitable decline began and unemployment increased, resentment began to build up. The French saw themselves as being deprived of jobs by the very people they had encouraged to come and do them. So the policy was reversed, and immigration was consciously slowed.

The *aide au retour*, a repatriation grant given to immigrant families wishing to return to their native country (particularly when they were also long-term unemployed) was introduced.

The type of immigrants allowed into France also changed: fewer single young men were admitted, but family groups were more favoured. In recent years there have been more entrants from eastern Europe, Latin America and Asia.

Residents of the **Départements d'outre-mer (DOM) and Territoires d'outre-mer (TOM)** sometimes seek work in France. These are not immigrants; the four DOM are Martinique, Guadeloupe, Réunion and Guyane and are, as their name suggests, part of France from the point of view of administration. The TOM, which include Nouvelle Calédonie and French Polynesia, are independent but maintain close links with France.

Immigrants who have been granted French nationality may have it withdrawn if they are convicted of a serious crime.

The situation outlined above has led to an **increase in racism in France**. In 1972 the *Front National* was formed by Jean-Marie Le Pen, a former army officer. He attracted a small but vociferous following and although he initially had little success in elections his followers have caused many problems within French politics and a great deal of actual harm in the streets through the racial violence they have fomented. Marches and protests have developed into riots, and racial hatred is unfortunately involved in a significant proportion of violent incidents, particularly in the streets of large cities.

In the presidential elections in 2002 he caused a political crisis by winning enough votes to take him into second position, which knocked Lionel Jospin out of the running and earned him the right to a head-to-head contest with Jacques Chirac. He lost, but the situation caused shockwaves throughout Europe.

Vocabulary for immigration and racism

l'immigration (f)	immigration	la politique	policy, politics
l'immigré	immigrant	la foule	crowd, mob
le ressortissant	national, immigrant	accueillir	to receive, welcome
le Beur	2nd generation North African	fuir	to flee
le travail au noir	'moonlighting'	se réfugier	to take refuge
le pays d'accueil	host country	s'insérer	to integrate
la terre d'accueil	host country	s'intégrer	to integrate
la frontière	border	s'installer	to settle
le réfugié	refugee	appartenir à	to belong to
l'asile (m)	refuge	régler	to put right
l'insertion (f)	integration	régulariser	to sort out
l'hébergement (m)	accommodation	rapatrier	to repatriate
le ghetto	ghetto	se deebrouiller	to cope
les moeurs (f)	customs	clandestin	secret, illegal
le patrimoine	heritage	au noir	illegal (job)
la diversité	diversity, variety	étranger, -ère	foreign
l'Hexagone (m)	France	maghrébin	from the Maghreb
le mode de vie	way of life	en situation irrégulière	without official papers
immigrer	to immigrate	muni de	provided with, having
émigrer	to emigrate	culturel, -elle	cultural
		divers	diverse, various
le racisme	racism	ethnique	ethnic
l'extrême droite	far right (politics)		
la xénophobie	hatred of foreigners	appeler	to call
le/la xénophobe	s.o. who hates foreigners	hurler	to yell
le préjugé	prejudice	injurier	to insult
les droits de l'homme	human rights	blesser	to injure

Vocabulary for immigration and racism (continued)

crier	to shout	jeter	to throw
haïr	to hate	c'est un sujet d'inquiétude	it's a matter for concern
exciter	to stir up	fomenter	to foment, stir up
attiser	to stir up	provoquer	to provoke
la bande	gang	menacer	to threaten
la haine (raciale)	(racial) hatred	intolérant	intolerant
l'agression (f)	attacks, mugging	insupportable	intolerable
l'attaque (f)	attack	raciste	racist
les injures (f)	insults	le/la lepéniste	supporter of Le Pen
la peur	fear	minoritaire	minority
la conduite	behaviour	de naissance	by birth
le comportement	behaviour	de souche	by origin
la culture	culture	naturalisé	naturalised
ne pas supporter	to be intolerant of	plein de préjugés	prejudiced
déchaîner	to unleash	en colère	angry
lancer	to throw, launch		

KEY POINT

- *immigré*: *immigrant* also exists; the difference is between the past and present participles. *Immigré* refers to someone who has already settled in the country.
- *Beur*: someone who was born in France but whose parents are North African by birth.
- *moeurs*: the *s* is pronounced on the end of this word.
- *fuir*: followed by a direct object: *il a fui l'oppression*.
- *préjugé*: the word *préjudice* should not be used in this context.
- *injures/injurier*: not 'injury/to injure'.
- *haïr*: see verb tables (pp. 74–76).
- *exciter/attiser*: *exciter* may be used with other passions, *attiser* is particularly associated with *haine*.
- *insupportable*: remember that words ending in *-able* and *-ible* are pronounced as though they had no *e* on the end.

2.6 Equality of opportunity

EDEXCEL	M4, M6
OCR	M4, M5
WJEC	M4, M6
NICCEA	M4, M5

The French government is working towards equality of opportunity for all: two important categories are women and the disabled. Laws are being considered and allowances have been introduced to improve the situation, but there is still some way to go.

Women

The French have in the past tended to be rather chauvinist, but they are making some effort to change. Promoting women to positions of importance began at the top, with several high-profile women being given senior posts in government.

Political reshuffles have not always favoured women ministers, however. In March 2000 one-third of the ministerial positions were held by women, but this was fewer than before and it was considered to be a retrograde step. Even so it is better than elsewhere.

> You may find a name you recognise being quoted in a different context if a ministerial reshuffle has taken place since the question was set.

Names to note in recent years have included:
Edith Cresson
Elisabeth Guigou
Martine Aubry
Ségolène Royal
Dominique Voynet

However, articles and interviews in the media make it clear that their path has not been easy and **they are still the exception rather than the rule**. A survey was carried out by the *Nouvel Économiste* of the heads of 65 major companies: they were asked: 'As far as your company profile allows, would you be prepared to appoint women to 30% of your top positions without any discrimination of salary, within three years?' The answers were interesting: 3 said yes, 22 said no and 40 would not commit themselves. All those who answered 'no' insisted it was not through sexual discrimination.

In fact, the area where most remains to be done is probably in the main workforce. As you have learnt already, the proportion of women unemployed is higher than men. More mothers than fathers take parental leave from work. Nevertheless, the position is vastly different from the one that existed at the end of the 1960s, when only 50% of women worked outside the home. The figure is over 80% now, and women make up 45% of the total workforce. **Employers are not allowed to pay women less than men for the same job.**

Women have had the right for some time to work at night in certain professions (e.g. health) but have been forbidden by French law to do so in many areas, including industry. This law has had to be changed to conform to EU policy.

Sexual harassment of women in the workplace is still quite prevalent.

Disability

The law requires money to be made available for training and integration (*insertion*) into employment, but not all disabled people have been able to take advantage of this. About 5% of those considered to be 'of working age' (under 60) work in a protected environment and just over twice that number in the ordinary workplace. Those who are unable, because of their disability, to find work are able to claim the *allocation aux adultes handicapés*, which also entitles them to free sickness insurance. Other allowances are available for the severely disabled who need regular care and there is help with fees for special education. Most companies are required to make 10% of their jobs available to the disabled, including *mutilés de guerre* (war wounded); the latter are also entitled to priority seats on buses and the underground. Money is also available to help with living expenses.

Vocabulary for equality of opportunity

l'égalité (f)	equality	concourir	to compete
l'égalité des chances	equal opportunities	faire concurrence à	to compete with
l'égalité des sexes	sexual equality	empêcher	to prevent
l'égalité des droits	equal rights	protéger	to protect
la condition féminine	the position of women	vivre sa vie	to live one's life
la catégorie	category	avoir accès à	to have access to
le changement	change	accéder à	to have access to
la main d'oeuvre	workforce	prendre des mesures	to take steps
le harcèlement sexuel	sexual harassment	bouleverser	to overturn
la pression	pressure	traiter d'égal à égal	to treat as equals
le handicap	handicap	être sur un pied d'égalité	to be on equal terms
l'invalidité (f)	disability	chauvin	chauvinist
l'incapacité (f)	disability	à l'extérieur	outside (the home)
les handicapés	the disabled	interdit	forbidden
les mutilés de guerre	war wounded	féministe	feminist
le fauteuil roulant	wheelchair	difficile	difficult
les béquilles (f)	crutches	handicapé	disabled
l'autonomie (f)	independence	total	complete
favoriser	to favour	partiel, -elle	partial
promouvoir	to promote	autonome	independent
permettre	to allow, permit	spécialisé	specialised
à travail égal salaire égal	equal work for equal pay	souffrant d'un handicap sévère	severely disabled

- *changement*: remember that *change* is only used in *bureau de change*.
- *handicap*: one of the few words beginning with *h* which does not have *l'*.
- *promouvoir*: a compound of *mouvoir* (see verb lists on pp. 74–76).
- *protéger, accéder*: both belong to the *espérer* group of verbs.
- *difficile*: no apologies for reminding you how to spell this word!

Useful acronyms for this topic (all sections)

- AFPA – Association pour la formation professionnelle des adultes
- ANPE – Agence nationale pour l'emploi
- ASSEDIC – Associations pour l'emploi dans l'industrie et le commerce
- DDASS – Direction départementale de l'action sanitaire et sociale
- DRASS – Direction régionale des affaires sanitaires et sociales
- DOM-TOM – Départements d'outre-mer/Territoires d'outre-mer
- HLM – Habitations à loyer modéré
- ILM – Immeubles à loyer moyen
- SMIC – Salaire minimum interprofessionnel de croissance
- UNEDIC – Union nationale pour l'emploi dans l'industrie et le commerce
- URSSAF – Union pour le recouvrement des cotisations de la sécurité sociale et des allocations familiales
- ZUP – Zone à urbaniser en priorité

You will not be expected to know exactly what these acronyms stand for unless you are studying them for the topic paper/discussion or for your coursework, but it is helpful to recognise what they are when you see or hear them. Most are self-explanatory. The DDASS and DRASS are the social services departments; the SMIC is the guaranteed minimum wage; people receiving it are known familiarly as *Smicards*. URSSAF deals with collecting social security contributions.

Progress check

When you have learnt the vocabulary for this section, write down the following key words, then check them with the lists.

Give the French for: district, neighbourhood, to commute, run-down, contribution, retirement, insecure, to be entitled to, widespread, job-seeker, to get unemployment benefit, to increase, at least, almost, social outcasts, volunteer, to despise, prejudice, heritage, to integrate

Give the English for: le harcèlement sexuel, la pression, l'autonomie, concourir, vivre sa vie, chauvin, de souche, minoritaire, exciter, la haine, la foule, déchaîner, maghrébin, l'asile, clandestin, muni de, maltraiter, marginalisé, les démunis, s'inscrire

Grammar

2.7 The Passive

Key points from AS

• **The Passive**
  AS Study Guide pp. 79–80

You learnt how to form and use the present tense of the passive for AS Level. For A2 you need also to be able to use other tenses; they are just as straightforward as the present. Many students panic when they try to form the passive, but there really is no need to do so as the construction is formed, word for word, in the same way as in English.

A verb is **active** if the action is being **performed by its subject**:

Le patron renvoie les ouvriers – 'The boss sacks the workers'. The verb is *renvoie*, active because the *patron* is performing the action.

A verb is **passive** if the subject is **having the action done to it**:

Les ouvriers sont renvoyés par le patron – 'The workers are sacked by the boss'. The verb is *sont renvoyés*, passive because the workers are having the action of sacking done to them by the boss.

Formation of other tenses

Don't confuse the passive with the continuous present or past tenses: 'They are taking on staff' is simply *Ils/elles embauchent* (present tense) and 'You were receiving' is *Tu recevais* (imperfect tense).

Use the appropriate tense of *être*, plus the past participle which **agrees with the subject** in the same way that an adjective agrees with a noun. There is no *avoir/être* divide; all verbs use *être* to form the passive. (In fact, verbs which take *être* in their compound tenses cannot be made passive; think of their meanings and you will see why. You cannot say 'they will have been arrived' or 'she was being comed'.)

The **future passive** uses the future tense of *être* plus the past participle:

L'argent sera payé demain – 'The money will be paid tomorrow'.

The **Imperfect passive** uses the imperfect tense of *être* plus the past participle:

Les immigrants étaient maltraités dans leur propre pays – 'The immigrants were mistreated in their own country'.

The **conditional passive** uses the conditional tense of *être* plus the past participle:

Il a dit que la situation serait réglée – 'He said the situation would be sorted out'.

The **perfect passive** uses the perfect tense of *être* plus the past participle:

Le mendiant a été arrêté par l'agent – 'The beggar was arrested by the policeman'.

The **pluperfect passive** uses the pluperfect tense of *être* plus the past participle:

Le vagabond avait été relâché deux heures plus tôt – 'The tramp had been released two hours earlier'.

The **future perfect passive** uses the future perfect tense of *être* plus the past participle:

Leurs papiers auront été contrôlés trois fois – 'Their papers will have been checked three times'.

The **conditional perfect passive** uses the conditional perfect tense of *être* plus the past participle:

Les immigrés clandestins auraient été mis en garde à vue – 'The illegal immigrants would have been taken in for questioning' (or 'have apparently been taken in for questioning').

The French for 'by' after a passive verb is always *par*.

2.8 Imperfect subjunctive

Key points from AS

- **Past historic endings**
  AS Study Guide
  pp. 125–126
- **Use of the subjunctive**
  AS Study Guide
  pp.111–112

The imperfect subjunctive is extremely rare in French now (the present subjunctive is normally used instead) but if you are reading an older set text or a very formal piece of prose you may meet it. Most parts of it are never used because they are so unwieldy and sound outdated. The whole verb is given below for reference purposes, but in practice you are unlikely to meet anything other than the third person singular (*il/elle/on*).

There are three groups of endings, linked with the endings of the past historic tense.

Verbs in -ai group	*verbs in -is group*	*verbs in -us group*
(que) je fouillasse	j'écrivisse	je dusse
tu fouillasses	tu écrivisses	tu dusses
il fouillât	**il écrivît**	**il dût**
nous fouillassions	nous écrivissions	nous dussions
vous fouillassiez	vous écrivissiez	vous dussiez
ils fouillassent	ils écrivissent	ils dussent

The exceptions, as with the past historic tense, are *venir* and *tenir*: *(que) je vinsse, tu vinsses, il vînt, nous vinssions, vous vinssiez, ils vinssent*

The most useful verbs to recognise in the imperfect subjunctive are: *eût* (from *avoir*), *fût* (*être*), *fît* (*faire*), *pût* (*pouvoir*), *prît* (*prendre*), *dût* (*devoir*) and *sût* (*savoir*). Examples:

> *Quoiqu'il dût quitter son emploi il n'était pas triste* – 'Although he had to leave his job he was not sad'
> *Je ne croyais pas qu'elle fût si courageuse* – 'I didn't think she was so brave'

Progress check

The passive

Translate into French (answers on p.154).

1 Contributions had been paid by the workforce.

2 Help will be provided by Restos du Coeur.

3 The homeless were rejected by society.

4 The refugees were quickly rehabilitated.

5 He was afraid that hatred would be stirred up by the crowd.

Translate into English:

6 L'appartement a été loué à un jeune couple.

7 Les allocations seront versées par la caisse.

8 Les chiffres auraient été améliorés cette année.

9 Les immigrés ont été menacés par les adhérents de Le Pen.

10 Le travail au noir ne serait pas toléré.

Imperfect subjunctive

From which verbs do the following come?
allât, contînt, fît, eût, connût, promît, bût, criât, fût, sût

How to answer

2.9 Sentence-completion

Much of the advice given in Chapter 1 about Q/A and grid-completion also applies to questions of this type.

You may need to add a single word or a short phrase to complete the sense. Because the sentence is started for you, there is an additional element to consider: your words must fit in with what is already there. So read the beginning of the sentence carefully, and don't include in your answer information that is given there. Even more than the 'trigger words' in Q/A and grid-completion exercises, **the words you are given here should lead you to the right part of the passage**. You must also make sure that your words continue linguistically from the first half; this will almost certainly mean adapting the words of the passage to fit in with the construction.

Here is an answer that could show comprehension but be wrong from the point of view of language:

> *Le taux de chômage a **diminution** au mois de juin.*

You have shown that you understood that there was a reduction in the rate of unemployment, but you would almost certainly be penalised for using a noun (*diminution*) instead of a verb (*diminué*). There is no excuse in this case, as *a* was already there and should have indicated that the perfect tense was needed.

2.10 Gap-fill

There are two types of gap-fill tests: (i) those in which you choose your own word (or short phrase) to complete the sense, and (ii) those in which you are given a list from which you have to pick the correct word. The first type counts as 'productive French' and is likely to be taken into account in any paper in which the quality of your written French is assessed; the second type usually counts as an 'objective test' and is not assessed for quality of language.

For both types it's very important to read the summary, including the gaps, before you start; not only will this help you with the structure of the sentences, but it will also aid your understanding the passage of which it is a résumé.

(i) As with sentence-completion, look at what has been stated already in the words preceding the gap. Then look at the words that follow the gap, particularly the one immediately after it. Take both these things into account when you choose your word to fill the gap.

Examples of incorrect gap-filling:

- *Le taux de chômage a atteint environ **à peu près** trois millions.*
  Environ, meaning 'about' is already there, so *à peu près* is unnecessary.

- *Les gens qui dorment dans les bouches de métro n'ont pas **sans domicile fixe**.*
  The negative is there already, so *sans* is wrong; *de domicile fixe* is the correct answer.

- *Les bénévoles **se souviennent** les problèmes de l'hiver dernier.*
  Here the word chosen has the correct meaning ('recall' or 'remember'), but *se souvenir* is followed by *de* so it isn't grammatically correct. The examiners were looking for *se rappellent*. However, if you have forgotten *se rappellent* and know that *se souvenir* is followed by *de*, it's almost certainly permissible to make a slight adjustment to the text; change *les* to *des*, and your language is correct (this wouldn't work, of course, in the case of a language-based exercise).

Check to see whether a particular idiom, or the subjunctive, is required.

One other thing to watch for in a gap-fill exercise is *le/la/les* and *leur* used as **pronouns**. It's tempting to assume that these are definite articles or the possessive adjective respectively, but this may not be the case. Look at the following example:

On va les _____ en leur _____ de l'aide financière.

The structure of the sentence shows that *les* must be the direct object pronoun and *leur* the indirect object pronoun; so the gaps would be filled something like this:

*On va les **aider** en leur **donnant** de l'aide financière.*

(ii) A list of words to choose from may include of a variety of parts of speech or consist of all the same type (usually adjectives or verbs). Each has its advantages and disadvantages.

- If you have several different parts of speech it should be easy to decide which words will not fit grammatically, and reject these immediately. Be careful, however, that you choose a word that reflects the meaning of the original passage; your choice might make sense but be incorrect in the context.

- If all the words are the same part of speech you should still be able to reject some immediately: a feminine plural adjective could not agree with a masculine singular noun, for example, and an *-ent* verb ending would be wrong after *nous*. But there is still a choice to be made, so the passage and the résumé must be read carefully. The list will usually contain more than the required number of words – in fact, up to twice as many as you need – so there are bound to be some that could fit in but are actually wrong.

Practice examination questions

1 Reading

This is an exercise based largely on statistics. Your answers must be in French, but there is no need to write full sentences. Because figures are involved it should be easy to find the place in the text where the answer is likely to be, but you will have to be very precise in your definition or you will give the wrong information. Check the answers carefully and see if you omitted any important factors.

Lisez le texte *La décrue continue* et expliquez EN FRANÇAIS les chiffres et les termes suivants, selon le sens du texte.

Exemple: 2 499 400 – nombre de chômeurs en février

CHÔMAGE: FORT RECUL EN FÉVRIER
La décrue continue
Le nombre des demandeurs d'emploi est le plus bas depuis 1991

Sur un an, 392 000 chômeurs en moins.

Pour la première fois depuis neuf ans, le nombre de demandeurs d'emploi est passé sous la barre des 2,5 millions. La décrue du chômage, amorcée à l'été 1997, s'est ainsi accentuée en février (–2,6%, soit 65 500 chômeurs en moins).

Fin février, 2 499 400 demandeurs d'emploi étaient inscrits dans les fichiers de l'ANPE, le niveau le plus bas depuis le printemps 1991, selon le baromètre officiel publié hier par le ministère de l'Emploi.

Le taux de chômage au sens du BIT (Bureau international du Travail), calculé différemment, a aussi reculé, passant de 10,5% à 10,2% de la population active, son plus bas taux depuis avril 1992. Son taux le plus élevé (12,6%) avait été atteint en juin 1997, au moment de l'arrivée de Lionel Jospin à la tête du gouvernement.

Sur un an, le nombre de demandeurs d'emploi de la catégorie 1 a reculé de 13,6%, représentant 392 200 chômeurs en moins, soit près de trois fois la baisse, déjà importante, enregistrée en 1998 (–135 200). Cette catégorie est constituée de demandeurs d'emploi immédiatement disponibles et à la recherche d'un emploi à durée indéterminée et à temps plein. "Le fait de passer sous une barre, même si elle est encore très élevée – nous en sommes conscients – est, pour le gouvernement, un profond encouragement à poursuivre sa politique économique et sociale", s'est réjoui le Premier ministre en visite à Toulouse. Dans ses dernières prévisions, l'INSEE table sur un taux de 10% fin juin. Le souhait de M. Jospin de voir "cette année un taux de chômage à un chiffre" pourrait se réaliser très vite. De son côté,

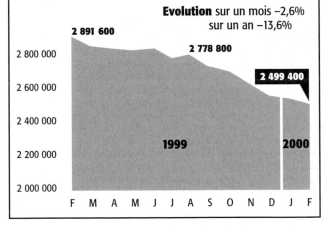

Chômage en France
Evolution mensuelle en demandeurs d'emploi

Evolution sur un mois –2,6%
sur un an –13,6%

2 891 600
2 778 800
2 499 400
2 800 000
2 600 000
2 400 000
2 200 000
2 000 000
1999
2000
F M A M J J A S O N D J F

la ministre de l'Emploi, Martine Aubry, a estimé que le gouvernement était "en train de gagner la bataille du chômage", grâce à "la politique de l'emploi" (35 heures, emplois-jeunes, loi contre l'exclusion) et à "la croissance forte du dernier trimestre 1999 qui se poursuit". Elle a souligné que la baisse du chômage intervient alors que "la population active s'accroit de 200 000 par an". La ministre s'est félicitée que la baisse du chômage profite à toutes les catégories de demandeurs d'emploi: le chômage de longue durée, le chômage des jeunes et "surtout que les emplois aujourd'hui sont des emplois moins précaires".

Remember that the comma (*virgule*) represents the decimal point in French: 2,5 is *deux virgule cinq* (2.5).

(a) 65 500
(b) 10,2%
(c) 13,6%
(d) catégorie 1
(e) 10%
(f) 200 000

Practice examination questions (continued)

2 Listening

Écoutez l'extrait au sujet du SMIC, puis complétez les phrases selon le sens du passage:

(a) Le SMIC varie .... (1)

(b) On trouve généralement des Smicards au sein des compagnies qui ne sont pas
.... (1)

(c) À cause des lois à propos de l'égalité des sexes, l'écart entre les hommes et les
femmes devient .... (2)

(d) La raison citée, c'est que les postes de responsabilité
.... (2)

(e) Le pourcentage des jeunes Smicards a
.... (1)

(f) Les jeunes se lancent plus tard dans le marché du travail parce qu'ils
.... (2)

(g) Quand ils deviennent plus vieux, ceux qui ont été payés au SMIC pendant leur
jeunesse .... (1)

3 Reading

Répondez EN ANGLAIS aux questions ci-dessous.

TRAVAIL DES FEMMES

L'égalité, même la nuit!

Après des années de résistance, la France s'apprête à appliquer la directive européenne autorisant le travail de nuit des femmes dans tous les secteurs d'activité, y compris celui de l'industrie. Au nom de l'égalité des sexes. L'occasion de réclamer une meilleure garantie d'encadrement... pour tous!

Elle se couche à l'heure où les autres se lèvent , se prépare à aller travailler quand la nuit commence à tomber, ne fait ses courses qu'à l'ouverture ou à la fermeture du supermarché du coin, confie son fils à sa nourrice le soir jusqu'au lendemain... L'emploi du temps de Christine n'est pas différent de celui de ses collègues de jour, il est tout simplement décalé. Cette jeune femme de 27 ans travaille de nuit comme aide-soignante dans une maison de retraite de la région parisienne. Ses horaires : 20 h – 6 h. Une vie à l'envers, à contre-courant... « Tout est une question d'organisation », assure-t-elle d'un ton tranquille. Dans les hôpitaux, les commissariats, les usines, les moyens de transport... plus de 800 000 femmes travaillent, habituellement ou occasionnellement, de nuit. Soit près de 8% des femmes actives, contre 22% des hommes. Beaucoup d'entreprises ont passé

outre à l'interdiction du travail de nuit féminin, toujours en vigueur dans certains secteurs professionnels, en particulier dans l'industrie, profitant de ce que le droit communautaire prévaut sur le droit français. Depuis des années, Bruxelles ne cesse de pointer du doigt ce qu'elle considère comme un facteur de discrimination, notamment en termes d'évolution de carrière. Le système de primes représente également un avantage considérable, surtout pour les plus bas salaires.

S'il accorde certains avantages, le travail nocturne a aussi ses revers, autant pour les hommes que pour les femmes. Notamment dans le domaine de la santé et de la sécurité. Pour sortir du chômage, nombreux sont les salariés prêts à endurer des conditions de travail plus que pénibles. Avec de tels horaires, difficile également de concilier carrière professionnelle et vie privée.

Examiner's tip

You should be able to use your knowledge of other topics when answering comprehension questions; in this case the chapters on law, on Europe or on politics may help you.

(a) Why has France had to change its laws relating to women working at night? (2)

(b) Describe the pattern of Christine's day. (4)

(c) What is her job? (2)

(d) What statistics does she quote? (3)

(e) Why have some firms felt able to employ women at night although French law currently forbids it? (1)

(f) What is the reason given by Brussels for the change in the law? (2)

(g) What other advantage may be gained by some workers? (1)

(h) What disadvantages of night work are mentioned? (3)

4 Reading and writing

Three of only 62 women among the 577 deputies in the National Assembly

Frenchwomen shun party parity

A LAW which demands an equal number of male and female candidates in French elections has hit a snag because women are proving extremely reluctant to become politicians.

When the much heralded *parité* law was ratified in June after fierce wrangling, it was described by Nicole Pery, the Secretary for Women, as "historic for women and their progress towards equality". But the law's critics denounced it as unworkable and parties across the political spectrum are beginning to agree. They have discovered that they need to recruit more than 40,000 women to stand as potential councillors in next year's municipal elections or face major fines.

"Parties are having to look to their campaigners and local supporters to fill the electoral lists," said Anne Hidalgo, an adviser to Mme Pery. "There's a lot of talk that politicians' wives will find themselves pressed into service, and no doubt that will be the case." Mme Hidalgo, who is standing for the first time in a southern Paris district, added: "We are encouraging professional women to think of themselves as potential politicians but they are often loath to think of themselves in that way."

But, just as many women are reluctant to start a political career, men who have grown used to the job are struggling to come to terms with the prospect of forced retirement. "The real problem is not with the women. It's with the men," Mme Hidalgo said. "They are not happy with being asked to make way for women."

The traditionally male-dominated world of French politics means that only 62 of the 577 deputies in the National Assembly are women.

That kind of statistic is now proving a major problem for political parties, whose claims to a reformed and modernised attitude convince few women – even those who have agreed to stand.

Lisez le passage *Frenchwomen shun party parity*, puis donnez EN FRANÇAIS les renseignements suivants.

(a) Loi dont il s'agit.

(b) Raison pour laquelle cette loi ne semble pas réussir.

(c) Situation qui existe pour les partis.

(d) Catégories de femmes visées comme candidates par les partis.

(e) L'opinion des hommes vis-à-vis de la situation.

(f) Résumez en français la situation mentionnée dans les deux derniers paragraphes. Qu'est-ce que vous en pensez?

Chapter 3

Les sciences et la technologie

The following topics are covered in this chapter:

- Scientific heritage of France and current research
- Satellites and space travel
- France and the technological revolution
- Ethical implications of scientific and technological advances

- Grammar: Inversion after adverbs; Revision: Present participle; reflexive verbs; idioms and other special cases
- How to answer: Non-verbal exercises

Science and technology

After studying this chapter you should be able to:

- understand how science and technology have developed in France
- identify the vocabulary you need to answer questions on these topics
- understand when to turn round verb and subject after adverbs
- use the present participle and reflexive verbs with more confidence
- improve your skill in non-verbal exercises

3.1 Scientific heritage of France and current research

| AQA | M4, M6 |
| OCR | M4, M5 |

France has always had an outstanding reputation in the sciences. In the 17th century there were Pascal, a mathematician, scientist and philosopher, and Fermat, the originator of the famous 'last theorem', a noted mathematician. In the 18th century came Lavoisier, who is generally considered to be the father of modern chemistry, followed by Gay-Lussac a chemist and physicist, and Ampère whose work on electrodynamics is well known. The Montgolfier brothers were pioneers in the field of balloon flight. The 19th century brought Becquerel, who first recognised that uranium emits radiation, and Perrin who worked on molecules and cathode rays. The 19th and 20th centuries have seen some of the greatest names in the history of science:

- Louis Pasteur, who is best known for his development of a vaccine against rabies and for inventing the process of pasteurising milk.
- Marie and Pierre Curie, who discovered radium.
- Their daughter Irène Joliot-Curie and her husband Frédéric who worked in the fields of artificial radiation and nuclear physics.
- Mandelbrot who has conducted distinguished research into fractal geometry.

In all, there have been more than thirty French Nobel prize winners for physics, chemistry and medicine.

Check the CNRS website (www.cnrs.fr) for the latest information

The French reputation for science continues to grow; superconductivity, molecular science and plate tectonics are just three of the fields in which researchers are currently engaged. The **CNRS** (*Centre national de la recherche scientifique*) oversees 1300 separate research units. Other institutes include the *Institut Pasteur*, the *Institut national de la santé et de la recherche médicale* (**INSERM**), and the *Institut de la recherche agronomique*, which is a centre for research into horticultural and agricultural matters (with particular emphasis placed on the study of vines).

Cité des Sciences et de l'Industrie

In order to celebrate France's past achievements in the sciences and to focus on the future, the Cité des Sciences et de l'Industrie was built in 1986 at La Villette in Paris. It covers a seven-acre site and offers exhibitions, shows, a planetarium, a space station, 'hands-on' exhibits, greenhouses, a vast cinema screen and many other attractions which open visitors' minds to the wonders of science. A monthly magazine *Science Actualités* is produced, and is linked with an exhibition area which is itself conceived like a magazine, with monthly 'editions' and daily and weekly news items.

Medical advances

The Institut Pasteur, founded by Louis Pasteur, is a centre for **biomedical research**. It has over twenty affiliated centres worldwide. It was at its centre in Paris that the HIV virus (*VIH* in French) was first isolated, and work continues on research into the virus, specifically aimed at finding a vaccine to fight Aids. At the INSERM research is being undertaken in the fields of **genetics, hormones and immunology**. In a drive to attract the best scientists it offers scholarships, prizes, lectures and training. There are also a number of commercially-funded research laboratories.

French researchers are playing an important part in deciphering the information transmitted by chromosomes; as a result of their work, progress has been made in the treatment by gene therapy of Alzheimer's disease.

Examiner's tip

If science is one of the topics in your specification, don't be afraid that you won't be able to understand the reading or listening passage; the language will not be too technical, and anyway most scientific words are very similar to the English. Terms such as 'genetic engineering', however, might be used as this is a matter of ongoing interest in the media.

Vocabulary for scientific and medical research

la réputation	reputation	le gène	gene
la renommée	fame	la génétique	genetics
les recherches (f)	research	le généticien	geneticist
la découverte	discovery	les manipulations génétiques	genetic engineering
la réussite	success		
la réalisation	fulfilment	développer	to develop
le progrès	progress	découvrir	to discover
l'unité (f)	unit	être occupé à	to be engaged in
le domaine	field, area	combattre	to fight
le chercheur/la chercheuse	researcher	entreprendre	to undertake
le pionnier	pioneer	jouer un rôle	to play a part
le scientifique	scientist	déchiffrer	to decipher
le savant	scientist, scholar	maîtriser	to master
le laboratoire	laboratory	alléger	to alleviate
la percée	break-through	réussir	to succeed
la mise au point	perfecting	réaliser	to achieve, fulfil
la lutte	struggle, fight	être atteint (de)	to suffer from
le but	aim, goal	mettre au point	to perfect, finalise
l'analyse (f)	analysis	être connu pour	to be known for
le vaccin	vaccine	se raviser	to change one's mind
la rage	rabies	célèbre	famous
le virus	virus	(bien) connu	well-known
la maladie	illness	éminent	distinguished
le/la malade	patient	génétique	genetic
la thérapie	therapy	génique	gene (adj.)
le sang	blood	thérapeutique	therapeutic
VIH	HIV	sanguin	(of) blood
le sida	Aids	scientifique	scientific
le clonage	cloning	dernier	latest
l'avancée (f)	step forward, advance	contaminé	contaminated
le remède	remedy, cure	à l'essai	on trial

- *réussite/réalisation*: *réalisation* is the carrying out of a project, which does not necessarily mean that it has succeeded in its aims. Both words might be translated as 'achievement'.
- *progrès*: usually plural.
- *scientifique/savant*: the first is used for a scientist at any level; *savant* refers to someone with an established reputation.
- *rage*: don't confuse this with 'rage'.
- *découvrir*: endings are like those of *ouvrir*.
- *alléger*: this might look like 'allege', but if you look closely at it you will see that it contains the word *léger*, 'light'.
- *génique*: used in the phrase *thérapie génique*, 'gene therapy'.
- *sanguin*: e.g. *groupe sanguin*, 'blood group'.

3.2 Satellites and space travel

OCR ▶ M4, M5

The *Centre national d'études spatiales* (CNES) was founded in 1961. Collaboration with the European Space Agency led to the development of the European rocket **Ariane**. Its launch site is near Kourou in French Guiana (*Guyane Française*) on the Atlantic coast of South America. The rocket has been used to launch many satellites, notably those of the SPOT (*Satellites pour l'observation de la Terre*) programme. In 1992 the Topex-Poséidon satellite, a joint venture with the USA, was launched; one of its tasks was to study the variation in the level of the oceans. Other countries pay to use Ariane to launch their satellites (or satellites with their research programmes on board), so that it becomes a commercial proposition and achieves some financial return for the huge costs of development.

Ariane was first launched in 1979; Ariane 5 launched a space observatory on its first commercial flight in December 1999. The first Frenchwoman in space was Claudie-Andrée Deshayes.

Impress the examiner: keep your eyes and ears open for details of the launching of the Ariane rocket; an up-to-date reference in a topic essay or discussion or in coursework is very valuable.

Vocabulary for satellites and space travel

i'ère spatiale	space age	les données	data
l'espace (m)	space	le/la spationaute	spaceman/woman
le satellite	satellite	l'astronaute	astronaut
la fusée	rocket	le/la cosmonaute	cosmonaut
l'engin spatial	spacecraft	lancer	to launch
la navette	shuttle	explorer	to explore
le lancement	launch	sonder	to explore
l'aire (f) de lancement	launch site	orbiter	to orbit
le base de lancement	space port	mettre en/sur orbite	to put into orbit
la rampe de lancement	launch pad	atterrir	to land
l'orbite (f)	orbit	amerrir	to splash down
l'observatoire (m)	observatory	alunir	to land on the moon
la spatiologie	space science	spatial	space (adj.)
les voyages interplanétaires	space travel	à bord	on board

- *explorer/sonder*: *explorer* is a general word, *sonder* is used more specifically. It also means 'to survey' or 'to take soundings of'.
- *atterrir/amerrir/alunir*: note the precise vocabulary associated with the place of landing.
- *astronaute* is used for Americans, *cosmonaute* for Russians.

3.3 France and the technological revolution

AQA	M4, M6
EDEXCEL	M4, M6
OCR	M4, M5
WJEC	M4, M6
NICCEA	M4, M5

Key points from AS

- **The Internet**
  AS Study Guide pp. 23–24
- **Education, training and work (IT)**
  AS Study Guide chapter 5

Examiner's tip

Try to find an example of a construction involving the use of new technology from an area you know well, if you are using this as a topic; a picture (or better still a photograph you have taken yourself) will really underline your interest in the subject.

Watch TV adverts for Renault as proof of this; they are a fruitful source of examples of the latest technology.

Despite the *fameux retard français* – the fact that the French are rarely the first to climb on the bandwagon of technological progress – when their imagination is caught they are eager to adopt new methods of communication and other technological advances. **Use of the Internet is fast becoming widespread commercially**, and is being extended into schools and the home. The delay in becoming involved in the Web can partly be put down to the success of Minitel, a system that has existed for many years in France. You will have noticed that many news reports and advertisements are followed by a telephone number and the Minitel number and code. Its services include directories, leisure activities, travel agencies and many other 'yellow pages'-type companies. Minitel is so successful that for some time the ordinary French person saw no need to use the Web. Now, however, use of the Internet is spreading quickly; you have only to open a French newspaper or magazine to see advertisements for access providers, recommendations for search engines, and reviews of websites. News items and advertisements now are more likely to conclude with a website or e-mail address than a Minitel code number.

The Internet is not, of course, the only advance in communications technology, or indeed of technology in general. The end of the 20th/beginning of the 21st century is a time of great progress, and if a country is to keep up with, or ahead of, its economic competitors it must adapt to new methods of working and introduce its own variations. So the electronics and telecommunications industries are extremely important. In this field a famous name is **Dassault**; the company is involved in projects of many sorts, including missile-guidance systems. **Alcatel** (now Alcatel-Alsthom), one of the foremost telecommunications companies in the world, is French. **Airbus Industrie** continues to win prestigious orders worldwide for its passenger jets.

Transport, urban and rail transport in particular, is an area in which France has traditionally been a leader. The TGV is an example of this, as is the Météor (the fast metro line) in Paris. Car companies have to compete in the world market by constantly updating their automobile technology. Several cities have introduced trams to help to solve their local transport problems.

New technology has also played a part in the building of many constructions in France in recent years; obvious examples are the Channel Tunnel, the Centre Pompidou and the Pont de Normandie, but there are many others.

Elsewhere, **digital technology** is becoming an important element of leisure in the home; and the *carte à puce* (smart card) was invented by a Frenchman.

Vocabulary for the technological revolution (All the vocabulary associated with the IT element of work and training in the AS Study Guide is also essential)

l'ère informatique	the computer age	l'internaute	surfer
la technologie	technology	la mise à jour	update
le retard	delay	le bouquet	package
l'essor (m)	expansion	la qualité du son	quality of sound
l'informatique (f)	computer science	le téléphone portable	mobile phone
l'électronique (f)	electronics	le lecteur de disques compacts	CD player
la carte à puce	smart card		
la technologie avancée	advanced technology	(s') étendre	to extend
le réseau	network	être engagé	to be involved
l'atout (m)	trump, asset	mettre à jour	to update
le défaut	failing	naviguer (sur Internet)	to surf (Internet)
l'avantage (m)	advantage	connaître un grand succès	to enjoy great success
l'inconvénient (m)	disadvantage	connaître un échec	to suffer a failure
l'ingénieur	engineer	communiquer	to communicate

Vocabulary for the technological revolution (continued)

l'ordinateur (m)	computer	séduire	to charm, appeal to
la puce	microchip	suivre le mouvement	to jump on the bandwagon
le clavier	keyboard		
le matériel	hardware	brancher	to plug in, connect
le logiciel	software	technologique	technological
la programmation	programming	démodé	outdated
la conception assistée par ordinateur	computer-aided design	à jour	up-to-date
		numérique	digital
les images de synthèse	computer graphics	numérisé	digitalised
la compétence en informatique	computer literacy	électronique	electronic
		de haute technologie	high-tech
la Toile (mondiale)	(world-wide) Web	de pointe	high-tech, latest
le site Web	website	sophistiqué	sophisticated
le fournisseur d'accès	access provider	innovateur, -trice	innovative
le moteur de recherche	search engine	fiable	accurate, reliable
le courrier électronique	e-mail	généré par ordinateur	computer-generated
le raccordement	connection (to telephone network)	initié à l'informatique	computer-literate

KEY POINT

- *courrier électronique*: several anglicised forms exist (*e-mail, le mel, le mél*) but it's more impressive if you can show that you know the proper French version.
- *bouquet*: 'package' in the sense of several things being offered together as an incentive to buy.
- *étendre, s'étendre*: the reflexive form is used when there is no object following.
- *électronique*: don't confuse this with 'electric'.

3.4 Ethical implications of scientific and technological advances

AQA	M4, M6
OCR	M4, M5

As with so many other topics in the AS and A2 specifications, the implications of scientific research and of the technological revolution for France and the francophone countries are very similar to those in the UK or indeed in the rest of the western world. You need, therefore, to understand what these implications are; once again, this underlines the importance of watching (or listening to) the news and reading a good-quality newspaper regularly. If you then learn the vocabulary associated with these subjects you should have little difficulty in understanding passages relating to them. You should also be able to discuss or write about them with confidence.

These are some of the issues that may arise:

- Is euthanasia justified if a disease is incurable and/or terminal?
- Is experimentation on animals justified if the quality of life for humans is likely to be improved as a result of the research?
- What are the moral implications of cloning?
- Is it right to spend billions of francs on building rockets when much of the world's population does not have enough to eat?
- Does the introduction of new technology mean that thousands of people are put out of work?
- Should research take place into producing weapons that will kill more people?
- Should access to the Internet be restricted for children on moral grounds?
- Is the Internet safe from the point of view of data protection?
- What are the risks of using a mobile phone while driving, cycling or walking?
- Does using a mobile phone on the train or in other public places infringe the personal liberty of other people in the vicinity?
- What are the risks of producing genetically modified food?

Examiner's tip

Remember that you may be asked to support a viewpoint with which you do not personally agree, so be prepared to present both sides of an argument.

Any of these topics would make an interesting subject for a discussion, essay or coursework, but most Awarding Bodies require you to relate it to France or a francophone country.

55

Vocabulary for ethical implications of scientific research

l'éthique (f)	ethics	mettre fin à	to put an end to
la moralité	morality	aborder	to tackle
la responsabilité	responsibility	créer	to create
l'intégrité (f)	integrity	modifier	to modify
le problème	problem	traiter	to treat
le dilemme	dilemma	manipuler	to manipulate
l'implication (f)	implication	se passer de	to do without
les retombées (f)	side-effects	interdire	to forbid
le sentiment	feeling	autoriser	to authorise, allow
le point de vue	point of view	condamner	to condemn
le risque	risk	approuver	to approve of
le danger	danger	réclamer	to demand
la souffrance	suffering	faire des expériences	to experiment
l'euthanasie (f)	euthanasia	tirer la sonnette d'alarme	to sound the alarm
la qualité de vie	quality of life	éthique	ethical
le clonage	cloning	moral	moral
la vivisection	vivisection	contraire à la morale	unethical
l'expérimentation animale	experimenting on animals	justifié	justified
		justifiable	justifiable
la greffe	transplant	indispensable	essential
l'éprouvette (f)	test-tube	essentiel, -elle	essential
le cobaye	guinea-pig	injuste	unfair
le site rose	erotic web-site	inacceptable	unacceptable
la pornographie	pornography	atroce	atrocious
s'opposer à	to oppose	dangereux, -se	dangerous
être d'accord avec	to agree with	cruel, -elle	cruel
justifier	to justify	à des fins (+ adj.)	with the purpose of
améliorer	to improve	la fin justifie les moyens	the end justifies the means
risquer	to risk		

Useful acronyms

OGM (*organismes génétiquement modifiés*) – GM products

ADN – DNA

- *responsabilité*: remember the *a* (not *i*) in the middle of this word.
- *problème*: it may look feminine, but this is a masculine word.
- *créer*: past participle is *créé*; don't leave the acute accent off the second *e*.
- *se passer de*: beware; when followed by *de* this does not mean 'to happen'.
- *autoriser*: it's sometimes easier to use this than *permettre*, which is followed by *à* with the person. Example: *Les expériences ont été autorisées*.
- *approuver*: no need for *de*; example: *je n'approuve pas sa conduite*.
- *expérience*: can be 'experience', but in a scientific context it means 'experiment'.

KEY POINT

Progress check

When you have learnt the vocabulary for this section, write down the following key words, then check them with the lists.

Give the French for: research, discovery, pioneer, to undertake, blood (adjective), HIV, space, data, on board, smart card, update, disadvantage, to be involved, to communicate, innovative, computer literate, side effects, suffering, to condemn, unethical.

Give the English for: déchiffrer, la percée, réaliser, la mise au point, la rage, sonder, amerrir, l'essor, le réseau, l'atout, le matériel, naviguer, numérique, fiable, le Sida, le cobaye, se passer de, améliorer, injuste, la puce.

Grammar

3.5 Inversion after adverbs

The verb and subject should be **inverted (turned round) after certain adverbs**. The most common of these are:

- *à peine* – 'hardly', 'scarcely'.

  À peine entendons-nous parler d'une invention que cette invention devient démodée – 'We scarcely hear of an invention before it becomes out-dated'.

- *aussi* – 'and so'.

  Le vaccin sera utilisé tout de suite, aussi va-t-il sauver la vie à beaucoup de malades – 'The vaccine will be used immediately, so it will save the life of many sick people'.

Always check to see whether *aussi* is followed by an inverted verb; if so, it must mean 'and so'.

- *peut-être* – 'perhaps'.

  Peut-être un remède pour le sida sera-t-il trouvé – 'Perhaps a cure for Aids will be found'.

  You can avoid inversion after *peut-être* by using *que* instead (*Peut-être qu'un remède sera trouvé*) or by placing it later in the phrase (*Un remède sera peut-être trouvé*).

- *sans doute* – 'doubtless', 'no doubt'.

  Sans doute la découverte exercera-t-elle une grande influence à l'avenir – 'No doubt the discovery will have a great influence in the future'.

- *toujours* – 'yet', 'nevertheless'.

  Toujours est-il que l'essor de l'électronique devient très important – 'Yet (the fact remains that) the expansion in electronics is becoming very great'.

There is, however, no inversion after *jamais* and *non seulement*, although verb and subject are turned round in English after 'never' and 'not only':

Jamais je n'ai entendu parler d'une telle expérience! – 'Never have I heard of such an experiment!'

Non seulement il disposait d'un nouvel ordinateur... – 'Not only did he have a new computer...'.

3.6 Revision: present participle

Key points from AS

- **Present participle**
  AS Study Guide p. 97

You should already feel confident about using *en* + **present participle**; if not, look again at the examples in the AS Study Guide.

The use of the present participle without *en* is less common, but you certainly need to be able to translate it into English; usually the ending -ing is required.

Réclamant la fin de l'expérimentation animale, les manifestants se sont adressés au PDG de la compagnie – 'Demanding an end to experimenting on animals, the protesters went to see the Managing Director of the firm'.

The present participle does not agree with the person to whom it refers; *manifestants* in the example above is plural, but *réclamant* does not change. Think of it as a verb.

More about reflexive verbs

Key points from AS

- **Formation and use of reflexive verbs**
  AS Study Guide pp. 27,64
- **Direct and indirect objects**
  AS Study Guide p. 65

The reflexive pronoun of most reflexive verbs is the direct object, meaning 'myself', 'yourself', 'himself', 'herself', 'itself', 'oneself', ourselves', 'yourselves', 'themselves'; the pronoun is not always required in translation:

> *Si les résultats de l'expérience sont inattendus, il faudra se raviser* – 'If the results of the experiment are unexpected, we'll have to think again'.

Apart from the verbs learnt as reflexives, i.e. with *se* as an integral part of their infinitive, there are some 'ordinary' verbs which may be used with a reflexive pronoun, which may be either a direct or an indirect object (there are implications for the agreement of the past participle in compound tenses). There are four possible meanings:

- 'myself', etc. (direct object)
- 'to (or for) myself', etc. (indirect object/dative of advantage)
- 'each other' – plural only (direct object)
- 'to each other' – plural only (indirect object/dative of advantage).

If a verb is used reflexively it takes *être* to form its compound tenses.

In French *s* is not added to surnames; there is no need for it, as the article with it (*les* or *des*) shows that that it is plural.

Examples:

Les scientifiques s'accusaient d'avoir oublié les principes de base – 'The scientists accused themselves of forgetting the basic principles'.

Elle va s'offrir un livre sur la vie des Curie – 'She's going to buy (for) herself a book on the life of the Curies'.

Ils se sont félicités sur les résultats – 'They congratulated each other on the results'. (This could also mean 'They congratulated themselves'.)

Au cours de nos recherches nous nous sommes écrit toutes les semaines – 'In the course of our research we wrote to each other every week'.

In the compound tenses, the past participle agrees **only when the reflexive pronoun is the direct object**; in *Ils se sont félicités*, *se* is the direct object of *féliciter*. There is no agreement with an indirect object: in *Nous nous sommes écrit*, *nous* is the indirect object of *écrire*.

Idioms and other special cases

There are many constructions and expressions which are **specific to one language.** You must recognise them when translating from French, and be able to use them with confidence at this level. You probably used some of them at GCSE and AS Level. Here are some of the most useful expressions.

Depuis/ça fait + present tense – 'has/have been (doing')

You would normally expect to use the perfect tense to translate 'have' or 'has'; but in fact the present is the logical tense to use because the action is still happening.

> *Ça fait cinq ans que les chercheurs travaillent dans ce domaine* – 'Researchers have been working in this field for five years'.

Depuis + imperfect tense – 'had been (doing)'

The construction is used with the imperfect tense (instead of the pluperfect which normally translates 'had') if, at the time of speaking or writing, the action was unfinished.

> *Depuis deux ans il essayait de convaincre son patron de l'importance des ordinateurs* – 'He had been trying to convince his boss of the importance of computers for two years'.

***Venir de* + infinitive – 'has/have just (done)', 'had just (done)'**

Like the constructions with *depuis* above, this can be used only with the present and imperfect tenses.

With the present tense it means 'have just' or 'has just':

Les scientifiques viennent de tirer la sonnette d'alarme – 'Scientists have just sounded the alarm'.

With the imperfect tense it means 'had just':

La fusée venait d'être lancée – 'The rocket had just been launched'.

This has nothing to do with being on the train!

***Être en train de* + infinitive – 'to be in the middle of (doing)', 'to be busy (doing)'**

Nous sommes en train d'installer un nouveau logiciel – 'We're in the middle of installing some new software'.

***Avoir beau* + infinitive – 'to do (something) in vain'**

Tu as beau me parler de l'expérimentation animale: tu ne me convaincras jamais! – 'It's no good talking to me about animal experimentation; you'll never convince me!'

***en vouloir à* + infinitive – 'to resent', 'to bear a grudge against'**

Je n'en veux pas aux médecins: ils ne sont pas responsables de la propagation de la maladie – 'I bear no grudge against the doctors; they're not responsible for the spread of the disease'.

Progress check

Translate into French (answers on p. 154).

1 He had been suffering from Aids for 18 months.
2 We have just heard that the scientists have made a breakthrough.
3 The astronauts are in the middle of surveying the moon's surface.
4 Last week the researchers gave information to each other.
5 The Montgolfiers supported each other.
6 Ask me anything; I'll show you how to find the answer on the Web.

Translate into English:

7 Vous avez beau essayer d'utiliser cet ordinateur; il ne marche plus.
8 Ne m'en veux pas! Ce n'est pas moi qui ai autorisé les essais.
9 Nous nous parlons rarement.
10 Sachant qu'il faudrait justifier ses résultats, elle avait rassemblé toutes les données.
11 Vous devrez effectuer les essais je ne sais comment.
12 Quiconque trouvera une solution au problème sera récompensé.

How to answer

3.7 Non-verbal exercises

You will certainly have had to deal with some, if not all, of these non-verbal test-types at AS Level. It is possible that they will also appear on A2 papers, as they are all valid ways of testing understanding; you will know if this does not apply to the exam for which you are entered.

Exercises of this sort are sometimes considered to be easier than questions for which full answers are required. This is not really the case, though it is true that you don't have to worry about how to express your own answer. Close attention to detail is needed, however; right or wrong answers may hinge on a single word, or a tense, or a negative; candidates who try to do these questions too quickly often don't do themselves justice. Good grades often depend on achieving at least three-quarters of the marks for these objective tests.

Some general dos and don'ts for all non-verbal exercises:

- Do read the instructions and follow them precisely.
- Do look at the example if there is one.
- Do take a minute to check that you have done the right thing.
- Don't leave gaps; if you can't work out the answer, put down one of the possibilities.
- Don't skim quickly through the statements, ignoring key words.

Vrai/Faux, Oui/Non, Tick/Cross

The simple True/False or *Oui/Non* exercise tends to be a thing of the past now, as an additional category has been added: a *?* if the answer is not definite, *pas mentionné* if it isn't stated at all, *pas toujours* if the action doesn't always happen. The change is partly to make the test more demanding, and partly to stop people obtaining marks by ticking all *Vrai* or all *Non* without bothering to read the passage, as a time-saving device.

You must read the statements very carefully, as well as the passage, and look for
- a change of tense
- a qualifier such as *toujours* or *fréquemment*
- a change from negative to positive or vice versa.

All of these might make the answer False, or at least uncertain. Remember that **tense may be implied as well as stated clearly**; *Il vient de trouver* refers to past action even though the tense of *venir* is present (see idioms p. 59), and future action may be expressed by the present tense of *aller* + infinitive as well as by the future tense itself. Time can also be indicated by such words as *demain, hier, l'année dernière*, etc., so be sure to revise them thoroughly. Do the same for 'quantity' phrases such as *plus de, moins de, au moins, environ, à peu près, presque*; they have a modifying effect on the statement or the passage and the examiner may wish to test your understanding of this. **Negative statements are notoriously difficult to deal with**; this may be because our natural reaction to 'not' is to think the answer must be 'no'. Double-check your answers to such questions; revise the negatives that may be used (AS Study Guide pp. 113–14).

If you have *ne...jamais* in the statement but the passage says *rarement*, the answer will be *Faux*. Never forget that *ne...que* means 'only' – the same as *seulement* – and that 'not only' is *pas seulement*.

A similar test is the tick-box exercise; here you have an additional problem to contend with. You may be asked, for example, to tick the six statements that apply, or the five attributes of a new piece of equipment. If you tick more than the number specified you will certainly lose marks; you could even lose them all if you don't follow instructions.

Multiple-choice

Multiple-choice tests may require you to choose a single word or a longer phrase that is closest in meaning to the original. Here, too, it pays to read the sentences very carefully; in addition to the type of mistakes mentioned above, you may be misled by **a word that is very similar to one in the passage.** Examples of words that have been confused in this way include *courir/courrier*, *doutent/redoutent*, *livre/livrer*, *maquis/marquis* and *bâton/bateau*.

Another easy mistake to make is to forget that **a word may have two different meanings**; think of *arrêter*, *cité*, *facteur*, *feuille*, *poste*, *tour*, etc. Some of these can be distinguished more easily because they have different genders, but this is not always the case. Check the context of the word very carefully, and don't jump to a conclusion too quickly.

One type of multiple-choice question asks you to make a judgement; you may have to summarise the tone of a passage.

Example: *La dame semble plutôt triste/résignée/peureuse.*

In this case you will have to look for clues throughout the text.

Matching

There are several types of matching exercise: you may have to fit together

- beginnings and endings of sentences
- headings and paragraphs
- statistics and definitions.

You are likely to be given a number of 'distractors' – there will be more answers than you need – so like some of the gap-fill tests it isn't just a simple choice. Again you must remember that your job is to show understanding of the passage; two halves of a sentence may fit together and make sense, but this may not be what the text says. As with gap-fill exercises, **the structure of the sentence may help you to eliminate some of the possibilities**, but this will not always work.

Matching headings to paragraphs requires a general understanding of the whole paragraph. In theory, matching statistics to definitions should be straightforward, because figures are easy to spot, but you will need to take into account the qualifying phrases and recognise the more general nature of words like *une vingtaine*, etc. Revision of numbers is vital here.

Find equivalents or definitions

This is not strictly a 'non-verbal' test, as you will have to write a few words; but they are words taken directly from the passage and are probably not taken into account when assessing quality of language.

The important thing is to find the exact equivalent – **include every element of the original phrase**, including the article if there is one. You are likely to lose marks for any element, however tiny, omitted or added; this is a pity if you have found the right phrase but have been careless about which part of it you use. An example from a recent paper was the phrase *à ceux qui continuent à refuser*; the answer required was *aux derniers résistants*. Leaving out *aux* meant that *à* had not been covered.

If you copy out a long phrase that includes the right words by chance, you will gain no marks because you have not shown proper understanding; and there is no excuse for copying incorrectly from the paper (in the case of a reading exercise). Take a moment to check what you have written.

If you are asked to find the single word that matches a definition given, the advice given above does not apply. The best way to prepare for this type of exercise is to look up some words of all sorts (nouns, adjectives, verbs, adverbs) in a French monolingual dictionary and see how their definitions are expressed. You will then know what type of word you are looking for.

Practice examination questions

1 Reading

For each of the reading passages below more than one question is set. Use any help you are given in the rubric and in the headings and sub-headings, as well as in the passages themselves. Some Awarding Bodies tell you where in the text to look for your answer.

RECHERCHE Après une formation à l'étranger
L'aide au retour des surdiplômés

Un certain nombre de jeunes diplômés français en biologie ou en médecine, souvent parmi les meilleurs, partent se former à la recherche médicale à l'étranger dans des grands laboratoires pendant deux ou trois ans. Le retour en France s'avère ardu, avec de grandes difficultés à trouver une place dans les structures publiques ou privées. La Fondation pour la recherche médicale a décidé de favoriser le retour de certains de ces « cerveaux » en leur assurant pendant deux ans des subsides.

Dr Martine Pérez

En 1997, 569 docteurs en biologie ou médecine ont choisi d'effectuer un séjour post-doctoral à l'étranger à l'issue de leur soutenance de thèse. Une grande majorité ont été en Amérique du Nord (340), 204 dans divers pays européens, 7 au Japon… Certains d'entre eux s'installent définitivement dans le pays d'accueil. Une majorité souhaite revenir en France. Et là, les choses se compliquent. Comment trouver un poste dans un laboratoire hexagonal quand on vit à l'étranger, alors que la concurrence est rude pour rentrer à l'Inserm ou au CNRS et que l'on n'a ni statut ni Sécurité sociale? Par exemple, pour l'année 1999 sur 440 candidats au concours de chargé de recherche de l'Inserm, 149 étaient en stage post–doctoral au moment du concours, dont 83 aux Etats-Unis. Il n'existe aucune procédure officielle pour aider ces jeunes diplômés à revenir travailler en France.

En 1997, la Fondation pour la recherche médicale a décidé de créer un fonds d'aide au retour. Ainsi, un conseil scientifique, composé de 26 membres, renouvelable par moitié tous les deux ans, analyse les dossiers des candidats qui souhaitent travailler en France. Pour l'année 1998, 59 demandes d'aide au retour ont été faites à la Fondation, et 24 ont été acceptées. Pour 1999, les chiffres sont similaires. Les critères de jugement des dossiers sont les études, les projets présentés et le laboratoire potentiellement prêt à intégrer le chercheur. Cette aide consiste en un soutien financier de l'ordre de 18 à 22 000 euros.

Mais ainsi que le précise Claire Dadou-Willmann, directeur général de la Fondation pour la recherche médicale: « *Nous n'avons pas la prétention de dire qu'une Fondation privée a les moyens de résoudre entièrement ce problème, mais elle peut donner un sens au mouvement.* »

Examiner's tip

Try using the passive in your answers to (c) and (e).

A Résumez en vos propres termes EN FRANÇAIS la situation qui existe pour les jeunes diplômés français en sciences, selon le premier paragraphe.

B Complétez EN FRANÇAIS les phrases ci-dessous, selon le sens du texte. Les réponses se trouvent dans les 2e, 3e, et 4e paragraphes.

   (a) Quoique quelques-uns des diplômés en sciences ....
.... , la plupart ....
.... (2)

   (b) Ce qui rend difficile l'entrée dans les centres de recherche en France, c'est qu'il y a beaucoup de .... (1)

   (c) Pour aider ceux qui veulent revenir, un fonds
.... (1)

   (d) Afin de choisir entre les candidats, les membres du conseil considèrent
.... (3)

   (e) Selon Claire Dadou-Willmann, le problème
.... (1)

2 Reading

You may find it helpful to read the information on France and the European parliament (Chapter 4) before tackling this question.

OGM : les Quinze maintiennent un moratoire de fait

Les ministres de l'Environnement ont décidé de durcir la procédure d'autorisations. La France s'est abstenue, estimant que le texte n'allait pas assez loin.

BRUXELLES : Pierre BOCEV

Après une nuit entière de discussions acharnées, les ministres de l'Environnement des Quinze réunis au Luxembourg ont fini par trouver un accord pour renforcer une législation européenne déjà ancienne sur la commercialisation des « organismes génétiquement modifiés » (OGM).

Leur tentative de rédiger également une « *déclaration politique* », qui aurait souligné leur refus commun d'accorder de nouvelles autorisations à ces produits avant d'avoir resserré les contrôles a néanmoins échoué.

La législation sur les aliments qui contiennent des OGM est déjà réglée par une directive (loi européenne) qui prévoit un étiquetage contraignant. Le débat au Luxembourg portait sur les conditions d'autorisation des OGM en tant que tels, notamment leur utilisation dans les semences.

Cet aspect fait lui aussi l'objet d'une directive, dite 90/220 mais elle est vieille de neuf ans et dépassée.

TROIS BLOCS DE PAYS

La « *position commune* » que les ministres ont adoptée pour adapter ce texte aux réalités nouvelles comporte un étiquetage plus explicite, interdit toute procédure simplifiée d'autorisation de produits réputés non nocifs, prévoit une évaluation préalable des risques et limite la durée des licences à dix ans.

Suivie par l'Irlande et l'Italie, la France a estimé que ces dispositions n'allaient pas assez loin, notamment en matière de traçabilité des OGM. Ces trois pays se sont abstenus, ce qui n'a pas empêché l'adoption du texte.

Ce projet de directive doit maintenant passer par le Parlement européen nouvellement élu qui, comme l'Assemblée sortante, fera l'objet d'un intense lobbying contradictoire de la part des environnementalistes et des grandes industries. L'entrée en vigueur de cette législation n'est de ce fait pas prévue avant 2002.

Examiner's tip

Read your translation when you have done it. If it doesn't make sense, it must be wrong!

A Traduisez en anglais le premier paragraphe du texte.

B Choisissez dans la liste ci-dessous un mot qui complète chaque phrase, selon le sens du passage. Vous avez le droit d'utiliser un mot <u>une fois seulement</u>. Attention! Il y a plus de mots que de phrases. Les réponses se trouvent dans les 2e, 3e et 4e paragraphes.

ancienne	étendues	prévues	risqués
défendu	limitées	pris	simple
différente	permis	réelle	utilisé

Examiner's tip

Read the instructions carefully. There is one question for which two answers are possible, but you will need one of them later in the exercise and you are not allowed to use a word more than once; this should make the decision easier for you. The endings will also help you to eliminate some of the incorrect choices.

(a) Selon une loi européenne déjà en vigueur, des contraintes en ce qui concerne l'étiquetage sont ....

(b) Au Luxembourg on a dû décider si l'emploi des OGM dans les semences devrait être ....

(c) Une directive .... à cet égard existe aussi.

(d) La situation à laquelle on doit faire face actuellement est

....

(e) Désormais il sera .... d'adopter une procédure rapide d'autorisation des OGM, les risques devront être

.... en compte, et les licences seront

.... à une période de dix ans.

Practice examination questions *(continued)*

Examiner's tip
Use your own words wherever possible: it will show that you have really understood the passage, and anyway there may be penalties for copying the exact words of the text.

C **Répondez EN FRANÇAIS aux questions suivantes. Les réponses se trouvent dans les 5e et 6e paragraphes du texte.**

(a) Pourquoi la France, l'Irlande et l'Italie n'étaient-elles pas d'accord avec les autres pays? (1)

(b) Comment est-ce que ces trois pays ont montré leur opinion? (1)

(c) Qui devra ratifier la directive? (1)

(d) Quels groupes essayeront d'influencer la décision? (2)

(e) Quand est-ce que la nouvelle législation entrera en vigueur? (1)

3 Listening

This passage refers to the introduction in the near future of a medicine which, as you are working on the exercise, is already available. Remember that it's your comprehension *of the passage itself* that is being tested.

Écoutez le passage au sujet du Relenza™, puis donnez EN FRANÇAIS les renseignements demandés:

(a) Détails du médicament (lieu d'origine, durée de recherches, étendue des essais). (3)

(b) Différence entre l'efficacité des anciens médicaments et le Relenza™. (5)

(c) Catégories de malades qui pourront bénéficier du Relenza™. (2)

(d) Autres détails (date de disponibilité, prescription, coût). (3)

4 Listening

Écoutez l'extrait sur un virus informatique, puis décidez laquelle des réponses s'accorde le mieux avec le sens du passage.

(i) (a) Beaucoup d'ordinateurs vont être contaminés.
(b) C'est à Washington que le plus grand nombre d'ordinateurs va être touché.
(c) Le virus s'est largement répandu.

(ii) Un homme à Minnéapolis a vu le message
(a) quatre fois
(b) quarante fois
(c) quatre cents fois

(iii) (a) En lisant la lettre d'amour indiquée on risque de contaminer son ordinateur.
(b) Pour sauver l'ordinateur il suffit de répondre à la lettre d'amour.
(c) Il faut attacher une lettre pour sauver son carnet d'adresses.

(iv) L'origine du virus
(a) est connue
(b) n'est pas connue
(c) est soupçonnée

(v) (a) 'I love you' est le seul message dont il s'agit.
(b) Le message varie de minute en minute.
(c) Il faut se méfier de plusieurs autres messages semblables.

(vi) Certaines compagnies ont
(a) arrêté la messagerie électronique
(b) coupé le courant
(c) refusé de laisser entrer le facteur.

Chapter 4

La politique

The following topics are covered in this chapter:

- *The political system in France*
- *The voting system*
- *The European Union*
- *France and the rest of the world*

- *Grammar: Verbs for A2*
- *How to answer: Translation and transfer of meaning*

Politics

After studying this chapter you should be able to:

- understand the French political system and France's position within Europe and the world
- identify the vocabulary needed to answer comprehension questions on the topic
- recognise and use more difficult verbs
- improve your translation skills

LEARNING SUMMARY

4.1 The political system in France

AQA	M4, M6
EDEXCEL	M4, M6
OCR	M4, M5

> The Fifth Republic dates from the time of Charles de Gaulle's presidency (1958) until the present day.

France is a republic; its head of state is the president. Its national anthem is the *Marseillaise*, and its slogan, adopted during the Revolution at the end of the 18th century, is *Liberté, Égalité, Fraternité*.

Structure

There are four levels of administration in France:
- the state
- the *régions*
- the *départements*
- the *communes*.

The state

Until recently the President was elected for a seven-year term, but following a referendum in September 2000 this has been reduced to five years. He is allowed to stand for re-election. Candidates for the presidency must be supported by at least 500 MPs. His official residence is the Elysée Palace.

The Prime Minister is officially appointed by the President, but the latter is expected to nominate one of the leaders of the party that has won the general election. This may lead to conflict if the President and Prime Minister are from different political parties, but in practice it is likely that both would present a united front to the rest of the world whatever their differences internally. Such a period is known as *cohabitation*: two recent examples have been those involving President Mitterrand and Prime Minister Jacques Chirac, and President Chirac and Prime Minister Lionel Jospin.

The *Assemblée Nationale* (formerly the *Chambre des Députés*) is the Lower House and consists of 577 *députés* (MPs) elected for a five-year term. Its equivalent in England is the House of Commons. It meets in the Palais Bourbon. Most of its sessions are open to the public; Question Time is televised on Wednesday afternoons.

The *Sénat* is the Upper House, consisting of 321 *sénateurs*. To be eligible for election a candidate must be at least 35 years old and is chosen by an electoral college of senior political figures in each *département*. One of its duties is to represent the *départements d'outre-mer* (DOM) and expatriates. The *Sénat* is not dissolved, so if the presidency is vacant (e.g. through resignation or death) it assumes temporary responsibility. Under normal circumstances, however, it is second in importance to the *Assemblée Nationale*.

The *régions*

> If you are talking or writing about a town in France, make sure you know which region and *département* it belongs to.

France is divided into 26 *régions*, of which four are the DOM (Martinique, Guadeloupe, Réunion, Guyane). The *régions* within France itself are large, and include such areas as Bretagne (Brittany), Basse-Normandie and Provence-Alpes-Côtes d'Azur (PACA).

The *région* is administered by the **conseil régional**, whose members are elected for six years. The *conseillers* themselves elect their president. This is currently the only area of French politics in which elections involve proportional representation.

The *départements*

There are 100 *départements*, four of them the DOM. Responsibility for running them belongs to the *préfet*, who is the representative of the state within the *département*, and the **conseil général**, whose members are elected for six years and whose president wields considerable power. The *départements* are similar to counties in the UK.

The *commune*

This is the smallest unit of local government. There are about 37 000 *communes* in France; their population varies from very small to very large. (see also Chapter 2). Paris, Lyon and Marseille are sub-divided into *arrondissements* for administrative purposes.

> The mayors of Paris and other major cities have greater powers.

The *commune* is run by the *maire* and the *conseil municipal*. The mayor has two functions: he is the representative of his *commune* to the state, and the representative of the state to his *commune*. One of his duties is to conduct marriages; without the civil ceremony a marriage is not valid in France even if it has taken place in church.

Vocabulary for the political system in France

l'État (m)	the State	le pouvoir	power
la république	republic	le décret	decree
le chef de l'État	Head of state	le débat	debate, discussion
le gouvernement	government	le porte-parole	spokesman/woman
la démocratie	democracy	se présenter	to stand (election)
la politique	politics, policy	entrer en lice	to stand (election)
le parlement	parliament	nommer	to appoint, nominate
le régime	(political) regime	diriger	to direct, lead
le conseil	council	démissionner	to resign
le système	system	dissoudre	to dissolve (parliament)
le mandat	mandate, term	siéger	to sit (committee, etc.)
le septennat	7-year mandate	débattre	to discuss, debate
le quinquennat	5-year mandate		
le ministère	Ministry	responsable	responsible
le ministre	minister	éligible	eligible
le sénateur	senator	provisoire	temporary
le député	MP	républicain	republican
le préfet	prefect	parlementaire	parliamentary
le conseiller	councillor	renouvelable	renewable

Vocabulary for the political system in France (continued)

le maire	mayor	politique	political
le maire adjoint	deputy mayor	en tant que	as, in the role of
la séance	session, sitting	entre les mains de	in the hands of
la session	session		

- *politique*: note the two possible meanings.
- *gouvernement, parlement, démocratie, républicain, responsable*: take great care with the spelling of these words.
- *ministère, ministre*: don't confuse these two very similar words.
- *maire*: take care with listening passages; the sound is exactly the same as that of *mère* and *mer* (those would be feminine, of course).
- *session, séance*: use the latter for a single sitting (of a committee, etc.).
- *dissoudre*: an irregular verb, like *résoudre* (see pp. 74–76).
- *en tant que*: equivalent to the contemporary English phrase 'wearing his (mayor's) hat'.
- *entre les mains de*: note the preposition – *entre*, not *dans*; *Le pouvoir est entre les mains du Président.*

4.2 The voting system

AQA	M4, M6
EDEXCEL	M4, M6
OCR	M4, M6

Women were given the vote in 1945.

The system in France, as in most other countries, is *suffrage universel direct*: everyone who is eligible to vote does so in person. The ballot is secret. Voters must be at least 18 (21 until 1974), of French nationality (except for European elections and town council elections) and must have registered on the electoral roll.

Most elections are conducted by the '*scrutin uninominal majoritaire à deux tours*':
- *scrutin* – voting
- *uninominal* – for one name
- *majoritaire* – a majority is required
- *à deux tours* – in two rounds.

This means that in the first round electors vote for their preferred candidate; if, when the votes are counted, one candidate has an **absolute majority** (more than all the other candidates taken together, i.e. 50% + 1 of the total number of votes) he/she is elected. If, as is more likely, no candidate has an absolute majority, there is a second round of voting; any candidate who has received fewer than 12.5% of the votes in the first round drops out at this stage. In the second round the candidate who has the highest number of votes (**a simple majority**) is elected. Elections take place on Sundays.

On matters of particular importance a **referendum** may be called. This consists of a question to which the voter has to answer *Oui* or *Non*. The range of matters on which referenda are permitted is small, but was extended in 1995.

Political parties

The French are generally interested in politics from an early age, and families are often shocked to discover how little their British exchange guests know about UK and European policies. In recent years there has been an increase in the number of political parties in France, though some have re-combined, notably the UDF. Even within the parties there may be several different factions. The main parties are currently:

- *Parti Socialiste* (**PS**) – left-wing.
- *Union pour la Démocratie Française* (**UDF**) – centre right. This consists of several smaller parties which united under one banner.
- *Rassemblement pour la République* (**RPR**) – right-wing.

There are several smaller parties, of which the most important are:

- *Parti Communiste* (**PC**) – sometimes called *Parti Communiste Français* (**PCF**).
- *Verts* – the ecology group includes several parties, one of which is *Génération Écologie*.
- *Front National* (**FN**) – cause of much of the racial violence in the streets of France.

During an election campaign parties must keep within a certain budget and must make their accounts available for scrutiny. There are restrictions relating to the number of posters that may be put up, and to where and for how long these may be displayed. Opinion polls on the anticipated result must not be published in the week leading up to a general election.

Examiner's tip

The popularity and importance of politicians changes from year to year; even so, it's useful to recognise the names of those who are in the public eye. Keep a list of those who are regularly in the news.

Vocabulary for the voting system

le suffrage	voting	voter	to vote
les élections législatives	general election	élire	to elect
l'élection partielle	by-election	être élu(e)	to be elected
le scrutin	ballot, poll	s'engager	to be involved
le droit de vote	franchise, right to vote	militer	to be actively involved
l'électorat (m)	electorate	s'inscrire à	to join (party, etc.)
l'électeur, l'électrice	voter	exprimer	to express
l'élu(e)	elected representative	croire à	to believe in
la campagne électorale	electoral campaign	garantir	to guarantee
la majorité absolue	absolute majority	dénoncer	to denounce
la majorité relative	relative majority	renouveler	to renew
le référendum (plural -s)	referendum	se rendre/aller aux urnes	to go to the poll, vote
la circonscription	constituency	s'abstenir	to abstain
le tour	round	subir	to suffer (defeat)
la voix	vote (individual)	remporter	to win (victory)
le parti	(political) party	majoritaire	in the majority
le panneau d'affichage	hoarding, billboard	municipal	municipal, town
le sondage d'opinion	opinion poll	cantonal	local, of the *canton*
le résultat	result	divisé	divided
l'adhérent (m)	supporter	actuel, -elle	current
le groupe de pression	pressure group	de droite	right (-wing)
le citoyen, la citoyenne	citizen	de gauche	left (-wing)
la démission	resignation	gauchiste	leftist
la défaite	defeat	centriste	of the centre
la victoire	victory	conservateur, -trice	conservative
l'homme/la femme politique	politician	extrême droite	far-right
		libéral	liberal
la représentation proportionnelle	proportional representation	vert	'Green', ecologist
		communiste	communist

KEY POINT

- *voix*: used in a precise sense in this context.
- *parti*: don't mis-spell this as *partie*; you will change the meaning of your sentence.
- *sondage*: often carried out by the organisation SOFRES.
- *élire*: a compound of *lire*.
- *garantir*: note that there is no need for *u* in the French spelling; the *g* is hard anyway before *a*.

4.3 The European Union

AQA	M4, M6
EDEXCEL	M4, M6
OCR	M4, M5
WJEC	M4, M6
NICCEA	M4, M5

France was one of the founder members of the *Communauté Economique Européenne*/CEE (European Economic Community, EEC in English) which later became the *Union Européenne*/UE (European Union, EU). The main stages in the development of this body were:

- 1957 – Treaty of Rome, setting up the EEC or 'Common Market', signed by Belgium, France, Germany (West), Holland, Italy and Luxembourg.
- 1963 – De Gaulle vetoes Britain's entry, largely because of its economic links with USA.
- 1967 – De Gaulle vetoes Britain's entry for the second time.
- 1973 – Denmark, Ireland and the UK join the EEC.
- 1975 – Heads of state and heads of government of EEC countries begin regular 'summit' meetings – European Council (*Conseil européen*).
- 1981 – Greece joins.
- 1986 – Spain and Portugal join the EEC.
- 1987 – Single European Act (*Acte unique*). European Council officially established.
- 1992 – Treaty on European Union (*Traité sur l'union européenne*), often known as the Maastricht treaty, signed by the twelve member nations.
- 1993 – The EEC officially becomes known as the European Union.
- 1995 – Austria, Finland and Sweden join the EU.
- 1999 – Eleven of the fifteen member states introduce the euro (single European currency). Those who do not join at this stage are Denmark, the UK, Greece and Sweden.
- 2001 – Treaty of Nice signed (see below).

Ten more countries (Cyprus, the Czech republic, Estonia, Hungary, Latvia, Lithuania, Malta, Poland, Slovakia and Slovenia) are due to join the EU in 2004, to be followed eventually by Bulgaria, Romania and possibly Turkey.

The aims of the **EEC** were to abolish trade boundaries and to set up a common agricultural policy (*politique agricole commune/PAC*). The **Single European Act** had as its objective the establishment of a single European Market which would allow people, goods and capital to circulate freely within the member states. The **Maastricht Treaty** widened the scope of the EU to include consumer protection, education and training, the environment, and social policies. It also gave the right to nationals of all member countries to vote in European and municipal elections in the country in which they are living. The **European Parliament** was given a greater role to play, and more cooperation was planned with regard to foreign and defence policies.

The Treaty of Nice laid down a number of new regulations, intended to simplify decision-making when the EU expands. Majority decisions will be accepted in a number of areas where formerly unanimous agreement was needed. However, talks on an EU constitution have led to considerable differences of opinion among the member states, and matters are not yet fully resolved (January 2004).

Single European Currency

France has been committed from the outset to the single European currency, and joined 11 other states in introducing the euro in January 2002. The currency is managed by the European Central Bank, which is answerable to the European Parliament. The main intention is to make trade between the member states easier because prices do not have to be transferred from one currency to the other, with subsequent reliance on differing exchange rates.

In view of the fact that the UK has not (at the time of writing) committed itself to the single European currency, comprehension passages could deal with the differences of opinion on this issue.

Common Agricultural Policy

This has been a source of conflict in several of the member states, and the cause of many of the strikes and protests that have been prevalent in recent years. The economics of the situation will probably be familiar to you if you are studying A Level Economics or Geography: as far as French is concerned, it is sufficient to understand that subsidies may be paid to farmers, among other things:

- to grow certain products
- not to grow certain products (or raise certain animals)
- not to grow anything at all in certain fields for a given period ('set-aside')
- to dispose of surplus quantities.

A surplus of products led to the 'milk lake', 'butter mountain', etc., which caused much annoyance to various groups of people: the farmers producing them, the customers who were not allowed to buy them cheaply, and humanitarian groups who felt that it was morally wrong to destroy quantities of food and drink which could be used to alleviate the plight of poorer countries and individuals. Milk 'dumping' is another aspect of the same problem. Many farmers have been put out of business because of EU rules.

European Parliament

The number of MEPs (Members of the European Parliament) varies according to the population of the member state. They are directly elected by the countries concerned. Under the Treaty of Nice, France has 72 members.

The full parliament meets in Strasbourg, in the Palais de l'Europe, sitting usually for one week in every month in public session. MEPs sit in political groupings, not in national units. There are a number of committees (*commissions*) which normally meet in Brussels. Most of the administration (*Secrétariat*) is based in Luxembourg.

Council of Europe (Conseil d'Europe)

This pre-dates the EEC; it was set up in 1949, and its headquarters are in Strasbourg. Its aim is a united Europe, but its powers are limited and it serves mainly as a setting for debate on issues of global importance and their relation to the member countries, of which there are more than thirty.

Vocabulary for the European Union

le traité	treaty	abolir	to abolish
l'accord (m)	agreement	mettre en place	to set up
le développement	development	établir	to establish
le droit	right	mettre en oeuvre	to implement
l'étape (f)	stage (in development)	prendre des mesures	to take steps
l'appartenance (f)	membership	fonctionner	to work, function
le membre	member	élargir	to widen
les pays membres	member states	renforcer	to strengthen
le partenariat	partnership	prévoir	to anticipate, plan
le partenaire	partner	appartenir à	to belong to
la monnaie unique	single currency	participer à	to take part in
la mesure	measure, step	favoriser	to favour
le but	aim, goal	privilégier	to favour
la frontière	boundary, frontier	concevoir	to think up
le délégué	delegate	préciser	to specify
la portée	scope, range	contester	to challenge, question
le bloc	block (political)		
le taux de change	exchange rate	économique	economic
la solidarité	solidarity	européen, -enne	European
la rivalité	rivalry	privilégié	favoured
le principe	principle	commercial	trade
la volonté	will, desire	large	wide, broad

Vocabulary for the European Union (continued)

la mise en place	setting-up	**prévu**	planned
la mise en oeuvre	implementation	**conçu**	designed, thought out
le surplus	surplus	**contestateur, -trice**	contentious, liable to
l'excédent (m)	surplus		opposition
la puissance	power		

- *puissance*: in the sense of 'France is a world power' in this context; not the same as *pouvoir*, which is the power wielded by someone.
- *appartenir, concevoir*: like *tenir* and *recevoir* respectively (see AS Study Guide).

4.4 France and the rest of the world

AQA	M4, M6
EDEXCEL	M4, M6
OCR	M4, M5
WJEC	M4, M6
NICCEA	M4, M5

History

France was one of the great colonial powers in the world at one time, and **retains close ties with most of its former colonies,** particularly countries in north, central and western Africa. Many of these countries have French as their main and/or official language. Others such as Vietnam, Cambodia, Laos, Syria, the Lebanon and Haiti have also been linked with France at some time.

One of France's most important colonies was part of Canada, which was 'discovered' by the French explorer Cartier in the 16th century. Another Frenchman, de Champlain, began the process of colonisation in the 17th century. There are still some people in Quebec who would prefer to see the French-speaking province separate from the rest of Canada: the *Front pour la Libération du Québec* (FLQ) was very active in the 1960s and 1970s, and the political party *Bloc Québecois* had some success in the elections in the 1990s. Quebec has its own government, similar to that of a state of the USA.

Also in the 1960s Algeria finally achieved independence from France. The Algerian war of independence had been waged since 1954, with the FLN (*Front de Libération Nationale*) planting bombs and kidnapping public figures who did not agree with them. The French troops, in their turn, reacted with brutality, and it was not until 1962, four years after the return to power of De Gaulle (and after much opposition to his plan for Algeria) that it finally became independent. There is still occasional unrest in the country.

Francophonie

Today over 100 million people speak French as their mother tongue: it is the ninth most-spoken language in the world. There are three aspects of *francophonie* that you will need to consider for the examination; all are linked with other topics.

- issues linked with francophone immigrants to France: culture, integration, exclusion, etc. (see Chapter 2).
- issues relating to other countries where French is spoken: travel and tourism (see AS Study Guide Chapter 2), conflict (see above and Chapter 6) and news items generally.
- the defence of the French language itself: there is considerable opposition to the anglicisation of words, particularly words entering the language as a result of new technology (see Chapter 3 vocabulary).

Examiner's tip

You may have to answer questions on a conversation in which one of the speakers is from a francophone country other than France. Such a passage will only be used if the speech is easy to understand. It would do no harm, however, to listen to TV and radio programmes involving such speakers so that your ear is tuned to more than one accent.

The Alliance Française is an organisation which exists to spread understanding of French language and culture worldwide. It offers courses and lessons in many countries.

Francophone countries include part of Belgium and Switzerland, Luxembourg, and the DOM-TOM, as well as those mentioned above.

The present-day and the future

In French UN is ONU (*Organisation des Nations Unies*).

France is **one of the five permanent members of the United Nations Security Council**, whose main object is to preserve peace. French is one of the six official languages of the UN, and one of its two working languages. UNESCO (the UN organisation for Science, Culture and Education) has its headquarters in Paris.

France is a member of NATO (North Atlantic Treaty Organisation, **OTAN** in French) which adopts and monitors defence policies by political and military means in time of war. France has not always agreed with NATO decisions, and withdrew from the military aspect of NATO in 1966 while retaining membership of the Alliance Atlantique and participating in peace-keeping manoeuvres. Reference is often made in the media to the ***casques bleus***, the blue-helmeted UN peace-keeping troops who may be deployed in times of conflict or disaster.

The *Ministère des Affaires Étrangères* is located at the Quai d'Orsay in Paris. Sometimes its address is used to represent the Ministry itself.

France has always had a fine record with regard to Human Rights (***les droits de l'homme***) and continues to promote these values whenever and wherever necessary. A significant proportion of the French budget is allocated to the developing countries and to humanitarian aid. One of its priorities is to support a ban on landmines. The medical charity *Médecins sans frontières* was established in France in 1971 to provide medical assistance wherever it is needed, in war and disaster zones.

Examiner's tip

The term *Tiers Monde* (Third World) is no longer used, having been superseded by *pays en* (*voie de*) *développement*, but in essays or discussion on the topic it would be impressive to show that you knew what the term used to be.

Vocabulary for France and the rest of the world

le lien	link, tie	**rapprocher**	to bring close together
les moyens (m)	means	**maintenir**	to maintain
les pays en voie de développement	developing countries	**retenir**	to retain
		détenir	to hold (power)
la diplomatie	diplomacy, tact	**soutenir**	to support
la paix	peace	**intervenir**	to intervene
l'appui (m)	support	**apaiser**	to calm
le soutien	support	**calmer**	to calm
l'aide économique	economic aid	**protéger**	to protect
la subvention	subsidy, grant	**promouvoir**	to promote
la détente	relaxation of tension	**s'opposer à**	to oppose
la rupture	break, breaking-off	**(se) consacrer à**	to devote to
l'embargo (m)	embargo (trade)	**aboutir à**	to result in
la sanction économique	economic sanction	**exploser**	to explode
la guerre	war	**se dérouler**	to take place
le conflit	conflict	**enlever**	to kidnap
la bombe	bomb	**kidnapper**	to kidnap
le désastre	disaster	**inonder**	to flood
le sinistre	disaster	**ancien**	former
la crise	crisis	**francophone**	French-speaking
le mine antipersonnel	landmine	**militaire**	military
le déminage	mine clearance, bomb disposal	**sinistré**	disaster-stricken
		universel, -elle	universal
l'enlèvement (m)	kidnapping	**mondial**	of/in the world
le tremblement de terre	earthquake	**culturel, -elle**	cultural
l'inondation (f)	flood	**humanitaire**	humanitarian
l'incendie (m)	fire	**expatrié**	expatriate
sous l'égide de	under the protection of		

- *paix*: don't confuse this when you hear it with *pays*, which has two syllables.
- *sanction*: remember the two distinct meanings of this word, in English and French; either 'approval' or 'punishment'.
- *sinistre*: refers to an event such as an earthquake or serious accident.
- *maintenir, retenir, détenir, soutenir, intervenir*: compounds of *tenir* and *venir*.
- *protéger*: one of the *espérer* group (see AS Study Guide).
- *promouvoir*: a compound of *mouvoir* (see p. 76).
- *ancien*: with this meaning it must be placed before the noun (AS Study Guide p. 49).

Progress check

When you have learnt the vocabulary for this section, write down the following key words, then check them with the lists.

Give the French for: democracy, council, spokesman, responsible, deputy mayor, opinion poll, defeat, conservative, to implement, single currency, delegate, European, peace, crisis, earthquake, humanitarian, universal, conflict, to protect, member states.

Give the English for: le député, diriger, subir, la circonscription, majoritaire, remporter, le traité, appartenir à, privilégier, large, contestateur, le soutien, apaiser, se dérouler, sinistré, les moyens, l'appui, prévu, le scrutin, élire.

Grammar

4.5 Verbs for A2

Key points from AS

- **Verb tables**
  AS Study Guide pp. 28–29

Note that in the table the Future and Conditional forms are given in the same column.

You will have met some of the verbs in the table below at AS Level, but you probably did not need to use many of them. For A2 your best course of action will be to learn their meanings and recognise their forms, and then refer to the table if you need to use them in your written and spoken French. You will soon discover which verbs are going to be most useful to you for your topic discussion and for your essay or coursework.

Infinitive	Present		Perfect	Future & Conditional	Imperfect	Past Historic	Present subjunctive	Present participle
Acquérir to acquire	j'acquiers	nous acquérons	j'ai acquis	j'acquerrai j'acquerrais	j'acquérais	j'acquis	j'acquière	acquérant
	tu acquiers il acquiert	vous acquérez ils acquièrent						
Atteindre to attain, reach	j'atteins	nous atteignons	j'ai atteint	j'atteindrai j'atteindrais	j'atteignais	j'atteignis	j'atteigne	atteignant
	tu atteins il atteint	vous atteignez ils atteignent						
Craindre to fear	je crains	nous craignons	j'ai craint	je craindrai je craindrais	je craignais	je craignis	je craigne	craignant
	tu crains il craint	vous craignez ils craignent						

Infinitive	Present		Perfect	Future & Conditional	Imperfect	Past Historic	Present subjunctive	Present participle
Croître to grow	je croîs tu croîs il croît	nous croissons vous croissez ils croissent	j'ai crû	je croîtrai je croîtrais	je croissais	je crûs	je croisse	croissant
Cueillir to pick, gather	je cueille tu cueilles il cueille	nous cueillons vous cueillez Ils cueillent	j'ai cueilli	je cueillerai je cueillerais	je cueillais	je cueillis	je cueille	cueillant
Fuir to flee	Je fuis tu fuis il fuit	nous fuyons vous fuyez ils fuient	j'ai fui	je fuirai je fuirais	je fuyais	je fuis	je fuie	fuyant
Haïr to hate	je hais tu hais il hait	nous haïssons vous haïssez ils haïssent	j'ai haï	je haïrai je haïrais	je haïssais	je haïs	je haïsse	haïssant
Inclure to include	j'inclus tu inclus il inclut	nous incluons vous incluez ils incluent	j'ai inclus	j'inclurai j'inclurais	j'incluais	j'inclus	j'inclue	incluant
Mourir to die	je meurs tu meurs il meurt	nous mourons vous mourez ils meurent	je suis mort(e)	je mourrai je mourrais	je mourais	je mourus	je meure	mourant
Mouvoir to move	je meus tu meus il meut	nous mouvons vous mouvez ils meuvent	j'ai mû	je mouvrai je mouvrais	je mouvais	je mus	je meuve	mouvant
Naître to be born	je nais tu nais il naît	nous naissons vous naissez ils naissent	je suis né(e)	je naîtrai je naîtrais	je naissais	je naquis	je naisse	naissant
Nuire to harm	je nuis tu nuis il nuit	nous nuisons vous nuisez ils nuisent	j'ai nui	je nuirai je nuirais	je nuisais	je nuisis	je nuise	nuisant
Résoudre to solve, resolve	je résous tu résous il résout	nous résolvons vous résolvez ils résolvent	j'ai résolu	je résoudrai je résoudrais	je résolvais	je résolus	je résolve	résolvant
Rompre to break	je romps tu romps il rompt	nous rompons vous rompez ils rompent	j'ai rompu	je romprai je romprais	je rompais	je rompis	je rompe	rompant
Suffire to be sufficient	je suffis tu suffis il suffit	nous suffisons vous suffisez ils suffisent	j'ai suffi	je suffirai je suffirais	je suffisais	je suffis	je suffise	suffisant
Suivre to follow	je suis tu suis il suit	nous suivons vous suivez ils suivent	j'ai suivi	je suivrai je suivrais	je suivais	je suivis	je suive	suivant

Infinitive	Present		Perfect	Future & Conditional	Imperfect	Past Historic	Present subjunctive	Present participle
Se taire to be silent	je me tais	nous nous taisons	je me suis tu (e)	je me tairai je me tairais	je me taisais	je me tus	je me taise	(se) taisant
	tu te tais	vous vous taisez						
	il se tait	ils se taisent						
Valoir to be worth	je vaux	nous valons	j'ai valu	je vaudrai je vaudrais	je valais	je valus	je vaille	valant
	tu vaux	vous valez						
	il vaut	ils valent						
Vivre to live	je vis	nous vivons	j'ai vécu	je vivrai je vivrais	je vivais	je vécus	je vive	vivant
	tu vis	vous vivez						
	il vit	ils vivent						

Remember that compounds and verbs with similar endings generally have the same forms as their 'pattern' verbs; for example,

- *conquérir* is like *acquérir*
- *plaindre* (*craindre*)
- *s'enfuir* (*fuir*)
- *poursuivre* (*suivre*)
- *joindre* (*craindre* and *atteindre*).

- *éteindre, peindre* (*atteindre*)
- *accueillir* (*cueillir*)
- *absoudre* (*résoudre*)
- *exclure* (*inclure*), but its past participle is *exclu*

Progress check

Give the French for: we shall acquire, they had reached, you feared, hating, I would have died, he was born, it is sufficient, you are following, she will have conquered, they were living.

Translate into English.

1 Le problème a été résolu.
2 Il faut que je rompe les liens.
3 La candidate s'est tue.
4 Il vaudrait mieux obtenir les papiers avant de quitter son pays.
5 La France accueillait des milliers d'immigrés.
6 Je suis convaincue de la nécessité d'adopter l'euro.
7 Les pouvoirs du parlement européen croissent d'année en année.
8 Il avait vécu seul pendant deux ans.
9 Je crains l'influence de l'extrême droite.
10 Cette mauvaise influence doit être éteinte.

How to answer

4.6 Translation and transfer of meaning

Translation is a precise skill; if your exam specification includes it, you will certainly have practised it throughout your course. 'Transfer of meaning' is not quite so rigorous; as long as you convey the main points of the text, a word-for-word translation is not required. There are, however, some elements that are common to both, and which apply from French into English and from English into French.

- **Look out for idioms**; if you don't recognise them you may misunderstand the sentence completely. They may be difficult to convey in the other language: 'it's raining cats and dogs' should not involve *chiens* or *chats* in French; instead, use an idiom such as *il pleut des cordes* which also conveys the force of the rain.

- **Check for *faux amis***; 'false friends' which look the same in both languages but which have different meanings. Examples: *assister à, actuellement, décevoir, disposer de, éventuellement, lecture, sensible*. You should make a list of these as you meet them during your course.

- **Don't leave out little words** such as 'often', almost', etc.; they may modify or change the meaning. In a detailed mark scheme they may even be worth a mark on their own.

Most important.

- **Learn vocabulary thoroughly**; test yourself from English into French as well as French into English.

Translation from French into English

Read the whole passage (or paragraph in which the sentence for translation appears) before you start; it will help you to understand the gist.

Recognise the different tenses; with the exception of a few constructions (*venir de, depuis*, the future tense with *quand*, the conditional expressing doubt, etc.) you will need to use the same tense as in the original. Candidates often ignore the pluperfect tense; while it's true to say that this tense is now used more often in French than in English, you are unlikely to be wrong if you translate it by 'had (done)'. If a distinction is made between the perfect and imperfect in French, you should reflect that distinction in your translation:

> *Le Président prononçait un discours quand il a reçu le message* – 'The President was giving a speech when he received the message'.

Details such as the definite article (*le/la/les*) may seem insignificant but could be important. Usually you will translate these as 'the', but sometimes they should be omitted; this is often the case with abstract nouns:

> *La violence a été le sujet de discussion* – 'Violence was the subject under discussion'.

Even with abstract nouns a translation of the article may be required; look at the following sentence:

> *La violence des jours précédents a été le sujet de discussion.*

Here the abstract noun is qualified; the translation is: 'The violence of the previous days was the subject under discussion'.

A wrong translation of *qui* or *que* may change the whole meaning of the sentence. Take particular care with *que*, as French word order is sometimes different from English:

Key points from AS

- **All tenses**
- **The article**
  AS Study Guide pp. 31–32
- **Relative pronouns qui/que**
  AS Study Guide p. 81

Les sanctions économiques qui mettent le pays à genoux – 'The economic sanctions that are bringing the country to its knees'.

Les sanctions économiques que soutiennent les pays membres – 'The economic sanctions which the member states support'.

Transfer of meaning from French into English

Here you are required to **convey the gist** (overall meaning) of a sentence or passage. In this case the vocabulary is most important; the way in which you express the meaning doesn't matter quite so much. Tenses still need care, as you may need to convey the order in which events have happened or are going to happen.

'Transfer of meaning' may be a free summary of a paragraph (*Résumez en anglais le contenu…*) or a guided summary in which you have questions or headings to help you. As always, look at the mark allocation, and before you complete your answer to one question look at the next so that your answers don't overlap. If you have to cross out some of what you've written, or draw arrows, your work may be difficult to read or may confuse the examiner.

For translation and transfer of meaning, your English must be **grammatical, natural, and accurately spelt**. Read your work through as you finish it, and remember the golden rule: **if it doesn't make sense, it must be wrong!**

Translation from English to French

It's unlikely that you will have to translate a long passage into French; most probably you will have to deal with a few separate sentences or a short paragraph. The important elements of translation are the same as those for any writing task in French: vocabulary and grammar. The examiner may wish to test your knowledge of precise points of language – passive, subjunctive, idiomatic phrases – so part of your preparation for any paper which involves translation into French should be a careful revision of all the language you have learnt. Obviously you must work on the grammar that you have learnt for AS and A2, but **it is often the basic points where mistakes are made** (verb endings and adjective agreement in particular), and if your written French is accurate it can make a tremendous difference to your grade.

Transfer of meaning into French

Again, accuracy is extremely important. You have more freedom to use your own words, so you can choose to express the meaning simply or use more complex language. The decision is a matter of confidence; you may feel that you can convey the meaning more safely if you keep the language straightforward. The meaning is, of course, your first priority; however good your French, if you haven't conveyed the required message it will be worth nothing. If you feel that you can use some of the advanced constructions you have learnt during the course your mark will be higher (provided that you have used them correctly and appropriately).

One danger of transferring meaning into French is that you may change the sense by using the wrong pronouns, particularly if you try to translate word-for-word. You should revise when and how to use indirect speech. Look at the example:

(Passage) The minister told us: 'We are considering introducing a new law so that you, the people of France, will pay no more taxes'.

(Task) Explain what the minister said.

(Answer) *Le ministre a dit qu'on envisageait l'introduction d'une nouvelle loi pour que nous autres Français ne payions plus d'impôts.*

Practice examination questions

1 Reading

This is a matching exercise. For hints on how to deal with it, see p. 61.

Faites accorder les paragraphes avec les descriptions. Attention! Il y a plus de descriptions que de paragraphes.

1

Le Chevallier recrée un groupe à Toulon

Le maire (ex-FN) de Toulon, Jean-Marie Le Chevallier, candidat à sa propre succession, a annoncé hier la création d'un nouveau groupe baptisé « Toulonnais d'abord », qui regroupera ses soutiens (« *sept ou huit élus* »), au sein du conseil municipal.

2

Rencontre Alliot-Marie, Madelin et Bayrou

Les présidents des trois partis de l'opposition, Michèle Alliot-Marie (RPR), Alain Madelin (DL) et François Bayrou (UDF), se rencontreront mercredi prochain pour discuter du projet de l'opposition et des élections municipales et législatives, à l'occasion d'un « petit-déjeuner de travail», à la Résidence Saint-Dominique à Paris.

3

Mexandeau (PS) contesté à Caen

L'ancien ministre Louis Mexandeau, député du Calvados, a été désigné jeudi soir tête de liste du PS à Caen pour les élections municipales, par 214 voix contre 165 à François Geindre, maire PS d'Hérouville-Saint-Clair. Mais sa victoire a été aussitôt contestée par son challenger, qui a dénoncé « *les conditions scandaleuses* » dans lesquelles le vote a été organisé. François Geindre a annoncé hier son intention de saisir la direction nationale du PS.

4

Les communistes russes « non grata »

Le PCF n' a pas invité de délégation du Parti communiste de la fédération de Russie au 30e congrès prévu du 23 au 26 mars à Martigues (Bouches-du-Rhône). Le secrétaire national du PCF, Robert Hue, a envoyé une lettre en ce sens à Guennadi Ziouganov, président du Parti communiste de Russie, dans laquelle il invoque des « *divergences majeures qui ne font que s'exacerber dans la dernière période* ». Il fait notamment allusion à la guerre en Tchétchénie.

5

La campagne du « non » de Pasqua

Charles Pasqua, le président du Rassemblement pour la France (RPF), a lancé, hier soir, la campagne du « *non au quinquennat* ». Au cours d'un meeting de la fédération du RPF de Paris, réunissant plus de 600 personnes, il a invité ses militants à constituer des « *comités pour le référendum* » pour « *s'opposer à l'adoption de cette réforme* ». « *Nous sommes pour un mandat de sept ans non renouvelable, pour la pratique du référendum* », a martelé M. Pasqua, en fustigeant l'attitude du président Jacques Chirac, ainsi que la cohabitation.

(a) Il s'agit d'une opposition à une loi proposée.

(b) On attend l'arrivée des délégués russes.

(c) On essaie d'empêcher une mauvaise influence à l'avenir.

(d) Quelqu'un cherche à être élu une deuxième fois.

(e) Une stratégie de collaboration va être mise en place.

(f) Il s'agit d'un candidat à la Présidence.

(g) Le Front national exercera une grande influence à l'avenir.

(h) On aurait utilisé des moyens moralement indéfendables pour atteindre le but désiré.

1	2	3	4	5

2 Reading

There are two different 'find the equivalents' questions and one short translation exercise set on this passage.

L'« alchimie » franco-algérienne.

Tout a été dit sur le caractère tumultueux des relations entre l'Algérie et la France.

Le dernier épisode en date, marqué par la visite du ministre français des Affaires étrangères, Hubert Védrine, dans la capitale algérienne, illustre la singularité des rapports entre les deux pays.

En fait, entre Alger et Paris, il y a toujours eu une succession de malentendus qui, pour préjudiciables qu'ils aient été pour les intérêts bien compris des deux pays, n'ont jamais entamé véritablement leur volonté d'inscrire leurs rapports dans la durée.

Point n'est besoin d'insister sur les raisons profondes du psychodrame qui entoure la coopération franco-algérienne. Près de quarante ans après l'indépendance de l'Algérie, les fantômes d'une décolonisation qui s'est faite dans la douleur sont toujours présents.

C'est à partir de cette réalité que les responsables algériens et français ont annoncé leur claire intention d'engager leurs pays sur une nouvelle voie.

Au-delà des premiers signes de ce que Hubert Védrine a appelé « l'alchimie franco-algérienne », dont attestent la réouverture prochaine des consulats et centres culturels français, ainsi que la promesse d'un accroissement du nombre de visas accordés aux nationaux algériens, les deux pays ont aujourd'hui de sérieuses raisons de consolider leur coopération. À y regarder de plus près et en prenant également en compte les importants flux migratoires entre les deux pays, cette coopération revêt même un caractère stratégique pour les deux partenaires.

A Trouvez dans le passage les phrases dont les expressions ci-dessous sont l'équivalent EXACT:

(a) rien ne reste à affirmer

(b) des difficultés n'ont cessé de surgir

(c) ça ne vaut pas du tout la peine

(d) si on examine plus attentivement le sujet

(e) le grand nombre de personnes qui se déplacent

B Trouvez les noms dont les expressions ci-dessous sont les définitions:

(f) le caractère original

(g) le passage à l'indépendance

(h) la participation à un projet commun

C Traduisez en anglais la phrase qui est soulignée dans le texte.

Practice examination questions (continued)

3 Writing

Lisez le passage au sujet d'un restaurant à Paris, puis écrivez en français 140–160 mots pour donner votre opinion sur ce que vous avez lu.

Paris 'speakeasy' restaurant defies EU food bans

Hidden away in an unfashionable corner of Paris, a clandestine restaurant is defying the edicts of Brussels by serving food long banned by the European Union.

Le Coin de Verre, buried in the eastern district of Belleville, does not advertise. From the outside, it appears to be permanently closed. A forbidding grill covers its entrance and, behind the front door, ancient drawn curtains suggest a gambling den or even a brothel.

But the rules broken here are all to do with food. The restaurant, which attracts its clients through word of mouth, is the headquarters of Appetit – a culinary resistance movement dedicated to flouting EU regulations on food safety in the name of traditional methods and good taste.

"Appetit is the abbreviated French acronym for the Association for the Protection of Traditional European Products Against the Imbecilities of National and International Technocrats," said the owner, Hugues Calliger.

"Brussels is so obsessed with hygiene and food safety that it is taking the fun and savour out of national and regional produce. In this restaurant we give people back the opportunity to make up their own minds."

You must express your own viewpoint, but these are the key points round which your answer should be constructed: the edicts of Brussels, banned by the EU, flouting EU regulations, obsessed with hygiene, make up their own minds.

Model answer

Dans l'article il s'agit d'un restaurateur qui refuse de suivre les règles imposées par Bruxelles, siège de l'Union Européenne, en ce qui concerne les conditions dans lesquelles la nourriture doit être préparée. Selon lui, les technocrates sont obsédés par l'hygiène à un tel point qu'on ne peut plus goûter librement les spécialités régionales et nationales. Certains produits, dont le fromage non pasteurisé, ont été interdits. Le restaurateur, lui, préfère laisser la décision aux clients: s'ils veulent courir le risque éventuel, on n'a pas le droit de les en empêcher.

Quant à moi, je suis d'accord dans une certaine mesure. Tout en admettant que je n'aime pas tellement l'idée de boire du lait qui n'a pas subi les contrôles dits 'de rigueur', je suis convaincue que le libre arbitre est un aspect très important de notre vie humaine. Si je refuse d'en boire, c'est mon affaire à moi. Il me semble que, bien que les responsables à Bruxelles aient mis en place des règles strictes, on devrait les contester pour que la liberté du choix soit rétablie.

Practice examination questions (continued)

Q 4

4 Listening

You are asked to correct the statements so that they reflect the sense of the listening extract. Some are straightforward, others require more thought.

Écoutez le passage au sujet de l'euro, puis corrigez les constatations ci-dessous selon le sens de l'extrait. Vous avez le droit d'utiliser les mots du passage si cela vous semble approprié.

(a) L'euro a perdu plus de 50% de sa valeur par rapport au dollar.

(b) L'explication de cette perte est évidente.

(c) Ceux qui vont partir en vacances aux États-Unis ne seront pas pénalisés.

(d) Les hommes politiques ont tous donné leurs réactions à la nouvelle.

(e) La monnaie unique a réussi à diviser l'Europe.

(f) L'Allemagne est indifférente à la dépréciation de l'euro.

(g) Les sentiments de Lionel Jospin à l'égard de la baisse de l'euro ne sont pas connus.

(h) Jacques Chirac pense que l'avenir de l'euro est discutable.

Chapter 5
L'environnement

The following topics are covered in this chapter:

- *Policy and pressure groups*
- *Nature and conservation*
- *Pollution*
- *Domestic waste and recycling*

- *Energy*
- *Grammar: More about verb construction*
- *How to answer: Other writing tasks*

The environment

After studying this chapter you should be able to:

- *understand French policy on conservation, pollution and energy*
- *recognise the vocabulary you will need to answer comprehension questions on these topics*
- *know how and when to use impersonal verbs and infinitive constructions*
- *improve your skill in various writing tasks*

LEARNING SUMMARY

5.1 Policy and pressure groups

AQA	M4, M6
EDEXCEL	M4, M6
OCR	M4, M5
WJEC	M4, M6
NICCEA	M4, M5

France's policy on the environment has been in place for 30 years, ever since concerns began to grow globally about the quality of air and water, the destruction of the rain forests, and the risk to endangered species. In 1990 the *Agence de l'Environnement et de la maîtrise de l'énergie (ADEME)* was set up, combining the functions of several organisations which had previously taken responsibility for these issues. Some towns have their own environmental plans, and individuals are becoming more involved. The overall responsibilty belongs to the *Ministre de l'environnement et de l'aménagement du territoire.*

Pressure groups such as Greenpeace and *Amis de la Terre* (Friends of the Earth) are active in France; both are international organisations, and both work towards more or less the same goals. Greenpeace is concerned largely with environmental problems on a world-wide scale: renewable energy, the oceans because they are the responsibility of no particular country, the risks inherent in the use of nuclear energy, GM foods. Greenpeace France uses this fact as its defence when people ask why it does not intervene in the matter of the Pyrenean bears and the Alpine wolves (see p. 84).

Amis de la Terre has as one of its principal campaigns the saving of the rainforests; it is also concerned about genetically modified foods, the risk of industrial pollution and the disposal of waste.

Although France has no tropical rainforests, the subject could still appear in exam questions because of the country's involvement with conservation issues.

Vocabulary for environmental policy and pressure groups

l'environnement (m)	environment	protéger	to protect
le souci	care, worry	préserver	to safeguard, preserve
l'inquiétude (f)	anxiety	intervenir	to intervene
la qualité	quality	exploiter	to exploit
l'atmosphère (f)	atmosphere	répertorier	to record, list
le risque	risk	impliquer	to involve
la question	issue, matter	à l'échelle mondiale	globally
le plan	plan	global	overall
l'individu (m)	individual	individuel, -elle	individual

Vocabulary for environmental policy and pressure groups (continued)

le groupe de pression	pressure group	**environnemental**	environmental
l'organisme (m)	organisation	**actif, -ve**	active
la campagne	countryside, campaign	**développé**	developed
le principe	principle	**principal**	main, principal
la réglementation	set of rules	**primordial**	essential, paramount
le développement	development	**efficace**	effective, efficient
la collectivité (locale)	(local) community	**intrinsèque**	intrinsic, inherent
l'assainissement (m)	cleaning up, decontamination		

KEY POINT

- *environnement/environnemental*; *développement/développé*: these words are often mis-spelt.
- *atmosphère*: must be used in this context (*ambiance* is not correct here).
- *individu/individuel*: don't confuse noun and adjective.
- *organisme*: *organisation* may also be used with a similar meaning.
- *campagne*: the risk of confusion is obvious; both meanings could make sense.
- *principe*: spell the English carefully; the noun 'principal' is a head teacher.
- *protéger*: remember the spelling of verbs ending in *-ger*; an extra *e* is needed before *a* or *o* (*nous protégeons, il protégeait*). A check of similar verbs should also remind you that the linked nouns usually end in *-ction* (e.g. *corriger/correction*).
- *exploiter*: remember the '*wa*' pronunciation of *-oi* in French.
- *global* is more general than 'world-wide'.

5.2 Nature and conservation

AQA	M4, M6
EDEXCEL	M4, M6
OCR	M4, M5
WJEC	M4, M6
NICCEA	M4, M5

At the moment there are seven national parks, six of them in France – Cévennes, Écrins, Mercantour, Pyrénées, Vanoise, Port Cros (Corsica) – and one in Guadeloupe. Six more are currently at the planning stage: these include one in Brittany and one in Guyane.

The existing national parks tend to be in remote mountainous areas which are sparsely populated, so access is not very easy and endangered flora and fauna can, in theory, flourish there. To fulfil a growing desire for a 'back-to-nature' place to roam at weekends and holiday times there are a number of *parcs naturels régionaux*, such as the Camargue and the Lubéron in Provence; there are also about 150 nature reserves. There are 400 protected species of plants.

Two of the issues that have been holding the interest of the media relate to the problems caused by bears in the Pyrenees and wolves in the Alps. The Slovenian bear was reintroduced in 1996 but there is much opposition from farmers because sheep and lambs have been attacked and killed; wolves cause similar damage. Rural France is still heavily involved in hunting; the range of birds and animals targeted is much wider than in the UK, and the bear is likely to be added to the list.

Special measures are in force to protect other species such as the Atlantic salmon.

The *parcs nationaux* are of particular importance for a large number of plants and insects. Some areas are designated as *Zones Naturelles d'intérêt écologique faunistique et floristique* (ZNIEFF).

Vocabulary for nature and conservation

le parc national	national park	les dommages (m)	damage
le parc naturel	nature reserve	la forêt tropicale	rainforest
la réserve naturelle	nature reserve	le déboisement	deforestation
la désertification	depopulation	détruire	to destroy
la sauvegarde	conservation	équilibrer	to balance
la survie	survival	(ré)introduire	to (re)introduce
le milieu	surroundings, environment	sauvegarder	to preserve, protect
l'habitat (m)	habitat	accéder à	to have access to
la flore	plant life, flora	éloigné	remote, distant
la faune	animal life, fauna	menacé	threatened
l'insecte (m)	insect	sauvage	wild
la plante	plant	peu peuplé	sparsely populated
l'espèce (f)	species	montagneux, -se	mountainous
la chasse	hunting	classé	classified, designated
la gamme	range	désigné	designated
l'ours/l'ourse	bear	en voie de disparition	endangered (species)
l'ourson (m)	bearcub	à l'état de projet	at the planning stage
le loup/la louve	wolf		

KEY POINT

- *habitat*: don't confuse this with *habitant*.
- *ours, ourson*: The *s* at the end is pronounced (as in *fils*). *Ourson* is also the French translation of Pooh (*Winnie l'ourson*).
- *détruire, introduire*: irregular verbs; endings are like those of *conduire*.
- *accéder*: one of the *espérer* group.

5.3 Pollution

AQA	M4, M6
EDEXCEL	M4, M6
OCR	M4, M5
WJEC	M4, M6
NICCEA	M4, M5

As in all industrialised countries, there is an increasing risk of pollution in France. This pollution may physically affect air, water and soil; another aspect of the problem is noise pollution, i.e. an unacceptable level of sound.

Air

Steps were taken some years ago to **decrease the use of CFCs**. Another contributory factor to atmospheric pollution is exhaust emissions from vehicles; nevertheless, of the industrialised nations France has the lowest rate of discharge into the atmosphere of carbon dioxide. In fact it succeeded in cutting its emissions of carbon gases by one third in the 1980s, but the increase in transport has reversed this to some extent. Factories are another source of air pollution (also of water pollution and the need for waste disposal: see p. 86).

You shouldn't need to know the scientific terms in French for ordinary comprehension purposes, but if you are studying Chemistry at A Level you might be able to bring in your detailed knowledge of the subject in a topic discussion or coursework.

The overall picture is that **sulphur dioxide emissions have decreased, lead has remained the same, and nitrogen oxide has increased**. A combination of sulphur and nitrogen oxides leads to acid rain, which is harmful to animal and plant life. Global warming is partly caused by the increase of carbon dioxide in the atmosphere.

Several solutions have been proposed, and some measures implemented:

- Drivers have been encouraged to reduce exhaust emissions by getting rid of older vehicles; a bonus was payable at the breaker's yard.
- The use of catalytic converters and unleaded petrol is now widespread.
- Diesel fuel is being more widely used.
- Car-sharing is encouraged.
- Electric cars are gaining in popularity.
- Smaller cars such as the 'smart car' are being promoted.

Look out for articles discussing the relative risks to health of diesel fuel; some think that diesel emissions may be as harmful as petrol fumes.

- Non-polluting public transport, particularly electric trams in large cities such as Strasbourg, is being introduced.

- Factories pay more taxes according to the amount of air pollution they create.

- An annual *sans voiture* day is observed in some cities and commuters are encouraged to use public transport.

An important weapon in the fight against pollution is the alarm system organised by **Airparif** in Paris and other large cities. An alert is automatically triggered when atmospheric pollution reaches a certain level. When this happens, the public is informed and restrictions are introduced depending on the level of the alert. In the worst situations, only vehicles bearing a green sticker (these would include electric cars and those which have a catalytic converter) may be driven. In Paris and Strasbourg, when pollution levels are very high, cars may be driven only on alternate days (organised by registration number). The situation is monitored daily by Airparif, which has a number of *stations de surveillance* to keep track of atmospheric pollution.

Soil

Soil pollution is a problem in some areas. These include:

- Mining areas (though these are decreasing; see p. 88).

- Agricultural areas, particularly those where intensive farming methods are used. The problem is the use of pesticides; not only do they pollute the soil, they may also damage the vegetation.

- Industrial areas: those in Northern France are the most affected.

- Fields next to motorways and near factories.

Soil pollutants include metals such as mercury, cadmium, lead, nickel and chrome. The CNRS, INSERM and scientists in the universities are working to find solutions to these problems.

Water

France is not short of natural water provision. In all there are almost 280 000 km of streams and rivers, plus canals. The *Agences de l'eau* monitor the water courses. Pollution of inland water and the water table is often caused by pesticides, the main culprit being **modern agricultural methods**. Factories polluting water courses are expected to pay for their cleansing; the scheme is known as *pollueur payeur*: the one who pollutes must pay. Grants may be available to help firms reduce or treat their effluent.

The sea and seashore is constantly at risk from **oil spillages**; the Channel and Atlantic coasts are particularly vulnerable. In 1999 oil slicks from the *Erika* polluted many of the beaches of Brittany and the islands off its coast. When a beach is affected by oil, a large-scale clean-up operation is quickly mounted. France is proud of the number of Blue Flag beaches it possesses (the blue flag is the emblem of a clean beach according to European standards).

Noise

Many awarding bodies have Transport in their AS specification, but as with other topics there are links with A2 and you should be aware that these issues could still appear at this level.

Noise pollution is generally linked to transport, particularly road and air transport. Other aspects may involve neighbours being annoyed by music being played too loudly, and workers running the risk of hearing loss because of noisy factory production lines.

Vocabulary for pollution

les effluents (m)	effluent, discharge	radioactif, -ive	radioactive
la pollution	pollution	la nappe d'eau	expanse of water
le polluant	pollutant	le pétrole (brut)	(crude) oil
les gaz d'échappement	exhaust gases	la marée noire	oil slick
les CFC	CFCs	le déversement	spillage
le plomb	lead	le mazout	oil
le monoxyde de carbone	carbon monoxide	le littoral	coast, shoreline
le mercure	mercury	le prélèvement	sample (water, soil)
l'azote (m)	nitrogen	le bruit	noise
les pluies acides (f)	acid rain	les nuisances sonores	noise pollution
l'effet (m) de serre	greenhouse effect	polluer	to pollute
la couche d'ozone	ozone layer	déclencher	to trigger, set off
le trou	hole	analyser	to analyse
la bombe aérosol	spray can	rejeter	to discharge
le carburant	fuel	dégager	to give off (gas etc.)
l'impôt (m)	tax	causer	to cause
le pot catalytique	catalytic converter	limiter	to restrict
le covoiturage	car-sharing	suivre de près	to monitor (situation)
le niveau	level	nuire à	to harm
la norme	standard	souiller	to soil, contaminate
la plage	beach	nocif, -ive	harmful, noxious
le produit chimique	chemical product	industrialisé	industrialised
le problème respiratoire	breathing problem	minier, -ière	mining (adj.)
l'asthme (m)	asthma	littoral	coastal
les hydrocarbures	hydrocarbons	potable	drinking (water)
le sol	soil	toxique	toxic, poisonous
le cours d'eau	watercourse	nuisible	harmful
le fleuve	river (large)	sourd	deaf
la rivière	river	souterrain	underground
le ruisseau	stream	selon	according to
le réchauffement de la planète	global warming	sans plomb	unleaded

KEY POINT

- *polluant, polluer*: there is no *t* in the middle of these words.
- *pétrole*: take care; in the context of the environment 'petrol' could well make sense (see next section).
- *nuisances*: the same applies to 'nuisance'.
- *nuire*: an irregular verb; see p. 75. Remember that it is followed by *à*.

5.4 Domestic waste and recycling

AQA	M4, M6
EDEXCEL	M4, M6
OCR	M4, M5
WJEC	M4, M6
NICCEA	M4, M5

France produces over 400 kilos of household waste per head of population per year, a total of 24 million tonnes per annum. The disposal of this waste is a particular problem in densely populated areas. Much of it is burned, and some of the burning produces energy which can be used.

A system of coloured containers has been introduced, so that individuals can sort their waste into separate categories (e.g. purple for plastic, green for glass, blue for paper and cardboard) and thus aid recycling.

For more information log on to www.recyclages.com

Firms must contribute to the cost of disposing of the packaging in which their products are sold, if this is not totally destructible or recyclable. France has set itself a target of recycling three quarters of all its packaging by 2002.

Vocabulary for recycling

les déchets (ménagers)	(household) waste	trier	to sort
l'enlèvement (m)	disposal (taking away)	recycler	to recycle
la destruction	disposal (destruction)	réutiliser	to re-use
le conteneur	container	réduire	to reduce
le recyclage	recycling	consommer	to consume, use
l'emballage (m)	packaging	compacter	to compact, compress
le traitement	treatment	gaspiller	to waste
le dépôt	dump, rubbish tip	jeter	to throw away
la décharge	dump	traiter	to treat
les ordures	rubbish	éliminer	to get rid of
le verre	glass	en plastique	made of plastic
le fer blanc	tin (cans)	recyclable	able to be recycled
la poubelle	dustbin	recyclé	recycled
le tri	sorting	vert	'green', ecological
les détritus	waste, rubbish	écolo(gique)	ecological

5.5 Energy

EDEXCEL	M4, M6
OCR	M4, M5
WJEC	M4, M6

The Superphénix fast breeder reactor (plutonium) began operating in 1986, but was shut down for economic reasons in 1998.

France has few fossil fuel resources of its own, so is very much dependent on imports for petrol and oil. A **network of 57 nuclear power stations** on the Loire and Rhône rivers has been developed, amid concerns by ecologists that the disposal of nuclear waste would be both difficult and dangerous. In fact France is second in the world (behind the USA) in the field of nuclear energy. As a result, it now produces about 50% of its own energy needs; this has doubled since the 1970s. Nuclear power accounts for 75% of its electricity production and 40% of its total energy consumption; EDF (*Électricité de France*) is one of the major electricity companies in the world. Nevertheless, the **long-term future of nuclear energy is currently being called into question**.

Other sources of energy include:

- coal – fast running out; mines in the Nord-Pas de Calais area have been shut down, and all others will be closed by 2005.

- oil – there are deposits in Brie and the Landes, but they provide only a tiny fraction of what is needed. Some North Sea oil is also available.

- natural gas – a little is produced in the south-west but it is rapidly becoming exhausted.

A fuel extracted from *colza* (rape seed) is used for buses in some cities.

The search for alternative sources of energy continues, but as yet only a small percentage is produced by these methods, in the following ways:

- aeolian (wind) power – on Atlantic and Channel coasts and the Rhône.

- geothermal – in the south-west, and heats a suburb of Paris.

- tidal – the Rance estuary in Brittany.

- solar – in the Pyrenees and Corsica, for use mostly in the Midi (South of France).

- hydraulic (water) – in the Alps, Pyrenees and Massif Central.

The high cost of imported fuel was the principal factor in the blockade of ports in summer 2000.

Ecologists are disappointed that more has not been accomplished in the field of alternative energy (it still amounts to no more than 2% of total energy production); they were hoping that nuclear power could be reduced, if not sidelined. People are urged to save energy by switching off machines when they are not in use, and by insulating buildings to conserve heat.

Vocabulary for energy

l'énergie (f)	energy, power	dépendre de	to depend on
les ressources (f)	resources	s'épuiser	to be exhausted
l'approvisionnement (m)	supply, provision	décevoir	to disappoint
l'importation (f)	importing	accomplir	to accomplish
l'essence (f)	petrol	disposer de	to have available
le pétrole	oil	utiliser	to use
le gaz	gas	user	to use up
le charbon	coal	suffire	to be sufficient
la houille blanche	hydro-electric power	chauffer	to heat
le gazoil	diesel	éteindre	to switch off
la centrale	power station	allumer	to switch on
les déchets nucléaires	nuclear waste	isoler	to insulate
les retombées	fall-out, side effects	insuffisant	insufficient
le besoin	need	de substitution	alternative (sources)
la consommation	consumption	éolien, -enne	wind (adj.)
le vent	wind	géothermique	geothermal
le gisement	deposit (oil, gas)	marémoteur, -trice	tidal
le réacteur	reactor	solaire	solar
le Moyen Orient	Middle East	hydraulique	hydraulic
la Mer du Nord	North Sea	renouvelable	renewable
le barrage	dam	décevant	disappointing
le blocus	blockade	déçu	disappointed
le marché	market	biodégradable	biodegradable
le chauffage	heating	électrique	electric
le mazout	oil for heating	énergétique	of energy
le fioul	fuel	nucléaire	nuclear
les matières premières	raw materials	à court terme	short-term
l'isolation (f)	insulation	à long terme	long-term

KEY POINT

- *décevoir*: this verb has the same endings as *recevoir*. A *faux ami*: not 'deceive'.
- *fioul*: a French (so more acceptable to the Académie Française) way to spell 'fuel'.
- *éteindre*: check the endings of verbs ending in *-indre* (p.74).
- *isoler*: can also mean 'to isolate'.
- *énergétique*: don't confuse with *énergique*, which means 'energetic'.
- *électricité, électrique*: these words are often mis-spelt.
- *suffire*: an irregular verb.

Progress check

When you have learnt the vocabulary for this section, write down the following key words, then check them with the lists.

Give the French for: environment, principle, to involve, individual (noun), survival, bear, endangered, pollutant, ozone layer, to restrict, level, harmful, recycling, to re-use, to accomplish, electricity, side effects, nuclear, renewable, insufficient.

Give the English for: global, primordial, l'assainissement, efficace, le milieu, la faune, le déboisement, sauvegarder, les nuisances sonores, l'impôt, le covoiturage, la norme, le ruisseau, la centrale, le tri, les déchets, user, écolo, la houille blanche, éolien.

Grammar

5.6 More about verb constructions

Devoir and falloir

In most sentences these two verbs are interchangeable: your choice when speaking or writing French will normally depend on which verb you find easier to use. Students sometimes find the meaning of the tenses difficult to remember; study the list below.

If you need to use the verb more than once you will impress your examiner if you can switch from one to the other.

Present: 'must', 'have to'
> *Je dois/il (me) faut réutiliser les sacs en plastique* – 'I have to re-use plastic bags'.

Future: 'will have to'
> *Ils devront/il (leur) faudra réduire leur niveau de consommation* – 'They will have to reduce their level of consumption'.

Imperfect: 'had to'
> *Nous devions/il (nous) fallait limiter l'utilisation de l'essence* – 'We had to limit the use of petrol'.

Conditional: 'ought to', 'should'
> *Tu devrais/il (te) faudrait recycler le fer blanc* – 'You ought to recycle tin cans'.

Perfect: 'had to', 'must have'
> *On a dû/il a fallu suivre la situation de près* – 'We had to/it was necessary to monitor the situation'.
> *Tu as dû avoir peur!* – 'You must have been afraid'.

Pluperfect: 'had had to'
> *Nous avions dû/il (nous) avait fallu intervenir pour protéger la flore* – 'We had had to intervene to protect plant life'.

Future perfect: 'will have had to'
> *Dans dix ans nous aurons dû/il (nous) aura fallu user toutes nos ressources* – 'In ten years' time we will have had to use up all our resources'.

Conditional perfect: 'would have', 'ought to have'
> *Elle aurait dû/il (lui) aurait fallu mettre en place des mesures de protection de la faune* – 'She ought to have set up measures to protect the wildlife'.

- You may have learnt *il faut* as 'it is necessary'. This is helpful in one way, because it reminds you that *il faut* is an impersonal verb (it can have no pronoun other than *il*), but it is not usually the best way to translate it into English as it is rather stilted.
- The negative of *falloir* means 'must not': *Il ne faut pas détruire la couche d'ozone*. For 'it is not necessary to' use *il n'est pas nécessaire de*.
- If the subject of the sentence is a noun you should use *devoir*: *Les besoins énergétiques devraient être pris en compte*.
- In the *falloir* sentences above, the pronouns have been bracketed. They are not strictly necessary, but it does clarify which person is the subject of the verb. The pronoun is the indirect object pronoun (*me, te, lui, nous, vous, leur*).

KEY POINT

Pouvoir, savoir and connaître

Pouvoir ('can') means 'to be able' or sometimes 'to be allowed to':
> *Tu peux m'expliquer les avantages du nucléaire?* – 'Can you explain to me the advantages of nuclear energy?'

Savoir may also mean 'can', in the sense of knowing how to do something:
> *Je ne sais pas lire la carte* – 'I can't read the map'.

In that sentence, 'can't read' could also have been translated as 'don't know how to read'. *Savoir* is used for knowing a fact or a skill; when 'know' is followed directly by a noun the verb *connaître* should be used. It is most often used with a person or place:
> *Tu connais le parc national à Port Cros?*

Impersonal verbs

You have known the 'weather' verbs (*il pleut, il neige, il fait beau,* etc.) since you began to learn French. There are also several other impersonal verbs besides *falloir* which are useful at A2 if you wish to improve the standard of your French. Some of them are 'normal' verbs which may be used with a full range of forms but which are often used in the *il* form with the impersonal meaning 'it' (or sometimes 'there'). They include:

* *Il semble, il paraît* – 'it seems'. Note that in parenthesis (between commas) this should be inverted: *la situation, paraît-il, devient insupportable.*

* *Il s'agit de* – it's about, it's a question of.

* *Il vaut mieux* – it's better.

* *Il existe* – there is/there are; used more often now, but still not as natural as *il y a.*

* *Il reste* – there remain(s): *Il en reste une vingtaine* – 'There are about 20 left'.

Students sometimes forget that the *a* of *il y a* is from *avoir*. The other tenses are:

future: *il y aura* – 'there will be'

imperfect: *il y avait* – 'there was', 'there were'

conditional: *il y aurait* – 'there would be'

perfect: *il y a eu* – 'there was', 'there were'

pluperfect: *il y avait eu* – 'there had been'

future perfect: *il y aura eu* – 'there will have been'

conditional perfect: *il y aurait eu* – 'there would have been'

past historic: *il y eut* – 'there was', 'there were'.

Verbs with different constructions

Key points from AS

* **Verbs followed by infinitive**
  AS Study Guide pp. 95–96
* **Indirect object pronouns**
  AS Study Guide p. 65

* As you have learnt, *commencer* is usually followed by *à* and *finir* by *de*. Both may, however, be followed by *par* if the English is 'by': *On doit commencer par analyser les prélèvements.*

* The construction used with verbs such as *dire, demander, conseiller* and *permettre* is very important at A2. You need: *à* + person, *de* + infinitive: *Demandez au ministre d'expliquer la situation.* If a pronoun is used it must be the indirect object pronoun: *Demandez-lui d'expliquer....*

* *Apprendre* uses *à* with the noun as well as with the infinitive: *Nous devons apprendre aux Français à recycler le verre (Nous devons leur apprendre ...).*

- Some verbs are followed by the indirect object of the person and the direct object of the thing. These include *apprendre, conseiller, demander, fournir, inspirer, permettre, refuser, reprocher.*

  Examples: *Elle lui a inspiré confiance; je lui ai conseillé la prudence: les centrales nucléaires ont fourni aux Français la plupart de leurs besoins en énergie.*

Infinitive as command

The infinitive may be used as a formal command, usually in written notices:
S'adresser au concierge – 'Apply to the caretaker'.

Progress check

Translate into English (answers on p. 154).

1 Vous devrez jeter les ordures dans la poubelle.
2 Il aurait fallu comprendre les risques plus tôt.
3 Il ne faut pas gaspiller nos ressources.
4 Elle a pu soutenir les demandes des Verts.
5 Ils ne savaient pas combien il y avait d'espèces.
6 Il semble que la situation devienne plus compliquée.
7 Il s'agit du trou dans la couche d'ozone.
8 Il y avait eu une vingtaine d'ours.
9 Je vous conseille de lui permettre d'y aller.
10 S'adresser au gardien.

How to answer

5.7 Other writing tasks

The assessment of your writing in French is carried out in several ways, depending on your particular exam:

- through the standard of the French you use when answering comprehension questions
- through explanation, short essays and articles written in the mixed-skill unit
- through the range and accuracy of your language in the Culture/Topics paper.

The third of these will be dealt with in Chapter 7.

You will know whether your exam requires you to answer any of the specific types of question below. Each type of task has its own characteristics and should not be attempted without preparation and practice; always answer according to your own strengths.

Explanation and paraphrase

You may have to show that you have understood a section of the passage by explaining it in your own words in French. It's very tempting to use a synonym for each word and assume that you have an exact equivalent, but this is rarely the case; in fact it's unlikely that you would be able to do this now that dictionaries are not allowed.

Look at this example:

> *Les accidents sont très fréquents dans les zones de fort trafic pétrolier* – 'Les sinistres sont très souvent dans les régions de grande circulation de pétrole'.

This contains errors (*souvent* is not an adjective; *région* and *circulation* are not the best words to use in the context) and it is difficult to understand – it certainly doesn't show that you have understood the original French. A good way to deal with individual phrases and sentences like this is:

* work out what it means in English
* think how you could express that meaning differently
* put it back into French.

So here, you would decide that the phrase means 'Accidents frequently occur in areas where there are many oil tankers' and express it as *Il y a souvent des sinistres là où il y a beaucoup de navires qui transportent le pétrole*. The French does not have to be sophisticated, but it should be accurate. Above all, it must make sense.

Adding your own opinion

Don't write *à mon avis je pense que*; firstly because it says the same thing twice, and secondly because you won't have the words to spare.

Usually, questions asking you to add your opinion are tacked on to the end of other questions on the same passage, so your answer will probably be fairly short. Try to use some variety; don't start each sentence with *Je pense que*. There are other possibilities; try *à mon avis, à mon sens, je trouve que, je crois que, il me semble que*.

Use topic-specific vocabulary to underline your understanding of the subject. It's best to use words other than those that are in the text, or at least to adapt them (*dépendre de* could become *dépendance*; *renouveler* could turn into *renouvelable* with a little manipulation).

This type of exercise will gain higher marks if you have used more sophisticated language (see list p. 114) but the number of words allowed means that you will have little scope to show what you can really do.

Essay or article

You should concentrate on three things: **content, structure and language**.

* **Content**: check whether your answer has to be based on a text or whether you have a free hand; in the latter case, check whether it must be linked directly to France (or a francophone country) or if it can be more general. If it has to be based on the text, spend a few minutes highlighting the particular points you intend to include. Otherwise, list the points you wish to make.
* **Structure**: present your points in a logical order, and use linking phrases to move from one to the next.
* **Language**: be accurate, particularly with basic grammar. Use the structures you have learnt during your course; subjunctive, passive, *après avoir* + past participle, *en* + present participle, pronouns, a variety of tenses and idioms, and topic-specific vocabulary.

Writing in registers

Some exams encourage you to be more original in your approach to the subject. You may have the choice of some of the following tasks:

* Dialogue: your style may be casual in tone, more like spoken French. **To get your points across within the word limit you will need to balance the conversation** carefully between question and answer. Check whether you need to use the *tu* or *vous* forms of the verb.

- Text of a speech: check the nature of your target audience and adapt the tone accordingly.

- Letter: informal (e.g. to a friend) or formal (e.g. to a newspaper or an official body). **Don't mix the two registers**, particularly in the beginning and ending formulae.

- Journalistic: you will need to capture the attention of the reader. Practise by reading French newspapers to get an idea of the style.

- Based on visual images + questions: use the picture as the basis for your answer, but take care to cover all the questions or you will be penalised.

- Work-related: this will probably be based on a letter, fax or memo. Look carefully at the stimulus, and identify the information that has to be conveyed and any vocabulary you may be able to use in your answer.

Whatever type of task you have to perform, there are three things to remember:

- Don't, unless it's absolutely necessary, do a rough version first. The time spent in copying it out is needed for the other questions. You might even leave out words or whole phrases in your haste.

- Do leave yourself a little time to check what you have written for accuracy (see list on p. 113). If you have only a few minutes left, concentrate on verb endings and adjective agreements.

- Keep within the word allocation you are given: check as you are writing that you are not going over the limit. The general advice given is that a 'word' is an item of French with a space on each side of it: so *les déchets* and *on nettoie* are two words each, *l'organisme* and *j'utilise* are each one word. Don't spend too much time counting; write at the end the approximate number of words used, but don't try to mislead the examiner by putting an obviously inaccurate total. Examiners quickly develop a 'feel' for the right length.

Examiner's tip

Before the exam, practise writing the correct number of words in your normal writing on a piece of paper of the same size as the exam stationery. You will be able to tell quite easily if your answer is getting too long, or if you haven't written enough.

Sample and practice exam questions

1 Reading

The five short paragraphs are concerned with different aspects of energy conservation and recycling. The questions on them are of different types; remember what you have learnt about how to answer each one as you attempt them.

LA VIE ECOLO

1. TRIER SES DECHETS

C'est un classique, on se l'entend dire et redire à longueur de temps. C'est pourtant le geste simple qui permet d'économiser le coût d'un tri en aval. Et permet le recyclage. En recyclant, on limite la pollution, on économise les matières premières et l'énergie. Pour faciliter ce tri, installez chez vous trois poubelles distinctes : une pour le verre, une pour le papier et une autre pour tout le reste.

2. UTILISER DU PAPIER RECYCLE

Il ne suffit pas de trier ses déchets, encore faut-il ensuite consommer recyclé. En plus d'être « écologiquement correct », le papier recyclé est élégant : lourd, coloré. Si vous ne le faites pas par civisme, faites-le seulement parce que le papier recyclé, c'est bien plus beau qu'une feuille blanche et lisse.

3. CONSOMMER MOINS D'ELECTRICITE

En y regardant bien, l'opération n'est pas si difficile. Baisser sa température de lavage de la machine à laver le linge de 90 à 60 degrés permet d'économiser 15% d'électricité par an. De même, il est important de dégivrer souvent son réfrigérateur (cinq millimètres de givre augmentent la consommation de 30%). Il faut aussi veiller à éteindre la télévision ou l'ordinateur lorsqu'on ne les utilise pas. Et à éteindre les lumières quand on quitte une pièce.

4. ROULER PROPRE

Si vous n'êtes pas prête à vous mettre au vélo, aux rollers ou aux transports en commun, adoptez quelques mesures basiques pour circuler en voiture en « limitant les dégâts » (les émissions toxiques qui saturent l'air de nos grandes villes et grignotent chaque jour un peu plus la couche d'ozone).

Poussés par les lobbies verts qui ont fait pression sur le législateur pour imposer des normes plus sévères d'émissions polluantes, les constructeurs automobiles sont désormais contraints de fabriquer des véhicules propres. Les modèles récents permettent de réduire les émissions polluantes de 20 à 30%.

Il faut aussi couper son moteur lorsqu'on est à l'arrêt, coincé dans un embouteillage. De toute façon, évitez de prendre votre voiture pour des petits trajets. Vous pouvez aussi opter pour un scooter, ou une moto 125 à conduire avec un permis A. C'est polluant, certes, mais nettement moins qu'une voiture. Et beaucoup plus pratique pour se garer! Reste aussi la location qui, tout bien calculé, ne revient pas plus cher que le coût d'une voiture (entretien + frais : 3 700F par mois).

5. CHAUFFER SANS EXCES

Au fioul, au gaz ou à l'électricité, le chauffage contribue à l'épuisement des ressources naturelles non renouvelables et à la pollution de l'air. Pour baisser sa consommation, il faut d'abord veiller à ce que les pièces soient bien isolées. Il faut aussi adapter les températures : pas la peine de chauffer une chambre à 22 degrés. 18 degrés conviennent parfaitement. Vous y gagnez, de surcroît, en qualité de sommeil.

(a) Les avantages du tri des déchets sont que la pollution

....

et que les matières premières et l'énergie

....

(b) Le papier recyclé est blanc et lisse. Vrai ou faux?

....

(c) Traduisez en anglais le paragraphe qui s'intitule *Consommer moins d'électricité*.

(d) Trouvez l'équivalent exact des expressions ci-dessous (*Rouler propre*):
   (i) des démarches élémentaires
   (ii) détruisent peu à peu
   (iii) afin de mettre en place une réglementation plus stricte
   (iv) quand on ne bouge pas
   (v) lorsque vous ne voyagez pas loin
   (vi) pas autant que

(e) Expliquez en français les expressions ci-dessous (*Chauffer sans excès*):
   (i) contribue à l'épuisement des ressources
   (ii) conviennent parfaitement
   (iii) vous y gagnez, de surcroît, en qualité de sommeil

Sample and practice exam questions (continued)

Q 2

2 Listening

Two short passages about pollution have been recorded on the CD. For the first one, you must correct the statements; for the second, answer the questions in French.

(i) **Écoutez le premier extrait, puis corrigez les phrases ci-dessous.**

    (a) Les habitants de la Bretagne devraient être contents.

    (b) On craint l'arrivée de nouvelles nappes de fioul.

    (c) Des nappes de fioul sont arrivées le premier décembre.

    (d) Heureusement on n'avait pas encore entamé le travail de nettoyage.

(ii) **Écoutez le deuxième extrait, puis répondez en français aux questions ci-dessous.**

    (e) De quelle ville s'agit-il?   (1)

    (f) Pourquoi les polluants ne sont-ils pas dispersés?   (1)

    (g) Quel conseil donne-t-on aux conducteurs?   (2)

    (h) Qu'est-ce qu'on leur dit pour les encourager à le faire?   (1)

    (i) Qu'est-ce qu'il y a comme restrictions pour les automobilistes?   (2)

3 Sample question – Writing

A votre avis, qu'est-ce qu'on devrait faire pour être plus écolo? Écrivez un maximum de 200 mots.

Model answer

On dirait que notre planète risque d'être détruite (1). Pas au pied de la lettre (2), bien sûr; mais notre santé va souffrir aussi bien que la qualité de notre vie. Pourquoi? (3) Parce que nous n'avons pas pris les mesures nécessaires pour la (4) sauver. En utilisant (5) trop les bombes aérosol qui contiennent les CFC nous avons fait apparaître (6) un trou dans la couche d'ozone. Les émissions qui proviennent des usines dans les pays industrialisés – en France, surtout dans le Nord (7) – ont causé des pluies acides qui, à leur tour, détruisent la flore et la faune, même les forêts.

Que faire pour résoudre le problème (3)? Premièrement (8), il faut qu'on interdise (9) les CFC: il est possible d'acheter (10) des produits qui n'en (4) contiennent pas. Deuxièmement, (8) il faut (11) mettre en place des normes plus strictes pour les usines afin qu'on les (4) empêche (9) d'émettre (10) des gaz toxiques; de cette façon l'atmosphère sera protégée (12) si ce n'est pas trop tard. Finalement (8), nous devons (11) trier (10) les déchets ménagers pour que nous puissions (9) réutiliser (10) ce qui (13) peut être recyclé (12). Si tout le monde fait de son mieux, nous pourrons réussir.

This is not perfect; the ending is rather trite, and in so few words it isn't possible to cover every aspect of the subject. However, the candidate has succeeded in using a wide range of topic-specific vocabulary, and there is good use of language.

The following points are worthy of merit:

1 first sentence attracts the reader's attention. It also includes a passive infinitive
2 idiom
3 asks a question, then answers it
4 use of pronouns
5 *en* + present participle
6 *faire* + infinitive
7 precise reference to France
8 clear structure
9 subjunctive
10 infinitive construction
11 another way of expressing the same thing
12 passive
13 *ce qui*

Now try to use some of the same constructions for the following question.

4 Writing

Écrivez un article, pour le magazine français de votre lycée, au sujet de l'avenir énergétique.

You will find a possible answer on p. 156.

Chapter 6
Questions diverses

The following topics are covered in this chapter:

- Religion and belief
- War and conflict
- Distribution of wealth
- Grammar: Indefinite pronouns and adverbs
- How to answer: Questions on listening passages

Miscellaneous issues

After studying this chapter you should be able to:

- answer questions about global issues such as religion, war, and the problems of the developing countries
- identify the vocabulary related to these topics
- understand how to use indefinite pronouns and adverbs
- increase your knowledge of some constructions involving verbs, pronouns and adverbs
- improve your listening skills

LEARNING SUMMARY

6.1 Religion and belief

| EDEXCEL | M4, M6 |
| OCR | M4, M5 |

The traditional image of religion in France is of a multitude of Catholic churches, processions of priests and the faithful on the occasion of the great church festivals, and children dressed for their *Première Communion*. Although this is still an important aspect of French culture, changes have taken place; **more people (20%) now say that they have no particular belief or no belief at all**, and – partly but not entirely because of the greater ethnic mix – **religions other than Christianity are becoming increasingly popular.**

At the beginning of the 21st century the situation (figures are approximate) is:

- 46 million French people are baptised Christians; the vast majority (about 45 million) are Roman Catholic, the rest are Protestant, mostly belonging to the *Église Réformée de France*. Only about 20% of baptised Catholics attend Mass regularly; a further 20% attend on feast days.

- 4 million are followers of Islam; just under one third of these are French nationals. About half a million fulfil the Islamic prayer requirements daily.

- 700 000 are Jews.

- 600 000 are Buddhists. As well as these, many people have adopted a Buddhist life-style because it appeals to them; they are particularly attracted to the calming effects of meditation and to the belief in karma and reincarnation.

- Various groups and sects, such as New Age and Scientology, have their supporters.

Officially the State is neutral as far as religion is concerned (*laïcité*) and the French are urged to be tolerant of religions other than their own. Religion is not taught as a subject in French schools. A few years ago the media seized on the case of two Muslim girls who were excluded from school because they wore their traditional dress; one reason given for the exclusion was that safety rules could not be followed in science lessons because of their head covering. The matter was front page news for some time. The matter resurfaced in 2003 when the government planned to ban the wearing of any overtly religious symbols.

There is a possibility that schools may be closed for Yom Kippur and Aïd-al-Kebir in future.

In practice, the Church still exerts considerable influence; many of the *jours de congé* are religious feast days (e.g. Ash Wednesday, Ascension Day, the Assumption, All Saints' Day). Factories, shops and schools originally closed on those days so that people could attend Mass; now there is less emphasis placed on the religious significance as many people use them simply as holidays. The organisation *Action Catholique* has connections with the workplace, professional associations and youth groups (including Scouts and Guides).

There is some concern about the 'crisis of faith' and the lowering of moral standards which some people feel is the result of turning away from religion. Overall, the number of priests is decreasing. Some of them, however, have a high profile in the media; one such is Cardinal Lustiger, who for many years has led a pilgrimage on Good Friday. Archbishop Lefebvre, who continued to celebrate Mass in Latin despite the changes made by the second Vatican Council, also had a considerable following. Those who continue to hold traditional Catholic beliefs are as devout as ever, and Lourdes is still a popular destination for pilgrims from France and elsewhere.

The situation as regards marriage fluctuates from year to year. Although there has been a huge increase in the number of *unions libres* (couples living together outside marriage – see also AS Study Guide Chapter 3) among some young people there is now a desire to preserve virginity until marriage. There is also more freedom now in the names that may be given to children; once it was expected that saints' names would be used, but there is much more influence from America and the UK now.

Examiner's tip

Moral questions, such as whether euthanasia should be permissible, are possible subjects for comprehension questions, particularly those to which you have to add your own opinions. It's a good idea to work out a response in French in advance.

Some years ago a mother complained that she was not allowed to call her daughter Marilyn. She compromised with the acceptable spelling of Marie-Line.

Vocabulary for religion and belief

le christianisme	christianity	l'abbé (m)	priest
l'Islam	Islam	le pasteur	minister, pastor
le bouddhisme	Buddhism	l'imam	imam
le judaïsme	Judaism	le moine	monk
le catholicisme	Catholicism	le religieux	monk
le protestantisme	Protestantism	la religieuse	nun
(le bon) Dieu	God	le monastère	monastery
la croyance	belief	le couvent	convent
la foi	faith	Père	Father (title)
la crise	crisis	Frère	Brother (title)
la moralité	morality	Soeur	Sister (title)
la vérité	truth	le gourou	guru
le croyant	believer	le jour de fête	feast day
le/la fidèle	believer	le mode de vie	way of life
l'adepte	follower	le pèlerin	pilgrim
l'assemblée (f)	congregation	le pèlerinage	pilgrimage
l'église (f)	church	croire	to believe
la messe	Mass	prier	to pray
la procession	procession	rendre un culte à	to worship
le cortège	procession	baptiser	to baptise
le défilé	procession	bénir	to bless
le rituel	ritual	chrétien, -enne	Christian
le rite	rite	catholique	Roman Catholic
l'office (m)	service (RC)	protestant	Protestant
le service	service (Protestant)	musulman	Muslim, Moslem
le culte	worship	bouddhiste	Buddhist
la cloche	bell	juif, juive	Jewish
la mosquée	mosque	hindou	Hindu
le temple	temple	religieux, -se	religious
la secte	sect	laïc/laïque	lay (not linked with religion)
la Bible	Bible		
le Coran	Koran	athée	atheist
la prière	prayer	agnostique	agnostic

Vocabulary for religion and belief (continued)

le tapis de prière	prayer mat	**fanatique**	fanatical
le prêtre	priest	**obsédé (par)**	obsessed (by)
le curé	parish priest	**spirituel, -elle**	spiritual
le pape	Pope		
le cierge	candle (church)		

- *foi*: remember the two other possible spellings of this sound (*fois* = 'time', *foie* = 'liver'). Take particular care not to confuse *crise de foi* with *crise de foie*!
- *cortège*: note that this is not just used for a funeral procession in French.
- *croire*: followed by *en* (*je crois en Dieu*) or *à*.
- *baptiser*: the *p* is not pronounced.
- *spirituel*: this word can also mean 'witty'; you will need to decide which is most likely in the context.

6.2 War and conflict

AQA	M4, M6
NICCEA	M4, M5
EDEXCEL	M4, M6 (current affairs, world-wide problems)
WJEC	M4, M6 (current affairs)

There has been no war in France itself since 1945; the study of the Second World War, including the Resistance movement, is a subject for topic discussion and essay or coursework (for advice see Chapter 8). For the purposes of comprehension questions, you should be aware of the following contemporary aspects of the topic:

- France's defence policy
- wars elsewhere in the world in which French troops may be concerned
- conflict involving dissident groups within France or on the borders.

Defence policy

This is stated as having three purposes:

- to defend the interests of the country
- to work towards the stability of Europe
- to put in place a global defence plan.

In general terms, the policy is one of **dissuasion**; France believes it should keep its forces and weapons at a level strong enough to deter other countries and make them realise that France is a force to be reckoned with.

France took part in the Strategic Arms Reduction Talks, and is in favour of the '**zero option**', a complete ban on nuclear tests of any sort. It was one of the first countries to sign an agreement to this effect, and as a result ceased its underground nuclear tests which had been taking place in French Polynesia. Factories producing plutonium and uranium were closed down and the Hadès missiles dismantled. A decision was also taken not to export nuclear materials to any country which had not agreed to allow its nuclear installations to be inspected by an international body. France is against the use of chemical and biological weapons and anti-personnel mines.

National Service has been phased out; technically it has been suspended, and could be reinstated if the need arose. This affects young men born after 31st December 1978. New regulations have been introduced to take the place of National Service. These include the addition to the school curriculum of the principles and organisation of defence, and a one-day course (for men born after

Two of the honours which may be conferred by the French government are the *Croix de Guerre* (established during the two World Wars) and the *Légion d'Honneur*, which is awarded as a military or civil decoration for services to the state.

There are plans for a European Defence Force under the command of Brussels which might be used in conflicts in which NATO is not involved. There is some disagreement about this.

31/12/1978 and women born after 31/12/1982) called *appel de préparation à la défense*. It will be possible to volunteer to do a *préparation militaire* of one year, which may be renewed annually for up to five years, or to join the reserve list of the army or *gendarmerie*.

French defence policy extends to the *sécurité civile*, the maintaining of public law and order within the country in the case of natural disasters; the purpose is to safeguard the network of essential services and to see that resources are properly allocated in times of crisis.

Wars elsewhere

Examiner's tip

Keep up to date with what is going on, particularly in Eastern Europe, and watch or listen for news that French troops are involved in any capacity in such conflicts.

France was opposed to the war in Iraq. In Europe, there is the possibility of **border conflicts** and those linked to ethnic groups. These may appear to be unrelated to your studies, but they could figure in comprehension questions, for several reasons (see also Chapter 4):

- France is heavily involved in NATO
- such conflicts may affect the stability of Europe
- there is often humanitarian cruelty on a large scale involved.

Dissident groups

Terrorism is a topic that is often in the news. From the French point of view, this tends to involve incidents relating to:

- Algeria, where there is still some anti-French feeling (see Chapter 4)
- Corsica, which is part of France but which has a vociferous independence movement (*Union Corse*)
- the Pyrenees, where violence on the part of Basque separatists sometimes spills over from Spain into France.

Vocabulary for war and conflict

la guerre	war	la répartition	sharing-out
la paix	peace	le mouvement	movement
le conflit	conflict	le/la rebelle	rebel
la lutte	struggle	le terrorisme	terrorism
la querelle	quarrel	le séparatiste basque	Basque separatist
la prévention	prevention	l'attentat (m)	attack (terrorist)
la stabilité	stability	les représailles (f)	reprisals
la stratégie	strategy	défendre	to defend
l'accord (m)	agreement	réduire	to reduce
la défense	defence	démanteler	to dismantle
la dissuasion	dissuasion, deterrent	inspecter	to inspect
la détente	relaxation of tension	dissuader (de + inf.)	to dissuade, deter
la trêve	truce	détourner (de + noun)	to deter
le partenariat	partnership	supprimer progressivement	to phase out
l'alliance (f)	alliance	rétablir	to reinstate, re-establish
les forces armées	armed forces		
les troupes (f)	troops	faire face à	to face up to
l'armée (f)	army	affronter	to confront
la marine	navy	se battre avec/contre	to fight
l'armée de l'air	air force	livrer bataille	to fight a battle
l'aviation (f) militaire	air force	combattre	to fight
la force de frappe	strike force	se rebeller	to rebel
l'affrontement (m)	confrontation	mener à bien	to see through (to a successful conclusion)
le combat	fight, action		
la bataille	battle	stratégique	strategic
le champ de bataille	field of battle	frontalier	border (adj.)

Vocabulary for war and conflict (continued)

le char	tank	chimique	chemical
les armes (f)	weapons	biologique	biological
le soldat	soldier	ethnique	ethnic
le missile (de croisière)	(cruise) missile	essentiel, -elle	essential
les alliés	allies	militaire	military
l'adversaire	adversary, opponent	blindé	armoured (vehicle)
l'ennemi	enemy	terrestre	terrestrial
l'unité (f)	unit	aérien, -enne	air (adj.)
le désarmement	disarmament	marine	sea (adj.)
la purification ethnique	ethnic cleansing	conventionnel, -elle	conventional
la cruauté	cruelty	sol-sol	ground to ground
le réseau	network	air-mer	air to sea
l'essai (m)	test	de la part de	on the part of, from
le compromis	compromise	onusien	of the UN
le couvre-feu	curfew	cessez-le-feu	cease-fire

> **KEY POINT**
>
> - *guerre*: don't confuse this with *guère* (with *ne*, a negative meaning 'hardly').
> - *défendre*: can also mean 'to forbid', but the context should make it clear.
> - *réduire*: irregular, like *conduire*.
> - *battre, combattre*: irregular verbs.

6.3 Distribution of wealth

AQA	M4, M6
EDEXCEL	M4, M6
NICCEA	M4, M5
OCR	M4, M5 (news items)
WJEC	M4, M6 (current affairs)

France and the developing countries

France is currently fourth in the list of world economic powers, helped to a large extent by its expertise in technology. Most of its trade is with its neighbours in Europe: Germany, UK, Italy, Belgium and Luxembourg, and Spain. Outside the European Union it trades mostly with the United States, Japan and Switzerland, and to a much smaller extent with the developing countries of Africa, Asia and Latin-America.

France supports international aid organisations such as UNICEF (United Nations Children's Fund), UNESCO (United Nations Educational, Scientific and Cultural Organisation) and the International Red Cross (*la Croix-Rouge*), and is in favour of alleviating or perhaps cancelling the 'Third World debt'.

In the 1980s the (then) EEC increased its aid to the less-developed nations. Because of its historical links with many of the countries of sub-Saharan (south of the Sahara desert) Africa, France has targeted its aid particularly towards those countries, often for specific projects all of which are intended to raise living standards. This aid consists of:

- money, in the form of grants and subsidies
- goods and materials
- personnel: consultants, technical experts and professionals such as teachers and medical workers.

Problems of the developing countries

Matters concerning the developing countries may appear in the exam under the heading of Global Issues or News items, even if they are not specifically related to France, because French personnel are involved.

Examiner's tip

As with most other topics, it's helpful to use what you know of the situation from the UK media. Common sense also plays an important part in comprehension questions on this topic.

A basic summary of the situation is that, in the countries concerned:

- birth rate and death rate are higher than elsewhere
- life expectancy is relatively short (40–50 in some African countries)
- infant mortality rates are high; in some countries more than 10% of children die within the first twelve months
- diet may be poor, leading to vitamin deficiencies
- floods or drought may lead to widespread disaster (destruction of crops, famine and death)
- water may be contaminated, leading to outbreaks of diseases such as cholera, yellow fever and dysentery
- working conditions may be poor and workers may be exploited by unscrupulous companies from other countries
- the greatest increase in population is likely to occur in countries that are least able to cope with it.

Passages are likely to concentrate on these conditions and possible solutions to them.

Terminology has changed several times in recent years, so the words used to refer to the topic may vary depending on the text you are reading. They could include:

- *Tiers monde* – Third World
- *Pays sous-développés* – under-developed countries
- *Pays (les) moins développés* – less/least-developed countries
- *Pays en voie de développement* – developing countries.

Vocabulary for distribution of wealth

French	English	French	English
l'économie (f)	economy	le soutien	support
le commerce	trade	l'outil (m)	tool
le secteur primaire	primary sector	l'analphabétisme (m)	illiteracy
le secteur secondaire	secondary sector (manufacturing)	l'état d'urgence	state of emergency
		le niveau de vie	standard of living
le secteur tertiaire	tertiary sector (services)	la qualité de la vie	quality of life
l'aide (f)	aid	la planification des naissances	family planning
la dette	debt		
les créances	debt	le planning familial	family planning
la croissance	growth	la tendance	trend
la subvention	grant, subsidy	annuler	to cancel
les biens	goods	devoir	to owe
les marchandises	goods	augmenter	to increase
l'expert	expert	diminuer	to decrease
l'expert-conseil	consultant	se nourrir de	to live on
l'ingénieur (m)	engineer	manquer	to lack
l'augmentation (f)	increase	contaminer	to contaminate
la hausse	increase	soutenir	to support
le taux de natalité	birth rate	améliorer	to improve
le taux de mortalité	death rate	éradiquer	to eradicate
la dénatalité	decrease in birth rate	supprimer	to suppress, eradicate
l'espérance de vie	life expectancy	souffrir	to suffer
le déclin	decrease, fall	haut	high
la diminution	decrease	élevé	high, raised
l'alimentation (f)	diet	bas, basse	low
la nourriture	food, diet	dans le dénuement	destitute
la pauvreté	poverty	pauvre	poor
la misère	poverty, hardship	misérable	wretched, destitute
la privation	hardship, deprivation	faible	weak
la détresse	distress	répandu	widespread
le manque	lack	agricole	agricultural

Vocabulary for distribution of wealth (continued)

l'insuffisance (f)	lack, insufficiency	épidémique	epidemic (adj.)
la carence	deficiency	endémique	endemic
les inondations	floods	sans scrupules	unscrupulous
la sécheresse	drought	illettré	illiterate
la faim	hunger	analphabète	illiterate
la famine	famine	insuffisant	insufficient
le désert	desert	affligé	distressed
la moisson	harvest	privé de	deprived of
la récolte	crop	soutenu	supported
l'épidémie (f)	epidemic		
la fièvre	fever		
le choléra	cholera		

KEY POINT

- *dette/créances*: these both mean 'debt', but the first is considered from the point of view of the person or country owing the money, and the second from the point of view of the person/country to whom the debt is owed.
- *alimentation*: 'diet' in the sense of what someone lives on; not a restricted diet, which is *régime*.
- *désert*: be sure to spell this properly; *ss* would change the meaning entirely.
- *planification des naissances* tends to be used of large-scale projects, *planning familial* for individuals.
- *devoir*: the original meaning of this verb is 'to owe', but it is much more generally used meaning 'to have to'.
- *soutenir, souffrir*: *soutenir* is a compound of *tenir*, and *souffrir* is like *ouvrir*.

Progress check: vocabulary

When you have learnt the vocabulary for this section, write down the following key words, then check them with the lists.

Give the French for: belief, crisis, nun, follower, pilgrimage, mass, to bless, agreement, struggle, to fight, to deter, chemical, tank, military, consultant, to improve, state of emergency, subsidy, famine, drought.

Give the English for: les biens, la carence, analphabète, manquer, la tendance, annuler, l'outil, le commerce, la cruauté, mener à bien, terrestre, la trève, affronter, l'adversaire, la paix, la répartition, prier, le cortège, le fidèle, l'office.

Grammar

6.4 Indefinite pronouns and adverbs

'Indefinite' in this context means those in which the **subject or object is not defined**. Look at the three sets of words below and read the examples; you should be able to see the precise shade of meaning in each case.

Quiconque, quelconque – 'whoever', 'any'

Quiconque means 'whoever' or 'anyone who':

> *Quiconque veut que la paix soit maintenue doit être tolérant des opinions d'autrui* – 'Whoever wants peace to be maintained must be tolerant of the opinions of others'.

Quelconque means 'any', but as the *quel* indicates it acts like an adjective so should be linked with a noun:

Adoptez une stratégie quelconque! – 'Adopt any strategy!'

N'importe (qui) – 'any(one) at all'

These expressions are used when it is not important 'who', 'what', 'how', 'where' or 'which':

N'importe qui veut alléger une situation si douloureuse ('anyone at all').

Tu dois essayer n'importe quoi pour les aider ('anything at all').

Nous devons mettre fin aux essais n'importe comment ('in any way we can').

Je peux travailler n'importe où ('anywhere at all').

N'importe quel requires a noun:

N'importe quelle église suffira – 'Any church at all will do'.

Je ne sais (qui) – 'some(one) or other'

Very similar to the *n'importe* list are the expressions meaning 'some- or other'. The implication this time is that the speaker doesn't know who, what, how, where or which; the examples will show you the slight difference in meaning between these sentences and those of the previous paragraph.

Je ne sais qui m'a conseillé de faire un pèlerinage ('someone or other advised me').

On va essayer je ne sais quoi pour l'aider ('something or other').

Mettons fin aux essais je ne sais comment ('somehow or other').

Il va travailler je ne sais où ('somewhere or other').

Elle est allée à je ne sais quelle église ('some church or other').

Negative without *pas*: *savoir, pouvoir, cesser* and *oser*

With these four verbs it is not always necessary to include *pas* in the negative. This usually occurs when the 'negative-ness' is less stressed.

savoir: particularly with the imperfect and conditional:

Je ne savais quoi faire – ('I didn't know what to do').

pouvoir: in the present tense (*je puis* form only – becoming rarer now. *Je peux* requires *pas*):

Je ne puis te dire combien tu m'as manqué – 'I can't tell you how much I've missed you'.

Je ne peux pas accepter une telle situation – 'I can't accept such a situation'.

cesser: when repetition is being stressed:

Les inondations ne cessent de causer des problèmes – 'Floods constantly cause problems'.

oser: *pas* is optional

Je n'ose en discuter avec le curé – 'I dare not discuss it with the parish priest'.

Je n'ose pas le faire – 'I dare not do it'.

Omission of *pouvoir*

With the verbs *entendre*, *voir* and *sentir* it is not always necessary to include *pouvoir* to translate 'can' or 'could'.

J'entendais pleurer les enfants qui avaient faim – 'I could hear the hungry children crying'.

Note also the subjunctive expression *À Dieu ne plaise!* – 'Heaven forbid!'.

Translation of 'how'

This may simply be *comme* (note the word order):
> *Regarde le vitrail: comme il est beau!* – 'Look at the stained glass. How beautiful it is!'.

Que may also be used in the same way: *Qu'il est beau!*

If 'how' really means 'in what way', use *comment*:
> *Le gouvernement ne comprend pas comment résoudre le problème* – 'The government doesn't understand how to solve the problem'.

And if it means 'how much', use *combien*:
> *Il est difficile de comprendre combien la situation est difficile* – 'It's difficult to comprehend how difficult the situation is'.

Progress check: grammar

Translate into French (answers on p. 154).

1 Anyone who doesn't believe in the existence of God is an atheist.
2 Wars anywhere at all in the world must be prevented.
3 We must do something or other to help them.
4 We could see the procession of the faithful.
5 Pilgrims constantly visit the grotto at Lourdes.

Translate into English.

6 Les scientifiques n'ont pas osé quitter le pays.
7 Vous savez combien les pays en voie de développement sont pauvres?
8 Que cette mosquée est belle!
9 Il faudra décider comment aider ces gens-là.
10 Je n'aurais pas cru qu'un tel désastre puisse se produire.

How to answer

6.5 Questions on listening passages

The problem with understanding spoken French rather than written French is that you can't always be certain exactly what the words are; so you have to help yourself by anticipating what you are going to hear and also by being aware of the sort of words that can mislead you.

Be prepared

To be one step ahead you need to know **what sort of words to expect**. This isn't as difficult as it might seem, particularly if the passage has a title or if you are given some information in the rubric about its content.

Imagine that your instructions read: *Écoutez l'extrait au sujet des inondations en Afrique.* You know that the passage will be about flooding in Africa so you should have a very good idea of some of the vocabulary that will be used:

- nouns such as *désastre, sinistre, faim, nourriture, manque, difficulté, épidémie, aide, expert*
- verbs such as *inonder, souffrir, contaminer, manquer*
- adjectives and participles such as *pénible, difficile, malade, privé de, misérable, affligé, insuffisant.*

Obviously you won't know precisely what the passage is going to say, but you will already have some pegs on which to hang your understanding of it.

The other way to help your positive understanding of the meaning is to **be aware in advance of the situation described**. This won't always work; the examiners might find a passage relating to an unusual incident that you couldn't hope to have read about. However, in the type of passage described above you should certainly have some knowledge of the situation.

Be alert

However well you know the topic and the vocabulary associated with it, there will almost certainly be some words – or more probably combinations of words – that you don't understand immediately. This is where it helps to be methodical. Ask yourself these questions:

- Does the apparent meaning make sense?
  If not, you have probably misunderstood one or more words. Some sounds can be misleading: distinguish between *pl* and *cl* (*place, classe*), between *u* and *ou* (*au dessus, au dessous*), and between *attendre* and *atteindre, dans* and *dont*.
- Does the word resemble nothing you have ever heard before?
  Try writing down all possible spelling combinations of the sound. As you look at them, you may realise what the word is. Take particular care with the sound *la*; you may think you have heard '*la cord*' or '*la liance*', for *l'accord* and *l'alliance*.

Be careful

Listen to **every word**. The little words that modify the meaning are very important (*à peu près, presque, au moins, plus de, moins de, ne…que*).

Don't jump to conclusions. Some words and phrases can easily be confused: there's a big difference between *la faim dans le monde* and *la fin du monde*, between *qui l'a mis* and *qu'il a mis* and between *plutôt* and *plus tôt*.

Revise numbers thoroughly. Listening passages often contain statistics which are a frequent source of error.

You should not confuse *mille/milliers/millions/milliards, deux/douze, trois/treize/trente, quatre/quatorze/quarante, cinq/quinze/cinquante, vingt-quatre/quatre-vingts,* the 60s and 70s, the 80s and 90s. In a telephone number even one incorrect digit will lose you the whole mark.

You have control over your cassette, and it can be tempting to listen over and over again to a particular phrase until you're quite sure you've understood it. However, time is a very important factor in mixed-skill comprehen-sion papers, and if you are having great difficulty with a question you should give it up and go on to the next. You would be very angry with yourself if you didn't attempt a question on which you could have done well, simply because you did not leave yourself enough time for it.

Sample and practice exam questions

1 Reading

Lisez le passage *Kosovo: Chirac avertit les deux camps* puis répondez aux questions suivantes EN ANGLAIS.

Le chef de l'État hier en Macédoine
Kosovo : Chirac avertit les deux camps

Il a rendu visite aux soldats français de la force d'extraction de l'Otan, commandée par le général Valentin.

KUMANOVO :
de notre envoyé spécial
Baudouin BOLLAERT

"J'ai voulu vous rencontrer parce que vous accomplissez ici, comme vos camarades en Bosnie, une mission essentielle pour la paix dans les Balkans"; Jacques Chirac a rendu visite, hier, dans leur base de Kumanovo, aux soldats français de la force d'extraction basée en Macédoine. Si un soleil éclatant a remplacé la pluie et le vent des derniers jours, l'endroit est aussi séduisant qu'une ville fantôme du Far West, les corbeaux et les vautours en moins…

La force d'extraction a été créée pour venir au secours, si nécessaire, *« des vérificateurs »* non armés de l'OSCE, chargés, après les accords d'octobre 1998, de veiller au cessez-le-feu dans la province du Kosovo toute proche. Commandée par le général Marcel Valentin, elle est insérée dans le dispositif de l'Otan et comprend 1923 soldats. Parmi eux, 850 Français, dont une trentaine de femmes.

Le cessez-le-feu est de plus en plus mal respecté. Jacques Chirac a donc lancé un *« avertissement solennel »* aux deux camps anfagonistes au Kosovo – les Serbes d'un côté, les Albanais de l'autre – pour qu'ils fassent *« le bon choix »* de la responsabilité, de la paix, et donc de l'Europe. Dans le cas contraire, a-t-il dit, *« ils s'exposeront à des conséquences politiques, économiques et militaires extrêmement dommageables »*.

Paragraph 1

(a) Why did Jacques Chirac want to visit the troops? (2)

(b) How has the weather changed? (3)

Paragraph 2

(c) What was the task of the unarmed OSCE forces? (2)

(d) Of what does the *force d'extraction* consist? (3)

Paragraph 3

(e) Summarise what Jacques Chirac said to the two opposing sides in Kosovo. (5)

Q 2

2 Listening

Notice as you read the questions that some of the words you might not have known are actually given to you.

Écoutez l'extrait à propos du Kosovo puis décidez si les constatations ci-dessous sont VRAIES (V), FAUSSES (F) ou si ce n'est pas mentionné (?).

	V	F	?
(a) Ce n'est pas la première fois que l'émissaire a essayé d'obtenir une amélioration de la situation.	…	…	…
(b) L'émissaire va rester à Belgrade jusqu'à demain.	…	…	…
(c) Selon la Russie, la mission est une bonne chose.	…	*F*	…
(d) Les grandes puissances ont décidé d'intervenir hier.	*√*	…	…
(e) On va envoyer des casques bleus.	…	…	*?*

Sample and practice exam questions (continued)

3 Listening

Écoutez le passage au sujet du Timor Oriental, puis répondez EN FRANÇAIS.

(a) Qui va arriver au Timor Oriental, et quand? (2)

(b) L'avion dont il s'agit vient de quel pays? (1)

(c) Cet avion, que va-t-il faire, et pourquoi? (3)

(d) Combien de temps a-t-on dû attendre la permission de le faire? (1)

4 Listening

Écoutez l'extrait à propos de la canonisation proposée d'une sainte, et trouvez les phrases qui sont l'équivalent exact des expressions ci-dessous.

(a) who became a Catholic

(b) does not agree with what has been decided

(c) it emphasises

(d) might in some way take over

5 Writing

Notice how this is not just a glorified monologue, with one of the speakers saying no more than '*Oui*' or '*Non*'. The examiner will not know whether you're telling the truth, so you should choose to write something you know you can express clearly in French even if it doesn't reflect your own opinion!

The tone is more familiar than that of a formal essay or speech.

Écrivez le texte d'une conversation (150 mots) entre deux jeunes personnes dont un(e) est pour la religion, l'autre contre.

Model answer

A À mon avis la religion ne vaut rien de nos jours. Les jeunes, surtout, n'en ont pas besoin.

B Je ne crois pas que ce soit le cas. La moralité est aussi importante que jamais.

A D'accord. Mais la religion et la moralité, ce n'est pas la même chose. Quant à moi, je ne crois pas en Dieu. Comment peut-on concilier l'idée d'un bon Dieu et la mort des enfants innocents, dans les sinistres en Afrique par exemple?

B Qui sait? Il y a des choses qui sont incompréhensibles. Mais si tu n'aimes pas la religion, tu pourras quand même suivre un mode de vie qui réduira le stress: le bouddhisme conseille la méditation, qui peut avoir un effet très calmant sur l'esprit.

A Ah oui? Je n'y connais rien. Comment est-ce que je peux en savoir plus?

B Viens avec moi jeudi prochain. Je la pratique depuis des mois déjà!

6 Writing

You will find a possible answer to this question on p. 156.

Vous êtes membre d'une équipe des Médecins sans Frontières, arrivée au sein d'un pays africain où il y a eu des inondations désastreuses. Écrivez à un(e) ami(e) français(e) une lettre dans laquelle vous lui décrivez ce qui se passe (150 mots).

Textes et thèmes littéraires

The following topics are covered in this chapter:

- *Knowledge of subject*
- *Organising your essay*
- *Quality of language*

Literature: topics and texts

After studying this chapter you should be able to:

LEARNING SUMMARY

- *write essays on literary topics, using an appropriate range of language*
- *identify the vocabulary and structures that will help you to do so*

It is not compulsory to study literature as part of the French A Level course. The option to do so remains, and for those who choose it there is a wide range of texts and topics to pick from. There are three main possibilities, depending on the exam you are doing:

- a choice of specific set texts (e.g. Colette: *Le Blé en herbe*)
- a topic studied through the means of literature (e.g. War in French literature); you may have a free choice of texts or the awarding body may specify them
- a topic studied through the work of one particular author (e.g. *La condition humaine dans l'oeuvre de Camus*).

There is a further choice between essay(s) as part of an end-of-course examination and coursework. For coursework there is additional advice in Chapter 9, but the general points in this chapter still apply (except those relating to length).

Most awarding bodies ask for essays of 250–350 words in French. OCR offers the alternative of a context question (see p. 121). Texts are not allowed in the exam. This word limit does not give you much scope to show an extensive knowledge of the text or topic, so it's important to know what the examiners are looking for. To do this you should check the Assessment grids in the specification document for your own exam; basically, however, you will be expected to:

Before you start, be quite sure that you understand the question. If not, choose another essay.

- show knowledge of the subject
- organise your essay properly
- write in accurate French with appropriate use of vocabulary and structures.

7.1 Knowledge of subject

AQA	M5
EDEXCEL	M5
OCR	M6
WJEC	M5
NICCEA	M6

When studying your text or texts you should consider:
- plot (including sub-plots)
- characters
- motivation for action
- setting/background
- style
- dramatic effectiveness (usually plays)
- versification (poetry).

Some of these may overlap in individual questions:

Choisissez une situation dans l'oeuvre que vous avez étudiée et expliquez comment l'auteur y montre le caractère du personnage principal. (character and plot)

Dans quelle mesure est-ce que le cadre du roman contribue à notre compréhension du thème? (setting and theme)

You will need to **back up your arguments with examples or quotations**, both of which must be **relevant**. Learn five or six short quotations; if you try to learn long ones you will probably get them wrong and anyway they will take the examiner's attention away from the point you are making. Choose them carefully – one for the main character, one relating to the theme, one that is a good example of the writer's style, one on an area that particularly interests you – but don't use them if they are not appropriate. It's not a good idea to put too many in the same essay; plan to use two or three if you can. The examiner wants to read what you think about the book, not a string of quotations joined together by a few comments.

Candidates sometimes learn three quotations which they are determined to include at all costs, but if they are not linked directly to what has just been written they are worse than useless.

7.2 Organising your essay

AQA	M5
EDEXCEL	M5
OCR	M6
WJEC	M5
NICCEA	M6

Every essay, however short, must have an **introduction** and a **conclusion**. The points in the main body of the answer should be made in a **logical order**, with **linking words or phrases** to lead from one point to the next.

Introduction and conclusion

It's always worth taking time to think about the introduction; this is the first your examiner sees of what you can do and it's a good idea to attract his/her attention by making an interesting or perceptive comment. The examiner will think 'Aha! This candidate has something interesting to say; this essay is likely to be worth reading'. Similarly, the conclusion is the final impression you are going to leave with the examiner, and you want that impression to be positive. So when you are writing your essay plan before you start, take some time to consider the introduction at least (the conclusion will most probably develop from what you have written in the body of the essay). It doesn't have to be long; you don't have words to spare for a long rambling paragraph anyway. **In your introduction try to refer to the question**, and bear it in mind as you begin each paragraph; if what you plan to say has no direct bearing on the question it will almost certainly be irrelevant.

In the conclusion you should not merely repeat what you have already said, but neither should you introduce any completely new points at this stage. It should be a 'conclusion' in two senses: as well as being a neat ending to your essay it should also **draw an inference or conclusion from what you have written** and thus show that you have answered the question appropriately.

Main body

Examiner's tip

Because of the word limit you will have to pick and choose carefully the points you are going to include; ideally you should hint at both the breadth and the depth of your knowledge. It might be worth making your main points and then putting in a pre-concluding paragraph, or even in the conclusion itself, a brief reference to items that are also relevant.

The structure of the main body of your answer will depend to a large extent on the wording of the question. You should keep a reasonable **balance**; if, for example, you are asked to compare two characters, you should write approximately the same amount about each of them. If you are given a quotation and asked *Dans quelle mesure êtes-vous d'accord avec cette opinion?* you will probably need to give points for and against it before deciding one way or the other. You could, of course, be totally in agreement with it or disagree with it completely, but you would have to support your opinion strongly as the words *Dans quelle mesure* indicate that the point being made is at least partly true. You will certainly have to give your own opinions; an essay at A2 Level must **go beyond the merely factual**.

Make sure that you understand what the following words and phrases mean, as used in essay questions:

- *Comment* – 'How?' *Par quels moyens?* – 'By what means?'
  Comment est-ce que Joffo réussit à nous communiquer l'ambiance de la guerre dans Un Sac de billes? You would probably discuss style, character and plot; you would not be able to go into great detail about any of them.

- *Quel* – 'What?'
  Quelle image de la jeunesse Pagnol nous présente-t-il dans La Gloire de mon père? This could be answered by reference to 2–3 episodes and how Marcel responds to them. Conclusions must be drawn about what this shows about young people, or Marcel at least.

- *Est-ce que* – asks a question which you must answer in your essay. *Est-ce que l'Avare vous semble plutôt comique ou tragique?* This essay should divide neatly into two halves; present the arguments for both sides, then decide which you favour.

- *Dans quelle mesure* – 'To what extent?'
  Dans quelle mesure Meursault est-il coupable du meurtre de l'Arabe? The conclusion will obviously depend on your own opinion, but even if you believe that Meursault is entirely guilty you should still indicate why some think that there are extenuating circumstances.

- *Pourquoi* – 'Why?'
  Usually linked with *à votre avis* or with another part to the question. *Pourquoi est-ce que Cyrano aime Roxane, à votre avis? Que pensez-vous de cet amour?* For this essay you would need to give at least two reasons why he loves her, with examples or quotations to illustrate the points you are making, and then add your own opinion in another paragraph.

- *Expliquez* – 'Explain'.
  Expliquez pourquoi, selon Pagnol, Manon veut venger la mort de son père. Comprenez-vous son point de vue? This needs a brief résumé of how and why Jean de Florette dies and how Manon reacts to it. The final section should be almost entirely your own reaction but a quotation or example will help.

- *Évaluez l'importance* – this is often another way of saying *dans quelle mesure*.
  Évaluez l'importance du rôle de Créon dans Antigone. Here you must agree that Créon is important; you have to say how important he is and in what way.

- *Comparez* – 'Compare'.
  Comparez deux personnages pris dans le texte que vous avez étudié. Lequel vous attire le plus? You have the choice of any two characters, but it obviously makes sense to choose two who have something in common or two who are completely different, so that you can draw a valid conclusion.

Link your paragraphs to each other as you write (for useful phrases, see list on p. 117), but don't fill your essay with pre-learnt phrases which are not appropriate and which use too much of your precious word allocation. There is little worse than an essay constructed almost entirely of such phrases with hardly anything related to the question.

You could link the paragraphs in a numerical fashion, with *premièrement, deuxièmement, finalement*. An essay which falls naturally into two halves could introduce the first half with, for example, *Considérons d'abord les aspects positifs*, and the second with *En ce qui concerne les aspects négatifs du sujet...* Conjunctions such as *de plus* or *en outre* ('moreover') – provided that you are actually going to add something to what you have said already – make sentences flow well into each other.

Aussi (when you mean 'and there's another point I should like to add') is not very good French.

7.3 Quality of language

AQA	M5
EDEXCEL	M5
OCR	M6
WJEC	M5
NICCEA	M6

As with any other writing tasks, you should be concerned with two aspects, **accuracy** and **range**.

Accuracy

To keep your work as error-free as possible, leave yourself time to check what you have written, looking particularly at basic grammar. The following types of error are frequently found in A Level scripts and are heavily penalised; in the column on the right you will find the chapter reference in the AS Study Guide so that you can check any you don't remember.

Key points from AS	*AS Chapter*
verb formation (e.g. the wrong future stem)	1,2,3,4,7
verb endings (particularly leaving the *s* off the *tu* form)	1,2,3,4,7
adjective agreement	2
infinitive – used wrongly or not used where it should be	5
pronouns – wrong one (often *lui* as the direct object) or in the wrong position	3,4
tense	1,2,3,4,7
singular/plural	1
qui/que	4
prepositions – omission, or the wrong one used	7
negatives – omission of *ne* or *pas*, or *pas* in the wrong place	1,4,6
other basics – writing such horrors as '*à les*' (except when *les* is a pronoun), '*beaucoup des*', '*le deuxième mai*', etc.	

Other types of mistake, such as gender and spelling and slight anglicism ('Englishness' of word order, etc.) are still important but don't usually count as individual errors; the mark for accuracy will be affected if, for example, your spelling is poor in general, or if you have several genders wrong, or if several 'spelling' accents are omitted. (Omission of the acute accent on the *é* of the past participle, or *a* written for *à* or vice versa, are serious mistakes.)

Range

The structures you learnt for GCSE Higher Tier are still very useful (see list on p. 114). You should also try to include some of the new constructions you have learnt for AS and A2: the conditional perfect and the subjunctive, for example, are both quite easy to incorporate particularly when you are expressing opinions:

> *J'ai l'impression qu'Antigone aurait préféré vivre.*

> *Je ne crois pas qu'Olga comprenne l'attitude de Hugo.*

Use of pronouns is always impressive; try to go beyond the direct object *le/la/les* and use *y* and *en*, perhaps with verbs taking *à* or *de*:

> *Quant au bonheur, Antigone y renonce* (*renoncer* is followed by *à* with the noun).

> *Vinca a des tâches à faire; elle doit s'en occuper ce matin* (*s'occuper* is followed by *de* with the noun).

Useful structures (references on the right are to the AS Study Guide)

Key points from AS	Chapter
après avoir/après être + past participle	5
venir de	1,2
depuis	1,2
other idioms	
en + present participle	5
passive	4
subjunctive	6
compound tenses	4,7
pronouns	3,4
relative pronouns including *ce qui, ce que*	4
interesting negatives	6
constructions using the infinitive	5

Examiner's tip

The best way to accustom yourself to literary phraseology is to read short extracts from literary criticism in French.

These structures, **if used correctly**, will improve your Quality of Language mark. You won't be able to use all of them in one essay, but try to include some at least. If you have to write more than one essay, use different structures in each in order to show the range of your language; for example you could use *bien que* + subjunctive in the first essay, *je ne crois pas* + subjunctive in the second.

You should also use an appropriate 'literary' vocabulary. The lists on pp.114–117 will help you to extend your range.

Vocabulary for essays on literature

(The words below are mostly general ones: you will certainly have covered any specific vocabulary related to your text(s) during your course.)

Nouns

la littérature	literature	l'intrigue (f)	plot
le genre	type (of literature)	le narrateur	narrator
l'oeuvre (f)	work, works (of lit.)	le protagoniste	main player/character
le chef d'oeuvre	masterpiece	le dénouement	end, unravelling
le roman	novel	le style	style
le roman à thèse	novel with a 'message'	l'esprit (m)	wit
la pièce (de théâtre)	play	l'émotion (f)	emotion
la comédie	comedy	le décor	scenery, set
la tragédie	tragedy	le portrait	portrayal
le conte	short story	l'ironie (f)	irony
le titre	title	la méthode (dont)	the way (in which)
le thème	theme	la façon (dont)	the way (in which)
le sujet	subject	le dialogue	conversation, dialogue
le rôle	part, role	l'analyse (f)	analysis
le fond	background	l'engagement (m)	commitment
le cadre	setting, background		(usually political)
le domaine	sphere	le rapport	relationship
l'ambiance (f)	atmosphere	les relations (f)	relationship
le ton	tone	le lien	link
l'auteur	author	le sens	meaning, sense
l'écrivain (m)	writer	la signification	meaning
le romancier	novelist	le résumé (m)	summary
le dramaturge	dramatist, playwright	l'extrait (m)	extract
le lecteur/la lectrice	reader	la citation	quotation
le spectateur/la spectatrice	spectator	le point de vue	point of view
le personnage	character	le chapitre	chapter
le caractère	character	la scène	scene, stage
le trait	characteristic	le but	aim
l'intérêt (m)	interest	l'effet (m)	effect

Vocabulary for essays on literature (continued)

la poésie	poetry	**le poète**	poet
le syllabe	syllable	**le vers**	line of poetry
la comparaison	comparison, simile	**le poème**	poem
le point culminant	climax	**la rime**	rhyme
l'apogée (m)	climax	**le rythme**	rhythm
la chute (dans le trivial)	anticlimax	**la strophe**	verse

KEY POINT

- *spectateur*: *les spectateurs* means 'the audience'.
- *personnage/caractère*: *personnage* is one of the characters in a work of literature (e.g. Hoederer, Joseph, Éliante); *caractère* is the character of that person.
- *dénouement*: not precisely a synonym for *fin*; it means the untwisting of the plot, but this is likely to be final only at the end of the play or book.
- *engagement*: in the field of literature, this usually means commitment to a cause by the author.
- *sens*: the final *s* is pronounced. The word is also used to mean the five senses.
- *signification*: there is no such word as 'significance' in French.

Vocabulary for essays on literature

Verbs

(s') exprimer	to express	**jouer le rôle**	to play the part
décrire	to describe	**faire le portrait de**	to portray
révéler	to reveal	**dépeindre**	to depict
sembler	to seem	**analyser**	to analyse
paraître	to appear	**signifier**	to mean, signify
lier	to link	**vouloir dire**	to mean
se dérouler	to take place, unfold	**refléter**	to reflect
dessiner	to draw	**évoquer**	to evoke
se dessiner	to stand out against	**expliquer**	to explain
raconter	to tell	**éclaircir**	to clarify
illustrer	to illustrate	**répéter**	to repeat
créer	to create	**réitérer**	to reiterate
concevoir	to imagine	**citer**	to quote
faire ressortir	to bring out (characteristic)	**s'identifier (avec)**	to identify (with)
se rendre compte	to realise	**susciter**	to arouse
souligner	to underline, emphasise	**éveiller**	to awaken
affirmer	to state	**déborder de**	to overflow with
incarner	to embody	**attirer l'attention**	to draw, attract
personnifier	to personify	**fournir**	to provide
critiquer	to criticise	**soutenir**	to sustain (interest)
commenter	to comment on	**transmettre**	to convey
frapper	to strike, impress	**faire allusion à**	to allude to
résumer	to summarise	**faire le récit de**	to recount

KEY POINT

- *décrire, soutenir, transmettre*: compounds of *écrire*, *tenir* and *mettre* respectively.
- *révéler/répéter/réitérer*: all belong to the *espérer* group.
- *paraître*: endings are like those of *connaître*.
- *se dessiner*: this means 'to stand out against a background', not 'to stand up for'.
- *créer*: the past participle is *créé*.
- *concevoir*: like *recevoir*.
- *incarner*: in theatre or TV this may simply mean 'to play the part of'.
- *dépeindre*: check the endings of verbs ending in *-eindre*.
- *vouloir dire, faire ressortir*: the second verb in each case remains in the infinitive.
- *fournir*: remember the construction: *fournir quelque chose à quelqu'un*.

Vocabulary for essays on literature

Adjectives

intéressant	interesting	**imaginatif, -ve**	imaginative
passionnant	exciting	**inventif, -ve**	imaginative, inventive
frappant	striking, effective	**vivant**	lively (style)
fascinant	fascinating	**clair**	clear
amusant	amusing	**précis**	precise
comique	funny, comic	**concis**	concise
tragique	tragic	**descriptif, -ve**	descriptive
dramatique	dramatic	**net, nette**	clear
choquant	shocking	**recherché**	elaborate
émouvant	moving	**complexe**	complex
symbolique	symbolising	**imagé**	full of imagery
philosophique	philosophical	**répétitif, -ve**	repetitive
éponyme	eponymous	**sophistiqué**	sophisticated
détaillé	detailed	**fade**	bland
objectif, -ve	objective	**étonnant**	astonishing
subjectif, -ve	subjective	**intelligible**	comprehensible
engagé	committed	**vraisemblable**	plausible, likely
réaliste	realistic	**invraisemblable**	implausible, unlikely
drôle	funny	**spirituel, -elle**	witty
ironique	ironic, ironical	**ennuyeux, -se**	boring, tedious
significatif, -ve	significant	**minutieux, -se**	thorough, detailed
croyable	believable	**abstrait**	abstract
incroyable	unbelievable, incredible	**concret, -ète**	concrete

- *passionnant*: note the double *n* in this word.
- *éponyme*: this refers to a character whose name is in the title, e.g. Thérèse Desqueyroux.

Vocabulary for essays on literature

To express an opinion

à mon avis	in my opinion	**je soutiens que**	I maintain that
d'après moi	in my opinion	**je considère que**	I feel that
selon moi	in my opinion	**je pense que**	I think that
à mon sens	in my view	**je crois que**	I believe that
je suis d'avis que	I am of the opinion that	**je trouve que**	I think that
en ce qui me concerne	as far as I am concerned	**je dirais que**	I would say that
quant à moi	as for me	**je suis d'accord**	I agree
pour ma part	for my part	**ce n'est pas le cas**	it's not the case
il me semble que	it seems to me that	**il paraît que**	it appears that
il semble que	it seems that	**...me plaît/plaisent**	I like...
ce qui me frappe le plus, c'est...	what strikes me particularly is...	**...me déplaît/déplaisent**	I don't like...
ce qui m'inquiète, c'est...	what worries me is that...	**il y a lieu de penser**	there's reason to believe

You will have noticed how many ways there are of saying the same thing. Show the range of your language by using a variety in your essays.

- *il semble que/il me semble que*: remember that the first of these takes the subjunctive, but the second does not.
- *je pense que, je crois que,* etc: these are followed by the subjunctive in the **negative and question forms only**.

Vocabulary for essays on literature

Starters, balancers and other useful phrases

non seulement... mais aussi	not only... but also
d'une part... d'autre part	on the one hand... on the other hand
d'un côté... de l'autre côté	on the one hand... on the other hand
il faut (également) noter que	one should (also) note that
il faut reconnaître que	we must recognise that
dans une certaine mesure	to a certain extent
ce qui plus est	what is more, moreover
il s'agit de	it's about
ou bien... ou bien	either... or
il y a le revers de la médaille	there's another side to the question/an opposing point of view

en règle générale	as a general rule	nul ne saurait nier	no-one could deny
à première vue	at first sight	il va de soi	it goes without saying
d'ailleurs	besides	de même	in the same way
de plus	also, moreover	certes	certainly
en outre	also, moreover	voilà pourquoi	that's why
cependant	however	par contre	on the other hand
néanmoins	nevertheless	en revanche	on the other hand
pourtant	however	par rapport à	in relation to,
à juste titre	rightly, justly		in comparison with
en réalité	in fact	à propos de	about
en fait	in fact	au sujet de	about
notamment	notably, in particular	à l'égard de	with regard to
de toute façon	anyway	quand même	all the same, even so
quoi qu'il en soit	regardless of that	par conséquent	consequently
toujours est-il que...	the fact remains that...	il en résulte que...	the result of this is that...

KEY POINT

- *il s'agit de*: this is an impersonal verb; its only possible subject is *il*. You cannot say '*la pièce s'agit de*'.

Progress check

When you have learnt the vocabulary for this section, write down the following key words, then check them with the lists.

Give the French for: masterpiece, short story, plot, wit, the way in which, sphere, relationship, meaning, character (in play or novel), chapter, effect, characteristic, poem, to express, to mean, to illustrate, to awaken, to depict, exciting, striking, symbolising, comprehensible, shocking, anyway.

Give the English for: en outre, en fait, quand même, certes, à mon sens, quant à moi, je soutiens que, émouvant, engagé, inventif, recherché, vraisemblable, décrire, se dérouler, concevoir, expliquer, citer, susciter, incarner, fournir, le vers, le dramaturge, le ton, l'ambiance, le décor.

Note: The sample essays each consist of one possible way of answering the question concerned. There may sometimes be a more elegant way of expressing the writer's sentiments, and this has usually been noted in the comments following each essay.

Sample questions and model answers

Examiner's tip

Before you start writing, take ten or fifteen minutes to produce a plan for your essay. It shouldn't matter whether this is in English or French (but if you don't finish the essay and want the examiner to look at your plan so that he/she can see what you were intending to include, it will probably only be taken into account if you have written it in French).

Because of the almost limitless number of texts set or allowed by the five awarding bodies, it is not appropriate to set practice questions. You will find in this section a number of sample essays of various types; read them and identify what is good about them.

1 Essay on classical play – Molière: *Le Misanthrope*
Theme: character.

Quel personnage vous a intéressé(e) le plus? Donnez vos raisons.

Plan

Introduction: Choix – Alceste: personnage principal/titre de la pièce/complexe

Main body: attitude envers la société/misanthropie/amour pour Célimène/ décision de quitter la société

Conclusion

Model answer

Le personnage qui me semble le plus intéressant de la pièce est Alceste. C'est lui qui est le personnage principal et qui, bien sûr, est le misanthrope du titre; de plus, je trouve son caractère assez complexe et, dans une certaine mesure, contradictoire. (1)

Alceste déteste la société du 17e siècle dans laquelle (2) il vit quotidiennement. Il ne peut pas en (3) accepter (4) l'hypocrisie dont (5) Célimène est l'exemple; elle parle d'Arsinoé dans des termes défavorables, mais change de ton lorsque celle-ci (6) entre en scène:

"Ah! Quel heureux sort en ce lieu vous amène?" (7)

Quand même il continue d'y (3) vivre (4). Peut-être aime-t-il (8) être en colère; on doit avouer (4) qu'à cause de l'ambiance du siècle il ne cesse (9) d'être (4) fâché.

Malgré sa haine de ses pairs Alceste est amoureux. On aurait cru (10) qu'il choisirait comme objet de cet amour quelqu'une comme Éliante qui n'a pas ces traits qu'il déteste tant, et à mon avis (11) un tel amour l'(3)aurait rendu (10) content – si tant est qu'il puisse (12) jamais être (4) content. Mais qui préfère-t-il? (13) Célimène, qui incarne tout ce qu'il déteste (14) chez une femme (15). On a l'impression que si elle n'avait pas été belle, il l'aurait rejetée. (10/16)

Alors il semble qu'Alceste soit séduit (17) par une femme qui ne saurait (9) le (3) rendre (4) heureux; tout en sachant (18) ce qu'elle (14) est, il ne peut pas s'empêcher (4) de l(3)'aimer (4), et cette contradiction m'(3)intéresse beaucoup.

Sa décision de quitter (4) la société me (3) semble typique de son caractère. Il paraît déterminé; rien ne (19) peut le (3) retenir (4). Quand même à la fin de la pièce on pense que Philinte va peut-être le (3) convaincre de changer (4) d'avis; donc cet homme qui nous (3) donne l'impression d'être si intransigeant est plus facilement persuadé qu'on ne l'aurait cru. (20/10)

Alceste est fort et faible à la fois; c'est pour cette raison que je le (3) trouve si fascinant.

Sample questions and model answers (continued)

1 Not a very exciting introduction, but the candidate has made it clear that she is going to answer the question relevantly.

2 Good use of the relative pronoun.

3 Use of pronouns.

4 Use of various infinitive constructions.

5 *Dont* used correctly is always impressive.

6 *Celle-ci* here means 'the latter'.

7 The quotation is properly set out.

8 Inversion after *peut-être*.

9 No need for *pas* here.

10 Use of the conditional perfect tense.

11 The candidate is including her reactions as she goes along.

12 This idiom requires the subjunctive: 'if indeed he can ever be'.

13 It's a good idea to ask a rhetorical question occasionally (but not too often or it will annoy the examiner).

14 Use of *ce que*.

15 *Chez* is used here to mean 'in'.

16 Agreement of the past participle with a preceding direct object (pdo).

17 Both subjunctive and passive.

18 Use of (*tout*) *en* + present participle.

19 *Rien* used as the subject of the verb.

20 Special use of *ne* (see AS Study Guide p. 114).

Examiner's tip

If you are studying a play or book that has been made into a film or is being presented on stage, try to watch a recording of it. Be careful, though, as a film version doesn't always coincide exactly with the original (this is the case in Pagnol's *La Gloire de mon père* and *Le Château de ma mère*).

2 Essay on 20th century text – Colette: *Le Blé en herbe*
Theme: setting/background

Dans le roman que vous avez étudié, dans quelle mesure est-ce que le cadre aide le lecteur à comprendre l'action?

Plan
Introduction: deux cadres différents – plein air, intérieur de la villa
Main body: plein air – Bretagne, mer, dunes – Vinca et Phil
              Villa – lourd, velours, rouge, or – Phil et Mme Dalleray
Conclusion

Model answer

Dans Le Blé en herbe, Colette présente au lecteur deux cadres très différents: premièrement la Bretagne qu'elle aimait tant, qui se caractérise par la mer et le ciel bleus (1) et les dunes de sable; deuxièmement, l'intérieur de la villa Ker-Anna qui, lourd et étouffant (1), forme un vif contraste avec le premier.

On dirait que le plein air représente les relations entre Vinca et Phil. (2) Ils se sont accoûtumés à rôder ensemble parmi les dunes et à pêcher dans les flaques laissées par la marée. Colette décrit minutieusement la flore et la faune (3) de la région. Ce n'est pas seulement la vue qu'elle éveille; nos oreilles mêmes sont à l'écoute quand elle décrit le crabe qui 'craqua comme une noix' sous les pieds de Phil, et nous sentons 'l'odeur d'esprit de lavande, de linge repassé et d'algue marine qui composait le parfum de Vinca'. (4)

Sample questions and model answers (continued)

On voit des liens entre Vinca et les choses de la nature. Elle a les yeux bleus comme la pervenche d'où (5) elle tire son prénom. Toute l'ambiance des jours ensoleillés souligne l'innocence: leur amitié et aussi l'amour véritable mais toujours innocent qui caractérise leurs relations au début du roman. Je ne crois pas que ce premier cadre nous fasse (6) comprendre (7) dans une grande mesure l'action du roman; à mon avis il fournit plutôt une ambiance contre laquelle (8) le cadre de la villa se dessine plus nettement.

De l'autre côté Ker-Anna, la villa qui a été louée (9) par Madame Dalleray, a une ambiance tout à fait sombre qui représente les relations entre Phil et la 'Dame en blanc'. Dès (10) son arrivée cette dernière paraît vouloir séduire (7) Phil. Lui, (11) toujours naïf, ne sait pas y (12) résister (7). Mme Dalleray n'aime pas la lumière du soleil (qui révélerait peut-être trop clairement son âge) (13); les rideaux sont en velours, les couleurs sont noir, rouge et or. Il s'agit donc de quelque chose de plus sophistiqué (14). Cette fois le sens qu'éveille Colette (15) chez ses lecteurs (16) est le toucher; on croit tenir soi-même le glaçon dans le verre d'orangeade que la dame (17) offre à Phil.

Face à une ambiance pareille Phil ne pourra pas refuser (7) ce qu'elle (18) va lui (12) offrir (7), donc le cadre de la villa me (12) semble bien nous (12) aider (7) à comprendre (7) ce qu'il (18) fait.

Colette a utilisé ses talents pour la description à deux buts différents; tous les deux ajoutent au plaisir que nous prenons au roman.

1 *Bleus* refers to both nouns (*mer* and *ciel*); *lourd et étouffant* agree with *intérieur*.

2 The candidate is giving his personal reactions during the course of his essay; this makes what he has to say more immediately relevant.

3 It's a good idea to use vocabulary learnt during the A Level course in your essay; 'culture' should never be considered to be separate from the rest of your studies.

4 This is a good way of integrating quotations when they follow on grammatically.

5 Correct use of relative pronoun.

6 Use of subjunctive after *je ne crois pas que*.

7 An infinitive construction.

8 Use of *laquelle* after a preposition.

9 Use of the passive.

10 An interesting preposition.

11 An emphatic pronoun.

12 Use of pronouns.

13 An interesting personal comment from the candidate.

14 Remember that *quelque chose de* is followed by the masculine adjective.

15 Note the word order here; it's good French to invert the noun and verb.

16 *Chez* used with people to mean 'in'.

17 Noun rather than *elle* is needed here because otherwise the reader might wonder whether it referred to Colette.

18 Use of *ce que*.

Sample questions and model answers (continued)

3 Context question – Camus: *L'Étranger*

Aujourd'hui, maman est morte. Ou peut-être hier, je ne sais pas. J'ai reçu un télégramme de l'asile: « Mère décédée. Enterrement demain. Sentiments distingués.» Cela ne veut rien dire. C'était peut-être hier.

L'asile de vieillards est à Marengo, à quatre-vingts kilomètres d'Alger. Je prendrai l'autobus à deux heures et j'arriverai dans l'après-midi. Ainsi, je pourrai veiller et je rentrerai demain soir. J'ai demandé deux jours de congé à mon patron et il ne pouvait pas me les refuser avec une excuse pareille. Je lui ai même dit: «Ce n'est pas de ma faute». Il n'a pas répondu. J'ai pensé alors que je n'aurais pas dû lui dire cela. En somme, je n'avais pas à m'excuser. C'était plutôt à lui de me présenter ses condoléances. Mais il le fera sans doute après-demain, quand il me verra en deuil. Pour le moment, c'est un peu comme si maman n'était pas morte. Après l'enterrement, au contraire, ce sera une affaire classée et tout aura revêtu une allure officielle.

J'ai pris l'autobus à deux heures. Il faisait très chaud. J'ai mangé au restaurant, chez Céleste, comme d'habitude. Ils avaient tous beaucoup de peine pour moi et Céleste m'a dit: « On n'a qu'une mère». Quand je suis parti, ils m'ont accompagné à la porte. J'étais un peu étourdi parce qu'il a fallu que je monte chez Emmanuel pour lui emprunter une cravate noire et un brassard. Il a perdu son oncle, il y a quelques mois.

> Don't spell *Meursault* incorrectly! Candidates often leave out the first *u*.

(a) Dans cet extrait, qu'est-ce qu'on apprend de l'attitude de Meursault?
(b) Qu'en pensez-vous?
(c) Commentez le style de Camus dans le passage.

> Model answer

(a) Meursault ne semble pas se soucier trop de la mort de sa mère. Les dispositions qu'il prend sont décrites d'une façon objective:

   "Je prendrai l'autobus de deux heures et j'arriverai dans l'après-midi."

Il paraît plus agité par la réaction de son patron quand il avait demandé à celui-ci deux jours de congé pour aller à l'enterrement.

La mort de sa mère n'a rien changé pour Meursault; sa routine reste la même:

   "J'ai mangé au restaurant, chez Céleste, comme d'habitude."

Il semble un peu surpris des condoléances de ceux qui mangeaient au restaurant; encore une fois, ce sont les aspects pratiques, surtout le besoin d'emprunter une cravate noire et un brassard, qui le troublent davantage.

> Try to identify examples of the use of infinitve constructions, the passive, a compound tense, the conditional tense used with the meaning of 'probably', pdo agreement, pronouns. Look up any vocabulary you didn't know and add the words to your own lists.

(b) Je trouve cette attitude très intéressante parce qu'elle est réitérée partout dans le roman; donc dès la première page on se rend compte du fait que cet homme n'est pas comme les autres, et qu'il ne ressent pas les émotions dites 'normales'. Il semble lui-même reconnaître ce fait quand il dit:

   "J'ai pensé alors que je n'aurais pas dû dire cela."

Ce qui paraîtrait chez les autres être la conséquence du choc qu'il a reçu – il n'aurait pas encore compris que sa mère est morte – s'avèrera être le vrai caractère de Meursault.

(c) Camus utilise des phrases courtes et un rythme plutôt saccadé dans cet extrait; il n'y a pas beaucoup de propositions subordonnées. On croit recevoir

Sample questions and model answers (continued)

The language of the answer is competent and reads quite well; although there is some repetition, much of the vocabulary is good. Note that there are no subjunctives; there is no point in forcing them where they are not natural or where the French is better expressed more simply (e.g. *'jusqu'à ce que nous finissions de lire le livre'* would be unnecessarily wordy here).

Model answer

This sample answer is based on one of the best-known 19th-century poems.

When writing about poetry you should take into account the style – rhythm, sound, rhyme, vocabulary – as well as the content. You will probably need to use some specialised vocabulary (see p. 115).

You should know by now the sort of language that is rewarded: see if you can identify at least fifteen examples of it in this answer. Notice also that the candidate has hinted at a deeper understanding of the subject by the reference to other poems and to her knowledge of Verlaine's life.

l'impression d'une liste de choses qu'il a faites et qu'il va faire, entremêlées de quelques réactions de sa part à ce que les autres ont dit. Tout cela me semble refléter admirablement le caractère de Meursault; il n'est pas complexe – du moins, c'est le cas au début – et puisqu'il est le narrateur le style doit montrer ce trait. Les deux premières phrases sont surtout choquantes et attirent tout de suite l'attention du lecteur; mais l'impression qu'elles nous donnent va durer jusqu'à la fin du livre.

4 Poetry appreciation

Choisissez un poème que vous aimez et expliquez pourquoi il vous a plu.

Verlaine: Le ciel est, par-dessus le toit

J'aime ce poème de Verlaine pour plusieurs raisons: il parle aux sens et aux émotions, et son ton mélancolique me plaît, surtout parce que je connais les circonstances sous lesquelles il l'a écrit.

Dans la première strophe Verlaine décrit, dans des termes simples, le ciel bleu et un arbre qu'il voit 'par-dessus le toit'. On comprend alors qu'il ne s'agit pas d'une vue ouverte, mais que pour une raison ou une autre cette vue est limitée. La deuxième strophe introduit deux sons qui sont liés au ciel et à l'arbre de la première. Ces sons ne sont pas forts: la cloche tinte doucement, le chant de l'oiseau est une plainte.

Il est intéressant de noter que dans ces vers les mots 'par-dessus le toit' et 'qu'on voit' sont répétés. Il semble alors qu'il s'agisse de quelque chose d'important; bien que le poète ne puisse pas voir clairement le ciel, le fait qu'il peut le voir est primordial.

En voyant le ciel et l'arbre et en écoutant la cloche et l'oiseau Verlaine se rend compte qu'une vie normale existe très proche de lui, et les bruits de la ville servent à lui rappeler une existence qui lui avait été retirée. Lorsqu'on sait qu'il a écrit ce poème en prison, tout devient plus clair; et la réaction qui se révèle dans la dernière strophe nous indique qu'il regrette son crime. On sait en effet qu'il avait repris sa foi, et la répétition des mots 'Mon Dieu' dans la troisième strophe souligne ce fait.

Ce poème me plaît donc à cause du caractère poignant de la situation du poète au moment où il l'a écrit; à mon avis il a réussi parfaitement à traduire ses propres émotions. Je trouve aussi que la structure – en quatre strophes avec des vers alternés de huit et quatre syllabes – est facile à lire et paraît moins froide que les alexandrins formels des autres poèmes que j'ai lus. Finalement, le vocabulaire qu'utilise Verlaine traduit bien le sens des mots: 'berce', 'tinte', 'plainte', 'tranquille' et 'pleurant' ont tous le son doux et lent et reflètent ainsi l'humeur du poète.

Chapter 8

Thèmes non-littéraires

The following topics are covered in this chapter:

- *AS/A2 topic areas*
- *Links with other A Level subjects*
- *Links with hobbies and interests*

Non-literary themes

After studying this chapter you should be able to:

- *write essays on non-literary topics, using an appropriate range of language*
- *identify the vocabulary and structures that will help you to do so*

LEARNING SUMMARY

You should also refer to the sections on Organising your essay and Quality of language in Chapter 7 (excluding the comments that relate specifically to literature).

If you have decided (or if it has been decided for you) to do the end-of-course essay as part of your exam, one or both of your answers may involve non-literary topics. If so, there are three possibilities:

- Your topic may involve further study of one of the areas already covered for comprehension purposes at AS or A2 Level (e.g. *les médias, la jeunesse, l'environnement, l'éducation, l'immigration*, etc.).

- You may be able to link your topic with knowledge gained from other A level subjects, e.g. geography and history, by writing about a region of France of your choice or about French history (usually the Second World War).

- You may have the chance to link the topic with your own interests, perhaps by studying the work of a French painter, composer or film director; these could also, of course, be part of your A Level studies as above.

8.1 AS/A2 topic areas

AQA	M5
EDEXCEL	M5
OCR	M6
WJEC	M5 (Independent/Guided studies options)
NICCEA	M6

The precise number of words allowed varies slightly among the awarding bodies, so check the requirements of your own exam.

The sub-headings may change from year to year, so check with your school or college.

You will already have learnt much of the vocabulary associated with these topics during your study of these topics within the course. It's unlikely, however, that you will have covered enough material merely from comprehension passages to be able to write a 250–350 word essay, so you will have to study the topic in greater detail.

Some of the exam specifications give sub-headings so that you know on which particular aspects of the subject you must concentrate. They might include:
- for Education: *contenu et diplômes; le bac professionnel*
- for La France multiculturelle: *Le Pen et la politique de l'extrême droite*
- for Les Français d'aujourd'hui: *les rapports entre les générations*.

It's extremely important that you **relate the topic to France** (for some subjects, a French-speaking country is allowed). This paper tests your knowledge of the culture and background of the country, not just your understanding of the topic in general. Just as quotations and examples are essential to underline your

Newspapers and the Internet are excellent sources of statistical information.

understanding of literature, so **facts and up-to-date statistics** relating to France are important in non-literary topics. They also show the examiner that you have taken the trouble to read round the subject.

Some of the vocabulary from the history section below may also be useful.

8.2 Links with other A Level subjects

AQA	M5
EDEXCEL	M5
OCR	M6
WJEC	M5 (Independent/Guided studies options)
NICCEA	M6

Key points from AS

- Vocabulary in AS or A2 Study Guides related to the topic you are planning to write about

The advantage of writing about a topic that you are studying in detail as a different part of your course is that you really understand the subject. The disadvantage is that you have most probably been studying it in English, so what you know about it has to be transferred into French; there is a risk that if you try to translate your notes – written perhaps in more sophisticated language than you can achieve in French on a specialised subject – your version will sound anglicised and may be difficult to understand. If you wish to use some of your notes, concentrate on conveying the gist of the meaning rather than translating.

Remember that your goal is to write in French that is comprehensible to a 'sympathetic native speaker **who knows no English**'.

For topics involving history you should of course be aware of the facts of the situation; other aspects to consider include:

- dates
- people involved (names spelt correctly!)
- reasons for what happened
- consequences
- the events set in a global context.

Vocabulary for history topic

l'époque (f)	time, era	expliquer	to explain
l'ère (f)	era	convaincre	to convince
le siècle	century	ajouter	to add
le résultat	result	contribuer	to contribute
la conséquence	result	saisir	to understand
le point de repère	landmark, reference point	surmonter	to surmount
la cause	cause	subsister	to remain (doubt etc.)
l'effet (m)	effect	établir	to establish
la crise	crisis	déterminer	to determine
le fond du problème	the basis of the problem	identifier	to identify
la tendance	trend, tendency	condamner	to condemn
la réponse	answer	approuver	to approve of
l'obstacle (m)	obstacle	s'aggraver	to get worse
le jugement	judgment	s'empirer	to get worse
le débat	debate	s'améliorer	to improve
l'argument (m)	argument (for/against)	à l'époque	at the time
le moyen	method, means	à l'époque actuelle	at the current time
l'étape (f)	stage	actuellement	currently
l'évidence (f)	evidence, proof	jusqu'ici	until now
la preuve	proof	jusque-là	until then
le doute	doubt	à cette époque-là	at that time
inquiétant	worrying	à ce moment-là	at that time
compliqué	complicated	aujourd'hui	today
répandu	widespread	de nos jours	nowadays
pertinent	relevant	les années quarante (etc.)	the Forties
persuasif, -ve	persuasive, convincing	dès le début	from the beginning
contestable	questionable	dès le départ	from the outset
inadmissible	unacceptable	à partir de	starting from
évident	obvious	la plupart du temps	most of the time
au fil des années	as the years go/went by	il y a + expression of time	ago
au fil du temps	as time passes/passed		

KEY POINT

- *moyen*: often used in the plural.
- *étape*: 'stage' in the development of a situation.
- *aggraver/améliorer*: used without *s* if they are followed by a direct object (*Cela a aggravé la situation*) but in the reflexive form e.g. *La situation s'est aggravée.*
- *actuellement*: a *faux ami* – not 'actually'.
- *il y a*: e.g. *il y a cinquante ans* – 'fifty years ago'.

As far as geography is concerned, the three English awarding bodies all offer the possibility of writing an essay on an area of France (WJEC specification includes it in the Guided Studies option). The main aspects you will need to cover are:

- chief characteristics of the region
- its geography
- its economy (including tourism)
- its history
- its culture and traditions (including gastronomy).

Key points from AS

- **Vocabulary for tourism**
  AS Study Guide Chapter 2
- **Vocabulary for leisure**
  AS Study Guide Chapter 4
- **Vocabulary for food and drink**
  AS Study Guide Chapter 6

If you know a region well, either because you have been there on holiday regularly or because you have been involved in an exchange, this is an excellent basis for covering the topic. Some awarding bodies have suggested in the past that you are unlikely to do well if you have not visited the region; this is not necessarily the case, but it will certainly help to add conviction to what you write if you can include comments based on your own observation.

Vocabulary for a region of France

(These are general words; you may need to learn specialised vocabulary that relates particularly to the area that you are studying.)

le trait	characteristic	**élever**	to breed, raise
le climat	climate	**mettre en place**	to set up
la campagne	country	**entrer en vigueur**	to come into force
la terre	land, earth	**privilégier**	to favour
la montagne	mountains	**favoriser**	to favour
la colline	hill	**s'accompagner de**	to be accompanied by
le fleuve	river (large)	**posséder**	to own
la rivière	river	**disposer de**	to have available, at one's disposal
le ruisseau	stream		
la côte	coast	**faire le tour (de)**	to go round
le rivage	shore	**augmenter**	to increase
le littoral	coast	**prendre l'essor**	to increase, take off
le champ	field	**se développer**	to develop
la plaine	plain	**prôner**	to sing the praises of
le lac	lake	**s'annoncer bien**	to be promising
le rocher	rock	**rural**	rural, of the country
la forêt	forest	**urbain**	urban, of the town
la mer	sea	**rocheux, -se**	rocky
la récolte	crops, harvesting	**montagneux, -se**	mountainous
le rendement	yield	**peuplé**	populated
les ressources (f)	resources	**peu peuplé**	sparsely populated
le patrimoine	heritage	**agricole**	agricultural
le changement	change	**industriel, -elle**	industrial
la production	production	**industrialisé**	industrialised
le produit	product	**littoral**	coastal
l'investissement (m)	investment	**touristique**	tourist
le réseau	network	**maritime**	maritime, coastal
le terroir	land, soil	**doux, douce**	mild
l'exploitation (f)	working (of land)	**élevé**	raised
la fabrication	making (in factory, etc.)	**ancien, ancienne**	old, ancient
le vignoble	vineyard	**moderne**	modern
la vendange	wine harvest	**oriental**	eastern

Vocabulary for a region of France (continued)

le commerce	trade	occidental	western
s'étendre	to stretch	principal	main
s'élever	to rise	laitier, -ière	dairy
conserver	to preserve	changeant	changing
couler	to flow	spécialisé	specialised
attirer	to attract	performant	successful
produire	to produce	financier, -ière	financial
investir	to invest	rentable	profitable
promouvoir	to promote	diversifié	diversified
assurer	to maintain, carry out	divers	diverse, various
de masse	mass (tourism)	prometteur, -se	promising

KEY POINT

- *mer*: no problem with the meaning in this context, but don't forget the other possible spellings of the same sound (*maire*, *mère*).
- *posséder*: one of the *espérer* group.
- *ancien*: remember its position: it means 'former' before the noun, 'ancient' or 'old' after the noun.
- *produire*: has the same pattern as *conduire*.
- *promouvoir*: a compound of *mouvoir* (see p. 75); the past participle is *promu*.
- *principal*: remember the masculine plural *principaux*.

8.3 Link with hobbies and interests

AQA	M5
EDEXCEL	M5
OCR	M6
WJEC	(Guided studies options)

In contrast to the first category of essay (8.1) the problem here may be to keep to the word limit; the chances are that this is a subject about which you know a great deal. It's all the more important, therefore, to **answer the set question properly** (it certainly won't be *Écrivez tout ce que vous savez sur...*) and to **select your material carefully**. You will already have narrowed your area of study for yourself; perhaps to 'Les Impressionnistes' or even just one of them, or to 'Debussy'; or the awarding body may have done it for you by specifying e.g. 'Le cinéma de Truffaut'. You should have no difficulty in finding examples to illustrate what you have to say, but do give titles in French (e.g. *Déjeuner sur l'herbe, Prélude à l'après-midi d'un faune, Le dernier métro*).

> Topic-specific vocabulary is particularly important here.

The questions set will of course vary according to the subject, but for all three principal topic areas (art, music, cinema) you should be able to:

Key points from AS

- **Leisure and the arts** *AS Study Guide pp. 74–78*

- give the chief characteristics of the painting, composition or film
- set the artist or his/her work in a wider context
- say why he/she is important
- give reasons why you like or dislike the work.

Vocabulary for art

le patrimoine	heritage	exposer	to exhibit
l'artiste	artist	exprimer	to express
le peintre	painter	inspirer	to inspire
l'école (f)	school (of painting)	exercer une influence	to exert an influence
le chef	leader	influencer	to influence
le paysagiste	landscape painter	peindre	to paint
le portraitiste	portait painter	dépeindre	to depict
la peinture	paint, painting	dessiner	to draw
la toile	canvas, painting	se spécialiser (dans)	to specialise (in)
le dessin	drawing	sentir	to feel
l'esquisse (f)	preliminary sketch	représenter	to portray, represent
l'exposition (f)	exhibition	faire le portrait de	to portray

Vocabulary for art (continued)

le salon	exhibition, show	appliquer	to apply (paint etc.)
la lumière	light	refléter	to reflect
la couleur	colour	révéler	to reveal, show
le ton	tone	esquisser	to sketch
la nuance	shade (of colour)	critiquer	to criticise
l'ombre (f)	shade, shadow	abstrait	abstract
le style	style	figuratif, -ive	representational, figurative
l'ambiance (f)	atmosphere, mood		
la beauté	beauty	symbolique	symbolic
le détail	detail	innovateur, -trice	innovative (person)
la tranquillité	tranquility	novateur, -trice	innovative (idea)
l'image (f)	image, picture	sensuel, -lle	sensual
le paysage	landscape	vif, vive	bright (colour)
le sujet	subject	sombre	dark (colour)
la technique	technique	morne	drab
l'effet (m)	effect	traditionnel, -lle	traditional
le développement	development	romantique	romantic
le pinceau	paintbrush	caractéristique	distinctive
la brosse	brush	subjectif, -ve	subjective
le coup de pinceau	brushstroke	objectif, -ve	objective
le trait de pinceau	brushstroke	naturel, -lle	natural
la critique	criticism, appreciation	à la mode	fashionable
le/la critique	critic	démodé	old-fashioned
(à) l'aquarelle (f)	(in) watercolour	à l'huile	oil, in oils

- *peinture*: a useful word; it can mean the paint itself, the finished picture or the painting of it.
- *exposition/salon*: a *Salon* tends to be a grand affair and is not used solely for art (*le Salon de l'auto* is the Motor Show).
- *critique*: remember that *la critique* need not be critical; also that the word may refer to a female critic.
- *peindre/dépeindre*: check the formation of these verbs (pp. 74–76).
- *sentir*: not a true -*ir* verb; its endings are like those of *partir* and *sortir*.
- *refléter*: one of the *espérer* group.
- *révéler*: also one of the *espérer* group; it also makes an interesting change of vocabulary from *montrer* (the *r* of which is often omitted by students, thus changing the meaning of the verb).

Vocabulary for music

(Some of the verbs and adjectives from the Art section may also be useful.)

la musique	music	composer	to compose
le genre	type (of music)	jouer	to play, perform
le compositeur	composer	interpréter	to perform
l'orchestre (m)	orchestra	improviser	to improvise
l'ensemble (m)	group of musicians	accompagner	to accompany
le choeur	choir	écouter	to listen to
la chorale	choir	entendre	to hear
le chef d'orchestre	conductor (orchestra)	enregistrer	to record
le chef de choeur	conductor (choir)	être dans le ton	to be on key
le premier violon	leader of orchestra	sortir du ton	to be off-key
les cordes (f)	strings section	chanter juste	to sing in tune
les bois	woodwind section	chanter faux	to sing out of tune
les cuivres (m)	brass section	diriger	to conduct
les percussions (f)	percussion section	léger, légère	light
le musicien	musician	fort	loud
l'instrumentaliste	instrument player	bruyant	loud
le chanteur	singer	sonore	loud
l'air (m)	tune	doux, douce	soft
la mélodie	melody	spontané	spontaneous

Vocabulary for music (continued)

l'oeuvre (f)	work	harmonieux, -se	harmonious
le morceau	piece	dissonant	discordant
l'harmonie (f)	harmony	harmonique	harmonic
la dissonance	discord	symphonique	symphonic
l'accompagnement (m)	accompaniment	polyphonique	polyphonic
le talent	talent	moderne	modern
le pionnier	pioneer	classique	classical
le concerto	concerto	trop haut	sharp (tone)
la symphonie	symphony	trop bas	flat (tone)
la sonate	sonata	faux, fausse	flat (tone)
la cantate	cantata	bémol	flat (key)
la rhapsodie	rhapsody	dièse	sharp (key)
le mouvement	movement	sans accompagnement	unaccompanied
l'opéra (m)	opera	a cappella	unaccompanied
l'opérette (f)	operetta	seul	unaccompanied
la chanson	song	chanté en choeur	choral
le ton majeur	major key	choral	choral
le ton mineur	minor key	en majeur	in a major key
l'interprétation (f)	performance	en mineur	in a minor key
la gamme	scale	do	doh, C
la musique de chambre	chamber music	ré	re, D
... d'ambiance	background music	mi	mi, E
... de scène	incidental music	fa	fah, F
... d'ascenseur	Muzak	sol	soh, G
... de supermarché	Muzak	la	lah, A
la fanfare	brass band	si	te, B
le leitmotiv	recurring theme		

- *compositeur, musicien, chanteur*: the feminine forms are *compositrice, musicienne* and *chanteuse* respectively.
- *jouer*: remember that this verb is followed by the appropriate part of *de* when an instrument is mentioned: *Elle joue du piano*.
- *accompagner*: followed by the correct part of *à* with an instrument: *Il l'a accompagné au piano*.
- *écouter*: NOT followed by *à*; and don't confuse it with *entendre*.
- *fort, bruyant, sonore*: *fort* refers to the extent of the sound, *bruyant* and *sonore* to the type of music.
- *bémol, dièse*: e.g. *en la bémol* – 'in A flat'.
- *sans accompagnement, a cappella, seul*: the first two refer to voices, *seul* refers to an instrument.
- *do, ré, mi,* etc: if you take middle C as 'doh' the rest follow logically. C can also be *ut*.

KEY POINT

Vocabulary for cinema

le grand écran	'silver screen'	jouer le rôle	to play the part
le cinéaste	film-maker	interpréter	to play the part
le cinéphile	film fan, enthusiast	incarner	to play the part
le mordu de cinéma	film buff	doubler	to dub
la vedette	star	réaliser	to direct
le réalisateur	director	mettre en scène	to direct
le metteur en scène	director	enregistrer	to record
le producteur	producer	réduire	to cut
le scénariste	script-writer	monter	to cut
l'acteur, l'actrice	actor	montrer	to show
le décor	set	faire voir	to show, make see
le plateau de tournage	film set	tourner (un film)	to shoot, make
le financement	funding	sous-titré	sub-titled
les fonds (m)	funds	surtitré	sur-titled
le budget	budget	en extérieurs	on location
le tournage	shooting, filming	contemporain	contemporary

Vocabulary for cinema (continued)

le filmage	filming	muet	silent (film)
la première	first showing, première	symbolique	symbolic
la distribution	cast list	divertissant	enjoyable, amusing
les droits d'adaptation	film rights	qui fait penser	which makes ... think
la censure	censorship	à faire penser	to make you think
la séance	showing, performance	réaliste	realistic
le long métrage	feature film	effrayant	frightening
le moyen métrage	medium-length film	frappant	striking, effective
le court métrage	(film) short	atroce	horrific
le documentaire	documentary	humoristique	humorous
le film d'animation	animated film	en gros plan	in close-up
le cameraman	cameraman	significatif, -ive	significant
la prise de vue(s)	camera work, shots	lourd de sens	significant (look)
l'équipe de prise de vues	camera crew	sous l'égide de	under the aegis of
le plan	shot	succès au box-office	box-office success
la cascade	stunt	qui fait recette	doing well financially
le cascadeur,	stuntman, -woman	le festival du cinéma	film festival
la cascadeuse		les effets spéciaux	special effects
la bande sonore	soundtrack	la musique de scène	incidental music
la lumière	light	le bruitage	sound effects
les éclairages	lighting effects		

See p. 116 for phrases to use when introducing your own opinions.

KEY POINT

- *vedette*: remember that there is no masculine form of this word.
- *cameraman*: the plural, if needed, is *les cameramans*; *caméra* is used for a film or video camera.
- *jouer le rôle/interpréter/incarner*: a chance to show the variety of your vocabulary if you need to use the verb more than once.
- *réduire/monter*: use *réduire* to mean 'cut in length', *monter* for 'to edit'.

- Remember that for all three types of topic you will be expected to give your own opinions. This is quite easy to do for the first type (e.g. *Je trouve que ces chiffres qui se rapportent au tabagisme sont scandaleux*) and very easy for the third (e.g. *Les Nymphéas de Monet me plaisent surtout à cause des couleurs qu'il a utilisées*). It's more difficult for the second, since you are dealing primarily with facts; the question will probably ask you to say what you think about a particular aspect, but if not you must be sure to include some personal reaction (e.g. *Cette attitude de la part du maréchal Pétain me semble peu intelligible*).

Progress check

History

Give the French for: judgment, proof, complicated, relevant, at the current time, ago, to identify, effect, to explain, century.

Give the English for: contestable, jusqu'ici, au fil des années, établir, s'empirer, l'étape, la crise, inquiétant, répandu, dès le depart.

Region of France

Give the French for: resources, to increase, agricultural, large river, industrial, mild, investment, to preserve, trade, to attract.

Give the English for: faire l'essor, le champ, le patrimoine, le produit, littoral, le vignoble, occidental, divers, promouvoir, prometteur.

Progress check (continued)

Art

Give the French for: painter, canvas, light, shade of colour, to express, to feel, to portray, abstract, natural, drab.

Give the English for: le pinceau, caractéristique, l'ombre, le paysagiste, refléter, à l'aquarelle, démodé, le ton, le Salon, exposer.

Music

Give the French for: composer, strings section, musician (feminine), tune, accompaniment, to conduct, classical, E flat major, harmonious, in a minor key.

Give the English for: chanter juste, spontané, le morceau, la dissonance, trop haut, interpréter, écouter, le genre, les cuivres, le pionnier.

Cinema

Give the French for: director, feature film, star, censorship, to make you think, stuntman, lighting effects, soundtrack, film set, shot.

Give the English for: le scénariste, le cinéphile, tourner, la distribution, effrayant, le grand écran, le cinéaste, qui fait recette, le bruitage, frappant.

Sample questions and model answers

The first essay is at the lower end of the word allocation, and has been written using only the facts given in the section on the Environment in the AS Study Guide. Try to work out where you could add more detail if you are allowed to exceed 250 words. The structure is quite simple, but clear.

1 (L'Environnement)
Est-ce que les Français se soucient de l'environnement?

Plan: Introduction – problème mondial mais mesures prises déjà en France
Main body – i) conservation (ii) protection (iii) recyclage
Conclusion

Model answer

La protection de l'environnement est un problème mondial. La France a été un des premiers pays à reconnaître (1) ce fait et à mettre en place (1) des mesures qui maîtriseraient (2) les choses qui ajoutent à la pollution de notre planète.

Premièrement les Français savent qu'il faut protéger (1) ce qui (3) existe déjà. On a donc créé des parcs nationaux qui fournissent un habitat approprié à la survie des espèces qui sont en voie de disparition. On y (4) consacre une partie assez importante du budget. Ces parcs attirent un nombre croissant de randonneurs, surtout le weekend et pendant les vacances.

Deuxièmement, on comprend qu'il est nécessaire (5) d'arrêter (1) la dégradation de l'environnement. Alors on a commencé à fabriquer des produits qui ne contiennent pas les CFC qui ont causé le trou dans la couche d'ozone. De plus, la compagnie Airparif surveille la qualité de l'air sur l'Ile de France et sur quelques autres grandes villes; si le niveau de pollution devient trop élevé, des mesures (dont (6) une réduction de vitesse pour les véhicules et de production pour les usines) sont déclenchées (7).

Troisièmement, on encourage les gens à recycler (1) tout ce qu'ils peuvent (3), surtout les déchets ménagers; un système de conteneurs en couleurs différentes a été établi (7) par certains conseils municipaux, et les Français les (4) utilisent volontiers.

Les groupes de pression, comme les Amis de la Terre, travaillent à l'échelle mondiale pour protéger (1) l'environnement, mais déjà en France elle-même on fait des progrès pour améliorer (1) la situation. On peut donc voir que les Français se soucient vraiment de l'environnement (8).

1   Use of constructions involving the infinitive.
2   The conditional tense is used to indicate that this is the purpose of the measures.
3   Use of *ce qui* and *ce que*.
4   Use of pronouns.
5   A change of vocabulary from the *il faut* of the first paragraph.
6   *Dont* here means 'including'.
7   Use of the passive.
8   This is a weak ending; the candidate has used the actual words of the question and would have done much better to express it in some other way. See if you can work out two or more different possibilities.

Sample questions and model answers (continued)

2 (L'Occupation)

Peut-on dire que le gouvernement Vichy était patriote?

Plan: Introduction – deux points de vue à considérer
        Main body – pour: ce que Pétain voulait
                    contre: Pétain pour Hitler, contre les Alliés
        Conclusion

Model answer

À première vue il semble impossible de dire que le gouvernement établi à Vichy sous le maréchal Pétain a été patriote, et en réalité je ne crois pas que ce soit (1) le cas. Néanmoins il y a des arguments à faire à ce propos. (2)

Lorsque, le 10 juillet 1940 (3), le pouvoir sur l'État français a été accordé (4) à Pétain, celui-ci (5) a annoncé son intention de créer (6) une Révolution Nationale dont (7) les mots-clé seraient Travail, Famille, Patrie (3). Il a mis en valeur les vertus traditionnelles; il prônait la discipline dans les écoles, il encourageait les familles nombreuses et il condamnait le divorce (3). On peut dire alors qu'il se voyait (8) vraiment comme patriote. (9)

Quand même (10) les Français qui habitaient dans la zone occupée traitaient Pétain de collaborateur; ils pensaient qu'il favorisait les Allemands, impression qui a été renforcée (4) quand une réunion a eu lieu entre Pétain et Hitler. Il considérait comme ennemis de la France la Grande Bretagne, les États-Unis, la Russie et, à l'intérieur du pays, les Juifs et les communistes. Il a introduit le Service du Travail obligatoire, (3) qui forçait les hommes à aller travailler (6) en Allemagne; pour y échapper (11/6) des milliers de gens se sont réfugiés dans les montagnes.

À l'époque aussi bien qu'aujourd'hui ce sont les membres de la Résistance et ceux qui les aidaient qui sont considérés comme des héros et des patriotes, parce qu'ils se battaient tout le temps pour libérer leur pays des armées allemandes. À mon avis le maréchal Pétain s'est dit (8) que ce qu'il faisait (12) était pour le bien de la France; mais je soutiens qu'il avait tort (13).

1 Use of the subjunctive.

2 The candidate has made it clear that he proposes to set out both sides of the question.

3 Dates and facts are essential in an essay relating to a historical topic.

4 Use of the passive.

5 *Celui-ci* used here to mean 'the latter'.

6 Constructions involving the infinitive.

7 The use of *dont* ('of which', 'whose') is always impressive. Check the word order.

8 'Ordinary' verbs used reflexively: 'he saw himself', 'he said to himself'.

9 The candidate has underlined the relevance of what he has just written and also summed up neatly the first half of his essay.

10 The other side of the question is introduced with an appropriate phrase.

11 Use of pronoun. Note that *échapper* is followed by *à* if someone is escaping from something in order to avoid it in the first place, but by *de* if he is escaping from something (e.g. prison) in which he already finds himself.

12 Use of *ce que*.

13 The candidate makes his position clear in the final sentence, but without repeating the words he has already used.

Sample questions and model answers *(continued)*

3 (Region of France)

Est-ce que la région que vous avez étudiée vous semble plutôt traditionnelle ou plutôt moderne? Donnez vos raisons.

Plan: Introduction – mélange des deux aspects
        Main body – (i) architecture/villes (Caen)
                    (ii) maisons/campagne mais Pont de Normandie
                    (iii) économie (surtout agricole)
                    (iv) culture (musique, musées)
        Conclusion

Model answer

La tradition et la modernité se réunissent en Normandie. Son architecture et son économie sont un mélange des deux; le sens de l'histoire est toujours présent aussi bien qu'un regard vers l'avenir (1).

Les villes normandes gardent un charme particulier qui provient d'une combinaison de leurs rues étroites bordées de vieilles églises et de hautes maisons et de leurs zones piétonnières nouvelles qui sont parsemées de petites places. À Caen, où le bombardement de 1944 a entraîné une reconstruction radicale (2), tout au milieu d'une ligne d'édifices modernes se trouve la Maison des Quatrans qui date du 15e siècle (2).

Dans la campagne normande on voit de rares maisons situées au milieu des champs de poiriers et de pommiers, où rien ne semble avoir changé depuis des siècles. Mais contre l'horizon près du Havre se dessine le Pont de Normandie, construction qui date de 1995 (2/3).

Les fruitiers sont un élément important de l'économie de la région. Le cidre et le calvados y (4) sont produits (5), quoique les méthodes utilisées pour les produire aient changé (6) par endroits. Néanmoins le rôle de l'agriculture est maintenant réduit en Normandie comme ailleurs; il s'agit de produits laitiers tels le beurre et le fromage (Camembert, Livarot) (7). En même temps des usines modernes se trouvent généralement dans les banlieues (8).

En ce qui concerne la culture (9), je suis d'avis que la tradition l'emporte (10) sur la modernité. Les galeries exposent les oeuvres des jeunes artistes, mais les Normands que je connais (11) aiment ce qui (12) est traditionnel. Les Arts Florissants, chorale bien connue qui est née à Caen, chante surtout la musique classique. En Normandie on est fier de sa culture: le musée de la dentelle à Bayeux (2) et bien sûr la tapisserie elle-même, attirent annuellement beaucoup de visiteurs.

Malgré les mesures qu'on a prises (13) pour rendre (14) la région plus moderne, je soutiendrais que ce sont les aspects traditionnels qui y (4) sont les plus frappants. (15)

This essay is rather long, and illustrates the difficulty of including enough facts to show that you know what you are talking about into 250–350 words. If excessive length is penalised in the exam taken by this candidate, she could take out the reference to Les Arts Florissants (16 words) and to the role of agriculture (12 words, but *aussi* would have to be added after *il s'agit* in order to keep the flow of the French).

1   This introductory paragraph makes it clear that both sides of the question will be considered.

2   Precise facts show that the candidate knows what she is talking about.

3   The two sides to the question are both covered in this paragraph.

4   Use of pronouns.

5   Use of the passive.

6   Use of the subjunctive.

7   Camembert is not very exciting, but the reference to Livarot is less obvious.

8 This is a very vague statement and should ideally be clarified by reference to the particular industries concerned. However, restriction on length makes it impossible to add any more detail here.

9 A good linking phrase to lead on to the next point (but it uses six precious words).

10 The *l'* is not translatable here; *l'emporte* has the sense of 'wins the day'.

11 A personal reference. The three words could be omitted.

12 Use of *ce qui*.

13 Pdo agreement.

14 Construction using the infinitive.

15 The candidate sums up her position in the final sentence; it bears out what she has said already.

4 (L'étude d'un artiste français)

Expliquez pourquoi l'artiste (metteur en scène, peintre, musicien) que vous avez étudié vous semble important. Décrivez les traits caractéristiques de son oeuvre.

Plan: Introduction: Offenbach – 'Mozart des Champs-Élysées'
  Main body: opérettes – Orfée – courageux
  Style
  Contes d'Hoffman
  Conclusion

Model answer

J'ai choisi d'étudier (1) la musique de Jacques Offenbach. Cet homme est généralement classé comme compositeur français, quoiqu'il fût né (2) en Allemagne. Rossini l'a appelé (3) 'le Mozart des Champs-Élysées' et d'après moi cette situation résume dans une certaine mesure son oeuvre (4).

On dirait que la plupart des compositeurs français ont produit la musique plutôt légère – tout en conservant (5) une tonalité plus émotionnelle – par rapport aux grands musiciens allemands ou autrichiens. Offenbach ne constitue pas l'exception, mais son oeuvre est tout à fait différente de celle (6) de ses contemporains. Il composait surtout des opérettes, dont (7) la plus connue est Orfée aux enfers. Le ton en (3) est presque satirique; Offenbach n'hésitait pas à ridiculiser (1) dans cette composition la conduite souvent méchante des dieux et des déesses de l'antiquité, mais en effet il utilisait ces derniers comme symboles des gens qui s'assemblaient autour de Napoléon III (8). À cause de cela il n'était pas toujours populaire chez ses contemporains, mais les spectateurs l'adoraient! (3) Je trouve qu'il était courageux de critiquer (1) de cette façon les moeurs du siècle, et à mon avis c'est un élément important du caractère de n'importe quel artiste (9).

Son style me plaît beaucoup; sa musique est spirituelle, mélodieuse et pleine d'humour. Prenons à titre d'exemple Orfée aux Enfers: on y trouve (3) un mélange d'airs joyeux (le galop, le Cancan) et de chansons réfléchies comme celle de l'ancien roi des Béotiens qui regrette la perte de son royaume (8). Les Contes d'Hoffman, oeuvre composée plus tard, est plus sérieuse mais retient les mêmes traits: mélodie chantante, facilité narrative, et maîtrise des nuances musicales.

Sample questions and model answers (continued)

Offenbach a été le précurseur des autres compositeurs d'opérettes dont la réputation est maintenant plus répandue – Strauss, Lehar et Sullivan par exemple – mais c'est lui qui a fait le premier pas sur la route.

1   Use of constructions involving the infinitive.

2   Use of the imperfect subjunctive.

3   Use of pronouns.

4   This statement is vague, and the candidate does not follow it up; it seems that he was simply keen to include a quotation he had learnt, whether it was relevant or not.

5   *En* + present participle.

6   Use of interesting relative pronoun.

7   Use of *dont* is always worth credit.

8   Evidence of having studied the subject – facts quoted in context.

9   The candidate has inserted his own comments as he goes along, a perfectly acceptable way of dealing with the question.

Chapter 9
Travail continu/ études guidées

The following topics are covered in this chapter:

- Pros and cons of coursework
- Choice of topic and essay title
- Practical points relating to coursework

Coursework/Guided studies

After studying this section you should be able to:

- make a sensible choice of title for your coursework essay(s)
- check that your work conforms to the rules of the awarding body

LEARNING SUMMARY

This chapter should be read in conjunction with Chapter 7 (literary topics) or Chapters 7 and 8 (non-literary topics).

9.1 Pros and cons of coursework

Many candidates offer coursework instead of writing an end-of-course essay. This has its disadvantages as well as advantages.

Pros:

- Presentation of your work should be very good.
- You can refer to grammar notes and dictionaries to check the accuracy of your French.
- You have time to find material to illustrate the points you are making.
- The choice of subject is yours.

If you have a free choice you must of course relate what you write to France or a francophone country.

This last point is the real advantage of coursework. Some centres may allow you a free choice; others make the decision about the topic for you but allow you to choose the aspect of it that you will write about.

Cons:

- Coursework has to be submitted earlier in the year, so the standard of your French at the time you are working on it may not be as high as at the end of the course.
- Because you are able to use a dictionary the moderator will expect a higher level of accuracy.
- Vagueness and triviality will be severely penalised because you have had several months in which to research the topic.

9.2 Choice of topic and essay title

It's very important to **convey your interest in the subject you have chosen**. Your own teacher will mark the work, but the marks will be moderated by the awarding body so you have to convince two people that you know what you are writing about. Enthusiasm is a great persuader! **An unusual approach** may impress your reader, who is likely to become bored if he/she has to read a dozen essays on the same subject. Be imaginative if you can; for example:

- If you have read *La Peste* and decide to write about the conditions in the town of Oran during the plague, take the part of one of the characters and write it as a diary instead of a straightforward account (choosing someone like Cottard or Père Paneloux would give it an unusual slant).

- If you are writing about the changes that have taken place in an area of France over a period of time, structure it as a conversation between a reporter and an older resident (but try to put some of your points into the questions or it will end up as an interrogation).

- If you are studying the French media you might consider producing the script of an advertisement for an imaginary product, together with an explanation of how and why you think it would appeal to a French television audience or readership.

- Suggest how you might adapt a novel to make a box-office hit in the cinema (perhaps in the style of a well-known director) or how you would stage a play in the theatre.

- Write about a working day in the life of your chosen musician or artist.

You may not be comfortable with this type of approach, in which case keep to the traditional 'account' format; you certainly won't lose marks by doing so.

If your centre allows you a free choice of topic you should really enjoy this aspect of the course. It's often a good idea to gear your choice towards your other A Level subjects; if you are studying the sciences, consider writing about the contribution made by French scientists (for some general points to follow up, see Chapter 3). Geography or economics students could bring real depth of understanding to the study of a region of France; history students could consider the reign of Louis XIV or the French Revolution.

Your own interests may lead you towards a topic: art or music, for example. The Impressionists are perhaps the obvious artists to study (but not the only possibilities; consider Watteau or Fragonard if you want to be different). In classical music there are composers such as Bizet, Fauré, Delibes, Satie, Debussy; in popular music stars such as Johnny Halliday, Sacha Distel, Charles Aznavour, Edith Piaf, Jacques Brel; in modern music Céline Dion and the rap groups IAM and MC Solaar. If you are not sure whether the subject is suitable, your centre will be able to check with the awarding body before you start.

If you choose any of these topics you must remember that this is A Level and that you must therefore consider the subject **in depth**; facts should be backed up with evidence in the form of quotations, statistics or some other form of illustration, and you should add your own opinions, giving reasons for your point of view.

Your essay titles might therefore include:

- *Dans quelle mesure est-ce que les scientifiques français ont réussi à améliorer la vie des hommes?*
- *Quels sont les facteurs qui ont influencé l'économie de la Normandie?*
- *La vie d'un courtisan sous le règne du Roi Soleil.*
- *Le rôle de Claude Monet dans le développement de la peinture.*
- *Claude Debussy: musicien impressionniste?*
- *Quelle est l'importance des groupes 'rap' dans la culture contemporaine?*

Examiner's tip

You will notice that several of these suggestions are in the form of questions. This is a good way of dealing with a coursework essay: to ask a specific question focuses the attention on the aspect of the topic you wish to cover. Discuss the wording with your teacher; if you decide to use a question as your title make sure that you answer it in your essay! These suggestions could also be used for topic discussion in the oral exam.

9.3 Practical points relating to coursework

Your centre should have a booklet setting out all the coursework regulations.

Word count

This is important; **you must not exceed the maximum number of words allowed**, and most awarding bodies will expect you to write an approximate total at the end of your essay. As with the comprehension writing tasks and topic essay, moderators can tell very quickly if the allocation has been exceeded, and will look with a jaundiced eye on a candidate who has produced five pages of closely-written French but appended '*701 mots*' (for an allowance of 700). However, as is also the case with the topic essay, you are unlikely to achieve the top grades if you are right at the lower boundary of the word allocation (unless you have a particularly concise style) so **aim for a total just within the upper limit**. Check the regulations for your own exam; often quotations are not included in the word count. Totals vary for the awarding bodies: some require one long essay (usually about 1200–1500 words), others ask for two shorter ones (perhaps 500–700 words) or you might be asked for one of each.

Content

You may be allowed to write two essays about different aspects of the same general topic (e.g. one on the economy of the region, the other on its traditions) or you may be expected to deal with two completely different topics. Also, some awarding bodies expect you to use two different topics for coursework and oral discussion.

Spell-checkers

You are not normally allowed to use French spell-checkers.

Word processing

This is generally welcomed – moderators sometimes find candidates' handwriting very difficult to decipher – but you should be aware that **typing errors still count as mistakes** (this includes omission of accents) so you should check your printed version carefully and amend by hand if necessary. Presentation is important (you have, after all, had a great deal of time in which to complete the work) so try to give a good impression. Double-spacing is often a good idea; try it and see how it looks.

Bibliography

You are normally required to **list your sources of information**. These may be books, magazine and newspaper articles, or radio and television programmes. Information researched via the Internet must be acknowledged; you should give the Website address in your bibliography, not just 'the Internet'. If you have based your essay on a conversation recorded while in France, you may need to include a transcript of the conversation (it will not be included in the word-count).

You should not, of course, copy out huge chunks and pass it off as your own work. Your teachers are required to sign a cover sheet stating that they believe the essay to be your own unaided work, and they are perfectly entitled to say that they think this is not the case; if so your work may not even be considered for a grade. Don't try to hoodwink your teacher or moderator; if one doesn't recognise your source, the other probably will. The awarding body may also make its own checks: if your coursework grade appears to be A but the grades in your other modules are D or E they may be checked again to see whether the A was really justified.

Examiner's tip

If your computer's word-processing program has an autocorrect system, check very carefully that it has not done something you didn't want it to do (e.g. correcting *dont* to 'don't'). Alternatively disable the autocorrect while you are typing in French – but only with the permission of the owner of the computer!

An attempt to translate an English article into French is likely to be unsuccessful also, because you will probably not have the skills required to do it well; the result will be either wrong or in poor French, or possibly both. In fact all the Coursework guidance booklets state that candidates are advised to use source material in French rather than in English.

Illustrative material

The sort of illustrative material you use will vary according to your topic; for some subjects it may not be appropriate at all, and you would certainly not be penalised for not using it. In any case, your moderator will not want to spend time cross-checking every sentence with a map or plan, for example; this would also have the effect of taking his/her attention away from the main body of your argument too frequently. So use material sensibly and sensitively.

> Remember that this material must not take the place of your own comments; it should only be used to reinforce what you are saying.

Good use of illustration might include:

- the picture or photograph to which you are referring
- a sketch or photo of a building to illustrate a style of architecture
- a drawing of a stage set or costume to illustrate your ideas about the production of a play
- an audio tape containing a brief example (perhaps played by you) of the music about which you are writing
- a video tape of part of the region that is the subject of your essay.

A final word of advice: **don't leave your coursework until the last minute**. This applies to all A Level subjects, of course, but is particularly important for a modern foreign language where you need to check the accuracy of what you have written or typed. Your final piece of work will be all the better if it reflects your studies during the course and not just the work you have done in the last three weeks, and you will do it better if you are more relaxed and not trying to complete it at the last possible moment.

Chapter 10

L'Examen oral

The following topics are covered in this chapter:

- *General conversation*
- *Conversation on topics*
- *Conversation based on a stimulus*
- *Presentation*

- *Interpreting*
- *Assessment of content*
- *Assessment of response*
- *Assessment of accuracy*

The oral examination

After studying this chapter you should be able to:

- *conduct a conversation on AS and A2 topics*
- *present a chosen topic*
- *understand how the oral exam is assessed*

LEARNING SUMMARY

Key points from AS

- **General advice**
  AS Study Guide Chapter 8

During the conversation, a 'Gallic shrug' of the shoulders, a '*bof*' or a French hesitation ('*euhhhhh…*') can all add to the impression of 'Frenchness' as long as you don't overdo it.

The content of the oral examination at A2 Level varies according to the particular exam you are taking, **but will include some or all of the sections below**. Make sure that you know exactly what you have to do; you can reduce the pressure of what many candidates consider to be a stressful experience by being familiar with all the aspects of your exam.

The examiner may be your own teacher, which is often an advantage as you don't have to face a stranger across the desk. An external examiner is a possibility for some exams; many candidates prefer this as they feel that they perform better in front of someone who doesn't know anything about them.

In either case, there are two important things to remember before you start:

- Try to forget the microphone and recorder and treat it as a conversation with a friendly adult.
- Say to yourself as you go into the examination room, "*À partir de ce moment je suis français(e)*", and react throughout as though you were that French person.

10.1 General conversation

The examiner may use *tu* or *vous* to you, but you must call him/her *vous*.

A general conversation based on general interests is likely to be used as a 'warm-up' session, to help you to relax as you talk about something that is really familiar to you, and will probably not last very long. All the topics you prepared for your GCSE oral could be useful here, so take some time to think out what you might say in answer to such questions as:

Parlez-moi de votre famille.

Quels sont vos intérêts?

Tu aimes la région où tu habites?

Ton collège/lycée te plaît?

Vous sortez souvent?

Quels sont tes projets pour l'avenir?

Tu connais bien la France?

In answering these early questions you should avoid the simple '*J'aime la natation*' or '*Je vais au cinéma avec mes amis*'. Such phrases may be used sparingly to start you off, but **move quickly to more sophisticated language**; these general questions give you the chance to show what you can do before you have to think more carefully about the content of your answers. When you reach the later stages of the exam you will find it less easy – though certainly not impossible – to use the complex structures you have learnt for AS and A2. Look at the examples below and see how the candidates have incorporated into their response some of the idioms and structures they have learnt.

> *Depuis l'âge de sept ans je m'intéresse au patinage.*
>
> *Je viens de rendre visite à ma copine française qui habite en Provence.*
>
> *Quoique ce lycée soit plutôt petit, je dirais que l'enseignement que j'y ai reçu a été très bon.*
>
> *Devenir astronaute, c'est mon rêve.*
>
> *Dès que j'aurai quitté le collège je travaillerai comme plongeur pour gagner de l'argent.*
>
> *Après avoir fini mes études je…*
>
> *En sortant avec ses amis le weekend on a l'occasion de se détendre, ce qui est important surtout quand on est stressé.*
>
> *Je ne pense pas que cette ville ait beaucoup à offrir aux jeunes.*
>
> *D'habitude nous nous entendons bien, tout en nous disputant de temps en temps – ce qui est normal dans la plupart des familles, à mon avis.*

Examiner's tip

Try to create a good balance between natural speech and complexity. Too many advanced structures may sound forced in the middle of a normal conversation.

10.2 Conversation on topics

AQA	M6
EDEXCEL	M4
OCR	M4
WJEC	M4
NICCEA	M4

These may be the A2 topics only, or could include those you studied for AS Level; check which applies to your exam.

Here, you should concentrate on using **specific vocabulary related to these particular subject areas** (see lists in each section of this book and, if applicable, the AS study guide). You have a real opportunity to show the examiner how much you know about these topics. You may have a chance to compare the situations in Britain and France, and you will certainly need to give your own opinions and reactions.

If you are allowed to choose your own topic area, you will be expected to have detailed factual knowledge of it; if not, a general understanding is all that is required. Use your knowledge sensibly; **material you have learnt for the purpose of understanding comprehension passages can now be used positively**.

Examples:

(La politique)

Examinateur: *La politique vous intéresse?*

Candidate: *Un peu, oui, mais pas autant que les jeunes en France.*

Ex: *Vous voulez dire?…*

Cand: *…que j'ai entendu dire que la politique est un sujet de discussion, voire de dispute, chez les ados en France. Il y a deux ans, la famille de ma corres a été choquée de découvrir que je ne connaissais pas le nom du premier ministre.*

Ex: *Du premier ministre français?*

Cand: *Non, anglais!*

Ex: *Ce n'est pas possible!*

You should give the name of the current prime minister at this point.

Cand: *Si, malheureusement. Mais maintenant je sais aussi que le premier ministre français s'appelle …………………; de plus, qu'il y a plusieurs femmes ministres, dont Elisabeth Guigou et Dominique Voynet. C'est mieux, n'est-ce pas?*

(Sciences et technologie)

Ex: *Tu as l'impression que les Français sont doués pour les sciences?*

Cand: *Ben oui. Depuis le dix-neuvième siècle les scientifiques français font un tabac; Marie et Pierre Curie, Louis Pasteur, par exemple.*

Ex: *Qu'est-ce qu'ils ont fait comme recherches?*

Cand: *Les Curie ont découvert le radium; Pasteur a trouvé un vaccin contre la rage et a donné son nom à la pasteurisation du lait, processus qu'il a inauguré.*

Ex. *Mais ils sont morts! N'y a-t-il rien de semblable à l'époque actuelle?*

Cand: *Si, les chercheurs dans les laboratoires en France travaillent dans le domaine de la biologie moléculaire.Et la France est un des partenaires dans la construction de la fusée Ariane qui a lancé des satellites dans l'espace.*

Ex: *À mon avis on dépense trop d'argent à de telles choses.*

Cand: *Je ne suis pas d'accord. Selon moi, il faut penser à l'avenir; en outre, les découvertes scientifiques sont très passionnantes.*

(Problèmes sociaux)

Ex: *Quels sont les problèmes sociaux les plus graves, à ton avis?*

Cand: *C'est une question difficile. Peut-être les SDF qui dorment dans les rues. Il faut que nous fassions quelque chose pour les aider.*

Ex: *Est-ce que le problème est plus répandu en France qu'en Grande Bretagne?*

Cand: *Euh… je ne sais pas. Dans ma ville il s'agit surtout des jeunes; il y a un homme d'une vingtaine d'années qui dort toujours dans la rue principale, son chien à côté de lui. Il demande doucement de l'argent, et je n'ai pas du tout peur; il a l'air triste. En revanche, en France j'ai vu des mères de famille avec leurs enfants qui mendient dans les rues et je me sens un peu menacée. Il semble que le problème soit différent dans les deux pays.*

(L'ordre public)

Ex: *Il vous semble que le crime devient plus répandu de nos jours?*

Cand: *Peut-être, oui. Mais je serais plutôt d'avis que le genre d'infraction est en train de changer, surtout parmi les jeunes. C'est à cause de la toxicomanie; ils doivent avoir de l'argent pour acheter de l'X ou de la cocaïne, donc ils se mettent à voler les radios dans les autos, à agresser les vieilles personnes dans les rues. C'est choquant, ça.*

Ex: *Avez-vous des solutions à proposer?*

Cand: *Non, je ne crois pas qu'il y ait de solution facile; s'il y en avait eu, on l'aurait déjà essayée. Je suppose qu'il faudrait mettre en place des programmes d'éducation dans les écoles, afin de persuader les jeunes de dire 'non' à la drogue dès l'enfance même.*

Notice how, in the four examples above, each candidate has used information that he or she has gleaned from studying the topic, and has in most cases related it specifically to France. A comparison with Britain is often a good way to bring in your own views on the subject. Some topics, such as *problèmes sociaux*, can be covered quite well with general vocabulary; others, such as *sciences et technologie* and *ordre public*, benefit very much from the use of vocabulary closely linked with the topic. The conversations read quite easily; if you listen carefully you will be able to identify a number of complex structures, but these have not been carried to extremes and the resulting conversations have a natural tone.

10.3 Conversation based on a stimulus

AQA	M6
OCR	M4
WJEC	M4
NICCEA	M4

There are various ways in which the awarding bodies deal with a conversation based on a stimulus; again, you must find out exactly what you have to do, but the general advice given below remains the same. There is always a period of preparation before the exam begins.

The main points to check are:

- whether the stimulus is in English or French
- whether the material is text only, a mixture of text and graphics, or in tabular form
- whether you have to begin by reporting on the content of the passage
- whether you are given specific questions to answer before a general discussion about the issues concerned.

You will not have to translate the material word for word; in fact your French will probably be much better if you don't try to do so. **Natural expression** is likely to sound much better than a stilted or anglicised version.

The first thing to do – and it's surprising how many candidates don't bother to do this – is to **read the stimulus passage right through to the end**. It's not a good idea to look at the first question (if there is one) and try to find the answer to it before you have had chance to assimilate the whole of the meaning.

Obviously there should be no problem in understanding a passage written in English, especially if you have been reading quality English newspapers and listening to radio and TV news so that you are familiar with the language of the issues being raised. If the passage is in French, you should still understand most of it; the intention is not to test your comprehension of the French, but your ability to comment on the topic. If there are a few words that you don't recognise, first **look to see whether their meaning is given at the end of the text**; if not, don't panic, because you very probably won't need them anyway. Concentrate instead on understanding the gist of the passage.

Then, when you have read it through to the end, you should think about conveying its meaning in French. This is the point at which you should read the specific questions that you have to prepare, if this is what your exam requires. **Look for 'trigger' words** – words that lead you to an equivalent phrase in the text and question – so that you can identify the precise place in the passage where the answer is; then **put that answer into your own words in natural, accurate French**. You may be allowed to make notes; these should not, however, be in the form of complete sentences because as soon as you begin to read aloud, your fluency (and probably your pronunciation) will deteriorate. You could look to see whether it's possible to incorporate **a subjunctive, a passive, a compound tense, or an idiom of some sort**, into your response.

If you have to report on the content without the guidance of particular questions, **pick out (by underlining or highlighting) the main points in each paragraph first**, and be sure that you can explain these; then go back and look at any supporting points or examples. At least you will have covered the whole of the content, however briefly, and will not have to search for the meaning of the last section while you are speaking.

If you are given no guidance at all as to how the conversation will proceed, you will need to decide what you think are the main points and decide how to put them into French; think back to your study of that topic and see how you can relate this passage to it. Work out also what questions seem to arise naturally from the material.

In all three cases, you should also prepare your own reactions to the content, together with reasons. This is often a good moment to include a subjunctive:

Je ne crois pas que ce soit le cas.

Je ne pense pas que l'auteur de l'article ait raison.

À ce que j'ai entendu dire, il semble que cela soit vrai.

If some or all of the material is in pictorial or tabular form, you will still need to study it carefully. You may need to practise saying numbers or percentages aloud; and make sure you know what the tables are actually saying by reading any introductory or explanatory sentences and/or the headings at the top of the columns.

10.4 Presentation

EDEXCEL ▶ M4
WJEC ▶ M4
NICCEA ▶ M4

Examiner's tip

Take care not to play all your cards at once, as you must leave something for the discussion later. Your task in the presentation is to show the examiner which aspects you would like to talk about in more detail, and so guide the conversation towards the direction you would like it to take.

If you have to give a brief presentation of your topic for discussion this will mean that you have chosen it yourself. So it's up to you to convey real enthusiasm; why would you have chosen it otherwise? An excellent way to begin is to give your reasons for choosing the topic in general, then for concentrating on one or more aspects of it. As you have had a chance to prepare this in advance, it will not be enough to say weakly '*parce que c'est intéressant*' (and certainly not '*parce que mon prof l'a choisi*'!). Try to relate it to yourself: Look at the two examples below, which could serve as the **introductory sentences to a presentation**:

(i) *J'ai choisi de parler au sujet des sciences et de la technologie parce que ce sont des choses qui deviennent de plus en plus importantes et aussi parce que c'est le domaine où je voudrais travailler à l'avenir. Il me semble que les découvertes qui ont été faites, et celles qui sont en train d'être faites, sont vraiment passionnantes.*

This can lead on to a discussion of what those discoveries are, how important they are and why.

(ii) *Il me semble que l'inégalité existe toujours dans la société dans plusieurs domaines, et je trouve ça dégoûtant. Ce qui me choque surtout, ce sont les problèmes des personnes handicapées en ce qui concerne l'emploi et l'insertion. J'ai un ami qui est dans un fauteuil roulant; il m'a fait voir les difficultés.*

Following this introduction you would expect to be asked to elaborate on the problems of disabled people and what is being done to counteract them.

In these examples the candidates have explained their choice of topic and made their interest clear, while opening the way for an informed discussion.

10.5 Interpreting

EDEXCEL ▶ M4

This is an alternative to the 'oral discussion of issues' and is a very specialised area. Two teachers, of whom one is a French speaker and the other is not, are present in the examination, and it is the candidate's task to convey the required information between the two.

Again, the important thing to remember is that it is not primarily a translation exercise. You may well be able to translate some phrases directly from one language to the other, and there is no reason why you should not do so if it is appropriate; but it is possible that some of the words and phrases used by the non-French speaker will not be able to be used as they are in French, so you will need to express them in a more natural way. So as with the stimulus passage, your job is to convey the gist of what the first person says. You must be careful not to leave out any important details.

There is a limited range of topic areas for this option. They relate to education, work, leisure and travel, so you know the sort of vocabulary you are likely to need, and you should learn it thoroughly. Assessment is, as for the other oral modules, based on transmission and quality of language, plus 'appropriateness of language'; this last element covers vocabulary, idiom and structures.

10.6 Assessment of content

For a conversation based on a stimulus, your marks for content will depend on your ability to convey the meaning of the passage competently, to answer the examiner's questions (prepared or unprepared) appropriately, and to engage in further discussion of the issues raised by it. Some awarding bodies also expect you to be able to cover other topics leading logically from it. You must be able to justify your point of view.

For the general conversation, some marks are awarded for your knowledge and understanding of the issues; as with the other aspects of the oral exam, it is also assessed for response, interaction and quality of language (see below).

10.7 Assessment of response

This may be divided into four separate elements: fluency, interaction, pronunciation and intonation.

Fluency

Candidates who are able to keep a conversation going without the slightest hesitancy or hesitation are rare, and there is no reason why you should not gain very good marks for fluency even if you have to stop and think for a moment before giving your answer. The trick is not to lose momentum or 'Frenchness'. Practise phrases that will allow you to think while you are speaking:

> *Bon, ben…je ne sais pas…euhhh… je pense que oui.*
>
> *C'est intéressant; je n'y avais pas pensé…Non, je dirais plutôt que…*
>
> *C'est une question difficile… Je ne sais pas s'il y a une réponse catégorique…*
>
> *Je ne crois pas qu'il y ait une réponse facile…*

Do not say 'um'! Remember the phrase you said to yourself as you began: *À partir de ce moment, je suis français(e)!*

If the examiner asks you a question that can be answered by a simple '*Oui*' or '*Non*' (this is unlikely) you should always extend your reply:

Ex: *Il vous semble que la condition féminine a changé récemment en France?*

Cand: *Oui, un peu. Dans le domaine de la politique il y a maintenant des femmes ministres: Élisabeth Guigou, par exemple. Quand même dans la plupart des familles rien n'a changé; c'est toujours la mère qui prépare les repas.*

This avoids the risk of the conversation sounding jerky, and is also valid as interaction with the examiner.

Ask the examiner a question occasionally (but remember to listen to the answer as you may need to respond to it). This will take the pressure off you for a few moments.

> *Voilà mon opinion à ce propos. Vous êtes d'accord, Monsieur/Madame?*

You will **lose** marks for fluency if your French is slow and halting, if you take a long time to reply to the examiner's questions, or if your response to them is short or disjointed. If you have not heard the question clearly, ask the examiner to repeat it:

> *Voulez-vous répéter la question, s'il vous plaît, Monsieur/Madame?*

> *Je n'ai pas entendu la question, Monsieur/Madame.*

Examiner's tip

You should always add *Monsieur* or *Madame*; firstly because it's polite, and secondly because it's part of the French culture to do so.

If you have not understood the question, ask for clarification; this all counts as communication, because you are communicating the fact that you haven't understood (though if you had to ask too often, the examiner might begin to wonder about your level of comprehension).

> *Je ne comprends pas la question, Monsieur/Madame.*

> *Je n'ai pas bien compris, Monsieur/Madame.*

Or in the case of a single word:

> ---------- , *ça veut dire quoi, Monsieur/Madame?*

Interaction

This is linked to fluency, but goes beyond it; it includes the **quality** of your response to the examiner.

As a general rule, **try to add at least two sentences of reasonable length in reply to each question**; the oral exam should not be a quick-fire question and answer session or an interrogation. If you can also include an example to back up what you are saying, your marks will be good.

To gain top marks you should be able to take the lead in the conversation; having answered the specific question you were asked, move on to a further development which arises naturally from what you have just said. The important point here is that it must be relevant; if you rattle off an answer to the question and then start to talk about something that appears to be unrelated to it, you are not responding well. Look at the two examples below; the first is bad practice, the second is much better.

Ex: *Tu crois que les gaz d'échappement nuisent à l'environnement?*

Cand: *Ah oui, les voitures ajoutent beaucoup à la pollution en ville. Je suis d'avis qu'on devrait recycler plus de déchets ménagers; pas seulement le verre, mais aussi le papier et les matières plastiques.*

This candidate obviously wishes to talk about the benefits to the environment of recycling waste, but there is no apparent link between the two parts of her answer. It should be possible to get to the desired outcome by a more circuitous but more relevant route.

Ex: *Tu crois que les gaz d'échappement nuisent à l'environnement?*

Cand: *Ah oui, les voitures ajoutent beaucoup à la pollution en ville. Le monoxyde de carbone est un grand problème, surtout pour ceux qui souffrent de problèmes respiratoires. Dans la région parisienne, Airparif surveille la qualité de l'air et des mesures sont déclenchées quand le niveau de pollution devient trop élevé. Quand même l'environnement peut être abîmé de plusieurs autres façons; le problème des déchets ménagers augmente tout le temps.*

This has the additional advantage of showing the candidate's knowledge of the topic in relation to France. She has directed the conversation towards the particular area she wishes to discuss, but has moved smoothly from one aspect to the other.

You will **lose** marks for interaction if you rely heavily on the examiner to keep the conversation going and if you volunteer very little or no additional information beyond a brief answer to the question.

Pronunciation

Key points from AS

• **Notes on pronunciation**
AS Study Guide p. 138

Does pronunciation matter?

• Yes, to the extent that you must **make an effort to sound French**.

• Yes, because poor pronunciation can prevent even a sympathetic native speaker from understanding what you are saying.

• No; provided that what you say is comprehensible, your pronunciation is only one aspect of your oral exam. Think of the people you know whose first language is not English: in most cases their speech is probably accented and yet you can understand perfectly well what they are saying.

What, then, is the standard that you should aim for? Ideally, of course, it should be impossible to tell that you are not French, and this must be your ultimate target. However, there are stages on the way to this level of competence, and examiners will give high marks – perhaps even full marks – to candidates who reach the sort of standard that can reasonably be expected of someone who has been studying the language at this level for the appropriate time. It doesn't have to be perfect.

How can you improve your pronunciation and set yourself on the road towards sounding French? Concentrate on three aspects, two of which are positive and one negative.

Vowels

Most of the French vowels are rounder (*â, o, ou*) or tighter (the rest) than their English equivalents, both in the way they are produced and in the sound that emerges. The best way to prove this for yourself is to repeat the examples on p. 148, stopping the CD at the end of each sentence so that the exact sound is in your mind. Try to notice the position of your mouth as you repeat the words. It's important to persevere with this; nothing makes your speech sound less French than anglicised vowel sounds, but on the other hand, correct vowels add enormously to the authenticity of your accent.

Nasal vowels are just as important; practise the examples and see how the position of your mouth and lips changes for *an/en*, *in*, *on* and *un*.

Consonants

These, too, must be kept more 'contained' than their equivalents in English; *t* and *d* are formed behind the teeth, *p* and *b* have the lips firmly closed before they are pronounced, *c* and *g* sound a little harder and more precise than in English. Remember to pronounce *r* at the back of your throat, as if it had an *h* before it.

Words similar to English

The temptation to pronounce these in an English way must be avoided. Endings such as *-isation*, *-able*, *-ible*, and words such as *alcool*, *intelligent* and *protection* must be carefully pronounced **according to the French rules**.

You must also take care not to pronounce the final *s* on the end of plural nouns (*tables*, *institutions*, etc.), with the exception of words such as *fils* (son/sons), *moeurs* and *sens* where a hard *s* is part of the exceptional pronunciation. Never pronounce the plural *-ent* on the end of a verb, but remember that it may be part of a noun (*l'enseignement*) or an adverb (*prudemment*) in which case it must be pronounced.

Sentences to practise

La tâche du gourou était difficile.

Les hindous et les bouddhistes n'ont pas les mêmes croyances.

Il faut trouver un compromis afin de réduire la tension.

Il n'est pas facile de déterminer la cause de la fièvre.

C'est un outil important contre la pauvreté.

Les nuances de sens qui se révèlent dans les expressions qu'il utilise sont significatives.

Son style est sensuel.

Le taux de production est très élevé par rapport à l'année dernière.

Quant au manque d'intérêt, c'est le principal ennemi de la technologie en France.

Dix moines ont accompagné les pèlerins.

Les inondations étaient terribles.

Le cortège a passé devant le café.

Actuellement la cuisine ethnique devient plus répandue.

Sa détresse était évidente.

La cuisine traditionnelle, qui est symbolique de la culture française, est vraiment remarquable.

La réalisation de ce projet, qui a pour but la protection de l'environnement, semble maintenant impossible.

Intonation

Examiner's tip

Listen to the passages on the CD with the transcript in front of you, so that you can see how this works; then try reading them aloud.

While you were practising the sentences to help your pronunciation, you probably noticed the intonation: that is, the way in which the voice goes up and down during the course of normal speech. If you listen again to the passages recorded for the first six chapters you will notice the same thing. Try to copy this; you will not sound silly, affected or odd, you will simply **sound more French**.

English can be a very monotonous language, but if you listen to other people you will realise how much more interesting they sound if they vary the tone. French is not – or should not be – monotonous, so it's important to make yourself sound more interesting by allowing the tone of your voice to rise and fall. It should rise when you are asking questions; try reading the sentences again, without changing the words but letting your voice rise at the end, and see how they automatically become questions.

Your voice should also rise slightly at intermediate points throughout a long sentence, falling only at the full stop. Practise this; you will probably start by overdoing it – not a bad thing – and will finally reach the correct level as it becomes natural to you.

10.8 Assessment of accuracy

The final element for which marks are awarded in the oral exam is **accuracy**.

Grammar

The obvious problem here is to find the happy medium between very accurate language and fluency; if you spend too long working out the precise form of words to use, your speech will become more hesitant. On the other hand, if you are very inaccurate your speech may be difficult to understand. Written French can be corrected later; spoken French, for better or worse, is best left alone once you have said it. Correct yourself only if you realise immediately that you have made a mistake:

Que disez-vous, Madame? – pardon, je voulais dire Que dites-vous, Madame?

The good news is that many 'mistakes' are not noticeable in spoken French. The *é* and *-er* sounds are indistinguishable; if you write '*je suis aller*' your French will be heavily penalised, but if you say it, it will still sound like *je suis allé(e)*, perfectly correct.

The bad news is that basic errors, particularly in verb formation and ending, are common in oral exams; perhaps the pressure of having to put their thoughts into French instantaneously thrusts grammar to the back of candidates' minds. Try to keep it at the front; it is important, and must not be neglected. Revision for an oral exam should always include grammar; if time is short, concentrate on verbs.

Structures

You should be incorporating the new structures you have learnt for AS and A2 Levels, as well as for Higher Tier GCSE, into your spoken French. They will gain you credit, but only if you use them correctly. There's no point in saying '*Après avoir considéré la situation, les aspects les plus importants sont…*' because *après avoir* + past participle must refer to the subject of the main clause. In this example the subject is *les aspects*, but presumably you were the one considering the situation, not 'the aspects'. Nor will you gain marks for the wrong formation of compound tenses. '*S'il avait voulu, il aurait venu plus tôt*' is no use; although there is a correctly formed pluperfect in the *si* clause followed by (supposedly) a conditional perfect, *venir* in fact takes *être* so it should have been *serait venu*. However carefully you have formed the subjunctive, it will do no good after *je pense que* because it is only used when *penser* is in the negative or question form. But don't despair; with careful revision and preparation you should be able to use enough complex structures to show the examiner that your language has developed well during the past two years.

Look at the useful structures for essays (p.114) and divide them into two lists: those you can incorporate into your presentation (it's helpful to work out a few sentences in advance, to sum up your opinions on each topic) and those that you hope to be able to include on the spur of the moment (e.g. subjunctive after *je ne crois pas que*). Then revise them all thoroughly so that the correct formation becomes completely natural.

Sample questions and model answers

1 French stimulus with questions as starting point for discussion

Comment protéger nos enfants d'Internet?

On vous demandera de participer à une discussion de ce texte avec l'examinateur/l'examinatrice.

Les questions ci-dessous seront utilisées comme point de départ à la conversation.

INTERNET VIE PRIVÉE

conseils pour protéger nos enfants d'Internet

Mieux vaut être réaliste. Il n'existe aujourd'hui aucun filtre pour éviter à nos enfants de tomber sur un site porno, négationniste ou grossier. Ce serait pourtant une erreur de les priver d'Internet. C'est un outil formidable, qui leur ouvre tous les domaines de la culture et qui est moins passif que la télé. Alors, pas de paranoïa, mais restons vigilants.

1. Installez l'ordinateur dans le salon plutôt que dans la chambre de votre enfant. Vous serez à proximité, vous pourrez ainsi surveiller du coin de l'œil et intervenir en cas de problème.

2. Essayez de découvrir l'univers Internet avec vos enfants. Naviguez, visitez les sites.

3. Sélectionnez une page d'ouverture destinée aux jeunes. Ainsi, le logiciel de navigation (Netscape ou Explorer) s'ouvre sur une page recensant des informations sélectionnées pour les enfants, comme www.club-internet.fr/selection/junior/

4. Dites-lui de ne jamais donner son adresse et son numéro de téléphone dans un forum de discussion en direct et conseillez-lui un forum de discussion surveillé. Chez Infonie, les forums de l'espace Infokids sont surveillés par un modérateur qui contrôle le contenu des conversations.

5. S'il reçoit des mails d'inconnus, informez votre fournisseur d'accès par mail. Et répondez à l'expéditeur en disant que, s'il recommence, vous porterez plainte à la police.

6. Au besoin, si vous êtes inquiet, rendez Internet inaccessible quand vous êtes absent. En retirant simplement le modem s'il est externe, ou en retirant le câble qui part vers la ligne téléphonique s'il est interne. Ce qui laisse à votre enfant l'accès aux CD-Rom et aux jeux.

(a) De quoi s'agit-il?

(b) À votre avis, est-ce que c'est un problème véritable?

(c) Que pensez-vous d'Internet?

Sample questions and model answers *(continued)*

Model answer

(a) Il s'agit de l'inquiétude que ressentent un grand nombre de personnes en ce qui concerne l'utilisation d'Internet par les jeunes enfants. Selon l'auteur de l'article, on aurait tort de refuser à l'enfant l'accès à la toile mondiale, parce que c'est un outil éducatif très important. On doit quand même être conscient des dangers, et le journaliste propose plusieurs solutions qui diminueraient les risques.

This has answered the first question in general terms; the candidate should now expect to be asked to elaborate.

Ex: *Donnez-moi des exemples.*

Cand: *D'accord; il conseille aux parents d'installer l'ordinateur dans un lieu quelconque où ils puissent le surveiller. Selon lui, les parents devraient naviguer et chercher sur le Web avec leurs enfants. Il faut surtout interdire aux enfants de donner leur adresse ou leur numéro de téléphone à qui que ce soit. Enfin, si on est vraiment inquiet on peut rendre Internet inaccessible aux enfants si on n'est pas là.*

The candidate has used some of the vocabulary from the passage, but has manipulated it so that it is not a direct 'lift' from the original article. (S)he has concentrated on three of the six aspects, which should be sufficient; if not, the examiner will ask for more.

(b) This is your opportunity to express your own point of view. It doesn't matter which side of the argument you support, as long as you can back it up. If you are undecided, it's probably best to go along with the opinion expressed in the text, as you will have more on which to base your comments. Expect some discussion of the issue.

(c) The last question is more open, and gives you the chance to show your knowledge of the topic in general. You could relate it to your own experience, but any facts and/or statistics you can include about the French attitude would be valuable.

Selon moi, c'est une chose fantastique. Cela nous ouvre tout un monde de connaissances et de communication. Les développements récents sont très passionnants: la vitesse avec laquelle on peut trouver des renseignements a augmenté, et on peut même accéder à Internet au moyen d'un téléphone portable. C'est notre avenir. Je sais que les Français n'en étaient pas fanas au début – peut-être à cause du Minitel – mais ils deviennent supporters et on peut lire des articles à ce propos dans tous les journaux.

Or:

Je ne suis pas vraiment doué pour l'informatique; ça me semble très ennuyeux. De plus, je trouve qu'Internet prend le relais des livres, et je n'aime pas ça. Il ne faut pas mettre de côté toute la culture de notre pays, et à mon sens on risque de le faire si on concentre trop l'attention sur les méthodes de communications électroniques. À ce propos je suis d'accord avec le fameux 'retard français'; c'est-à-dire qu'au début les Français résistent à quelque chose de nouveau, surtout sur le plan technologique.

Sample questions and model answers (continued)

2 English stimulus with reporting and discussion

If your exam does not ask you to summarise the content first of all, you should still expect to be asked questions on the text so the same sort of skills are required.

Résumez le contenu du passage.

Young offenders help themselves at Paris airport

De Gaulle baggage plundered daily

by JULIAN COMAN

in Paris

JUVENILE offenders employed under a job creation scheme as luggage handlers at Charles de Gaulle airport, Paris, are behind a spate of thefts of luxury goods such as Louis Vuitton bags, Chanel perfume and Armani suits.

Although airport officials last week attempted to play down the crime wave, British Airways confirmed that there was a serious problem.

"A rather significant number of losses had been noted at Paris, which is a cause for concern, because Charles de Gaulle is a vital airport for us," a BA spokesman told *The Sunday Telegraph*. The airport is BA's leading European destination.

And Air France, which flies 72,000 passengers in and out of the airport daily, says that on average 1,300 customers file complaints every day, the majority of which refer to missing goods. Items stolen in recent months range from designer clothing to mobile phones, portable computers and luxury perfumes.

The thefts are being blamed on an ill-advised youth employment scheme, devised two years ago, when airport authorities decided to expand Charles de Gaulle by creating two new runways.

Local left-wing councils in the rundown surrounding area objected on environmental grounds. To save the £270 million project – which will maintain Charles de Gaulle's position as the eighth busiest airport in the world – the airport offered to give the lion's share of the new jobs created to local unemployed youngsters.

However, new recruits included juvenile offenders, some of whom were offered a choice between a prison sentence or a job at the airport. Nearly 4,000 unemployed youths from one of the city's most deprived suburbs were taken on as part of the scheme.

Sample questions and model answers (continued)

It's a good idea to sum up the content in one sentence first, before going into the detail. It's probably best then to deal with the article in order, so that there is less risk of leaving anything out.

Model answer

Il s'agit de l'aéroport Charles de Gaulle à Paris, où des jeunes criminels ont volé les affaires des voyageurs.

Ces jeunes gens participent à un projet de création d'emplois, c'est-à-dire qu'on a créé les postes de bagagistes pour eux. Ils volent les articles de luxe, dont (1) les sacs Louis Vuitton, le parfum Chanel et les vêtements haute couture. Quoique les officiels de l'aéroport aient dit (2) que ce problème n'est pas très répandu, les responsables de British Airways ne (3) sont pas d'accord; ils ne sont pas contents, car selon eux l'aéroport Charles de Gaulle est essentiel pour la ligne aérienne (4), étant (5) sa destination principale en Europe.

Quant à la compagnie Air France, elle a dit qu'en moyenne 1300 clients sur 72 000 se plaignent chaque jour d'avoir été volés (6). Il s'agit aussi de téléphones et d'ordinateurs portables.

Les vols seraient (7) le résultat d'un projet peu judicieux qui a été conçu (6) il y a deux ans (8) quand on a décidé de créer (9) deux nouvelles pistes à l'aéroport. Face aux objections de la part des conseils municipaux de gauche – pour des raisons environnementales – les responsables de l'aéroport ont proposé d'offrir (9) la plupart des postes qui seraient créés (6) à des jeunes gens au chômage. Pourtant, quelques-uns de ceux qui ont été embauchés (6) étaient des jeunes délinquants auxquels (10) on avait offert (11) le choix entre ce travail et la peine de prison. On avait embauché (11) presque 4000 jeunes chômeurs qui habitaient les banlieues défavorisées.

1 Use of *dont* meaning 'including'.

2 Subjunctive after *quoique*.

3 Use of pronoun.

4 Specific vocabulary related to the topic.

5 The present participle used in a similar way to English.

6 Use of the passive.

7 Conditional tense meaning 'are thought to be, but there's no proof'.

8 *Il y a* + time phrase means 'ago'.

9 Infinitive construction.

10 *À* + the correct part of *lequel* = 'to whom'.

11 Use of the pluperfect tense.

Possible conversational spin-offs for this article might include:

- *Pensez-vous que des projets de création d'emplois comme celui-ci soient une bonne idée?*

- *Est-ce que la prison est la meilleure sanction pour les jeunes délinquants? Pourquoi (pas)?*

And as a link to move on to other topics:

- *Est-ce que la vogue des articles de luxe est une bonne chose?*

- *Croyez-vous que voyager en avion soit la meilleure façon de se déplacer?*

See if you can think of any more subjects for further discussion that might arise naturally from either of the passages.

Progress check answers

Chapter 1
Future perfect and conditional perfect tenses
1 Quand/lorsque le commissaire sera arrivé nous pourrons continuer l'enquête.
2 Ils sont en retard: il y aura eu un accident.
3 À cinq heures ce soir/À 17 heures nous aurons fini d'interpeller les suspects.
4 Tu m'aurais cru/vous m'auriez cru si je te/vous l'avais dit plus tôt?
5 Pourquoi est-ce qu'il aurait fait une telle chose?
6 Ils auraient été mis en garde à vue.
7 As soon as you have given your evidence you will have to leave the courtroom.
8 The victims will have arrived at the hospital in 20 minutes' time.
9 She is dead; she must have killed herself.
10 I wouldn't have thought she would want to do it.
11 If you had been braver you would have come with me.
12 The rate of violence has apparently increased to an unacceptable level.

Pdo
1 Les portraits-robots? Non, il ne les a pas encore regardés.
2 Les plaintes qu'ils ont déposées ont déjà été examinées.
3 Quels visages as-tu/avez-vous reconnus?

Chapter 2
Passive
1 Les cotisations avaient été payées par la main d'oeuvre.
2 L'aide sera fournie par Restos du Coeur.
3 Les SDF étaient rejetés par la société.
4 Les réfugiés ont été vite réhabilités.
5 Il craignait que la haine ne soit/fût attisée par la foule.
6 The flat was let to a young couple.
7 (The) allowances will be paid by the office.
8 The figures would have been improved/have apparently been improved this year.
9 The immigrants were threatened by Le Pen's supporters.
10 Moonlighting would not be tolerated.

Imperfect subjunctive
Aller, contenir, faire, avoir, connaître, promettre, boire, crier, être, savoir

Chapter 3
Idioms
1 Il souffrait du Sida depuis dix-huit mois.
2 Nous venons d'entendre que les scientifiques ont fait une percée.
3 Les astronautes sont en train de sonder la surface de la lune.
4 La semaine dernière les scientifiques se sont donné des renseignements.
5 Les Montgolfier se sont soutenus.
6 Demandez-moi n'importe quoi; je vous montrerai comment trouver la réponse sur le Web.
7 There's no point in trying to use this computer, it's not working any more.

8 Don't be cross with me/hold it against me! I wasn't the one who authorised the tests.
9 We rarely speak to each other.
10 Knowing she would have to justify her results, she had assembled all the data.
11 You'll have to carry out the tests somehow or other.
12 Anyone who/Whoever finds a solution to the problem will be rewarded.

Chapter 4
Verbs for A2
nous acquerrons, ils/elles avaient atteint, tu craignais/vous craigniez, haïssant, je serais mort(e), il est né, il suffit, tu suis/vous suivez, elle aura vaincu, ils vivaient.
1 The problem has been (re)solved.
2 I must break the ties.
3 The candidate was silent (not 'killed herself; that would be s'est tuée!).
4 It would be better to obtain the papers before leaving one's country.
5 France used to welcome thousands of immigrants.
6 I am convinced that we must adopt the euro.
7 The powers of the European parliament grow from year to year.
8 He had lived alone for two years.
9 I fear the influence of the far right.
10 This bad influence must be extinguished.

Chapter 5
1 You will have to throw the rubbish in the dustbin.
2 You ought to have understood the risks earlier. (Any personal pronoun will do here)
3 We mustn't waste our resources.
4 She was able to support the demands of the ecologists.
5 They didn't know how many species there were.
6 It seems that the situation is becoming more complicated.
7 It's about the hole in the ozone layer.
8 There had been about twenty bears.
9 I advise you to allow him/her to go (there).
10 Apply to the warden.

Chapter 6
1 Quiconque ne croit pas à l'existence de Dieu est athée.
2 Il faut empêcher les guerres qui ont lieu n'importe où dans le monde.
3 Nous devons faire je ne sais quoi pour les aider.
4 Nous voyions/on voyait la procession des fidèles.
5 Les pèlerins ne cessent de visiter la grotte à Lourdes.
6 The scientists did not dare to leave the country.
7 Do you know how poor the developing countries are?
8 How beautiful this mosque is!
9 We'll have to decide how to help these people.
10 I wouldn't have believed that such a disaster could occur.

Practice examination answers

Chapter 1

1   Listening – Yves Godard

1 soupçonné   2 partir/monter/disparaître   3 sang
4 véhicule   5 laissé   6 sont/se trouvent   7 vivent
8 soit morte   9 état   10 montrent/indiquent
11 quinzaine   12 soit/puisse être   13 détestait
14 résoudre   15 endroit   16 quitté   17 étudier
18 l'argent   19 facile   20 bateau/voilier

2   Listening

(a) Against the rise (1) of delinquency (1).
(b) To denounce the lack of security (1) to get his voice/the towns-people's voice heard (1).
(c) Terror had reigned (1), windows had been broken (1) in the town hall (1) and the glass front (1) of the multimedia library had also suffered (1).
(d) In January 1998.
(e) That someone had broken windows/caused damage (1) but was free two hours later (1).
      They think that delinquents are going unpunished (1).
(f) People should make their voices heard more loudly (1) and react more strongly (1).
(g) They dare not go out in the evenings (1) because there are gangs roaming about (1).
      They are completely stressed (1).

3   Reading (Patrick Henry)

(a) ? (b) V (c) ? (d) F (e) V (f) F (g) F (h) V (i) F   (j) F

4   Reading (Nice, Luynes, Avignon)

(a) Nice, Avignon   (b) Nice, Luynes, Avignon
(c) Nice, Luynes   (d) Luynes   (e) Nice, Luynes   (f) Nice

Chapter 2

1   Reading – La décrue continue

(a) baisse/diminution du nombre de chômeurs en février
(b) pourcentage actuel de la population active sans emploi selon le BIT
(c) diminution du pourcentage de demandeurs d'emploi de catégorie 1 sur douze mois
(d) personnes qui cherchent un poste à temps plein, sans limite de temps, et qui peuvent commencer tout de suite
(e) taux de chômage prévu par l'INSEE pour la fin du mois de juin
(f) augmentation annuelle du nombre de gens qui peuvent travailler

2   Listening – SMIC

(a) selon l'inflation
(b) (très) grandes
(c) plus petit/étroit (1) au fil des années (1)
(d) sont ouverts (1) aux femmes (1) OR sont acceptés (1) par les femmes (1)
(e) baissé/diminué
(f) poursuivent plus longtemps (1) leurs études (1)
(g) continuent à être payés de la même façon/reçoivent toujours le salaire minimum
(Note: an answer that means the same is equally acceptable)

3   Reading – L'égalité, même la nuit!

(a) To comply with a European directive (1) on sexual equality (1).
(b) Gets up when others are going to bed (1). Is getting ready to go to work as night falls (1). Does her shopping only just as the local supermarket is opening or closing (1). Gives her son into his nanny's care from evening until the following day (1).
(c) Care assistant (1) in an old people's home (1).
(d) More than 800 000 women work at night, regularly or occasionally (1). This is about 8% of working women (1) compared with 22% of men (1).

(e) European law takes precedence over French law.
(f) The current situation discriminates against women (1) in terms of their career (1).
(g) There may be a bonus system.
(h) Health and safety (1) some take a night job in less than ideal conditions (1). It may cause problems in private/home life (1).

4   Reading and writing – Frenchwomen shun party parity

(a) Il faut avoir un nombre égal d'hommes et de femmes comme candidats aux élections.
(b) Les femmes ne semblent pas vouloir poser leur candidature.
(c) Ils doivent recruter plus de 40 000 femmes pour les élections municipales de l'an prochain; sinon ils devront payer des amendes.
(d) Celles qui soutiennent les campagnes électorales régionales et les femmes des hommes politiques.
(e) Ils ne sont pas contents de devoir céder la place aux femmes.
(f) Le cadre politique français est jusqu'ici dominé par les hommes; il n'y a que 10% de femmes députés à l'Assemblée Nationale. Les femmes – même celles qui sont prêtes à poser leur candidature – ne semblent pas être convaincues par les partis qui disent que leur attitude a changé.

(Don't forget to add your own reaction.)

Chapter 3

1   Reading – L'aide au retour

A   Après avoir obtenu leur diplôme en sciences, certains docteurs français quittent la France pour suivre une formation en recherches médicales dans les grands laboratoires ailleurs. Quand ils veulent revenir en France deux ou trois ans plus tard ils rencontrent des problèmes parce qu'il n'y a pas assez de places disponibles. Une organisation a donc mis en place un système d'aide financière.

B   (a) veuillent rester à l'étranger (1), préfèrent rentrer en France (1)
     (b) candidats/concurrence
     (c) a été établi/mis en place
     (d) les études faites par chaque candidat (1) les projets qu'il présente (1), le laboratoire qui va peut-être l'embaucher (1)
     (e) ne sera pas entièrement résolu

2   Reading – OGM

A   After a full night of heated discussion, the Environment ministers of the Fifteen (members of the EU) meeting in Luxembourg finally came to an agreement to reinforce European legislation that existed already about the marketing of genetically-modified organisms. However, their attempt to draw up also a 'declaration of policy', which would have underlined their common refusal to grant new authorisation for these products before controls were tightened, failed.

B   (a) prévues (b) permis (give yourself the mark if you've put défendu, but you must then mark it wrong in (e))
     (c) ancienne (d) différente (e) défendu, pris, limitées.

C   (a) Elles croyaient que les mesures devraient être plus strictes.
     (b) en s'abstenant (c) le parlement européen (qui vient d'être élu) (d) les écologistes (1) et les (représentants des) grandes industries (1) (e) en 2002/pas avant 2002

3   Listening – Relenza

(a) Laboratoires britanniques/Glaxo-Wellcome (1), dix ans (1), 6000 patients.
(b) Les antibiotiques (1) calmaient les douleurs (1) et baissaient la fièvre (1), tandis que le Relenza™ stoppe le virus (1) et l'infection (1).
(c) Les personnes qui ont plus de 12 ans (1) et moins de 65 ans (1).
(d) À partir du mois d'octobre (1), il faut le prescrire dans les 48 heures après l'apparition des symptômes (1), il sera remboursé par la Sécurité Sociale à partir de l'hiver 2000/2001 (1).

4   Listening – Virus 'I love You'

   (i) c   (ii) c   (iii) a   (iv) c   (v) c   (vi) a

Chapter 4

1   Reading – 5 paragraphs

1 d   2 e   3 h   4 c   5 a

2   Reading – Alchimie franco-algérienne

A   (a) tout a été dit (b) il y a toujours eu une succession de malentendus (c) point n'est besoin (d) à y regarder de tout près (e)
les importants flux migratoires

B   (f) singularité (g) décolonisation (h) coopération

C   This situation was the starting point from which the Algerian and
French leaders announced their clear intention of committing
their countries to a new course.

4   Listening – l'euro

(a) L'euro a perdu près de 15% de sa valeur par rapport au dollar.

(b) Il ne paraît pas y avoir d'explication rationnelle.

(c) La situation pénalise seulement ceux qui vont passer les vacances
aux États-Unis.

(d) Seuls ceux qui sont contre l'UE ont donné leur réaction.

(e) Elle n'a pas suscité le choc fédérateur que certains prévoyaient.

(f) Tous les pays sauf l'Allemagne semblent indifférents à la dépréciation de l'euro.

(g) Lionel Jospin s'est montré peu satisfait.

(h) Jacques Chirac croit que l'euro repose sur une base solide OR J.C.
croit que la tendance va être renversée à la longue.

Chapter 5

1   Reading – La vie écolo

(a) est limitée; sont économisées

(b) Faux

(c) If you look closely at it, it isn't so difficult to do this. Lowering
the washing temperature of your washing machine from 90 to
60 means that you save 15% electricity per year. Similarly, it's
important to defrost the fridge frequently (5mm of frost increases consumption by 30%). You should also make sure that you
switch off the TV or the computer when they are not in use. And
switch off the lights when you leave a room.

(d) (i)   quelques mesures basiques

(ii) grignotent chaque jour un peu plus

(iii) pour imposer des normes plus sévères

(iv) lorsqu'on est à l'arrêt

(v)   pour des petits trajets

(vi) moins que

(e) (i)   aide à user les sources d'énergie

(ii) ça suffit pleinement

(iii) il y a aussi l'avantage que vous dormirez mieux par con-
séquent.

2   Listening – pollution

(a) Les Bretons ont raison d'être découragés.

(b) De nouvelles nappes de fioul sont déjà arrivées.

(c) Elles sont arrivées premièrement en décembre.

(d) Malheureusement on avait déjà passé des semaines à nettoyer
les plages.

(e) (Il s'agit de) Paris.

(f) Parce qu'il n'y a pas de vent.

(g) De laisser leur voiture au garage(1), de prendre les transports en
commun (1).

(h) Le stationnement résidentiel sera gratuit.

(i) La vitesse est réduite (1) de 20 km (1).

4   Writing

Les sources d'énergie traditionnelles s'épuiseront bientôt. 'Bientôt',
ça veut dire peut-être dans les vingt ans à venir. Comment – et où –
en trouver d'autres?

Il y a une trentaine d'années la France a construit un parc de centrales nucléaires. Cependant les Verts ne les aiment pas, et je dois
avouer que je suis d'accord. Il existe toujours le risque d'accidents et
de retombées. Le charbon vient d'être épuisé; les gisements de gaz
et de pétrole ne dureront pas. Il faut donc que nous soyons plus
courageux. Tournons-nous plutôt vers des sources énergétiques dites
'de substitution'.

De quoi s'agit-il, alors? Premièrement, de l'énergie éolienne. Le vent
est un élément tout à fait naturel, qu'on utilise déjà sur le littoral
atlantique. Deuxièmement, l'énergie solaire peut être captée, surtout
là où le soleil brille beaucoup, comme dans le Midi. Il est possible
d'exploiter aussi la puissance des eaux, dans des centrales maré-
motrices. Même la chaleur qui se trouve dans les sols peut fournir de
l'énergie géothermique.

À mon avis ces méthodes, quoiqu'elles ne soient pas encore très
répandues, devront être utilisées à l'avenir pour produire l'énergie
plus naturelle.

Chapter 6

1   Reading- Kosovo

(a) Because they were carrying out a mission (1) that was essential
for peace in the Balkans (1).

(b) It had been raining (1) and windy (1) but the sun was now shin-
ing brightly (1).

(c) To check that the ceasefire was being upheld (1) in the neigh-
bouring province (1).

(d) There are 1923 soldiers (1), 850 of them are French and about
thirty of these are women.

(e) They must make the right choice (1) for responsibility, peace and
therefore for Europe (1).

If not (1) they would risk political, economic and military consequences (1) that would be extremely damaging (1).

2   Listening – Kosovo

(a) V   (b) ?   (c) F   (d) F   (e) ?

3   Listening

(a) les casques bleus/les troupes de l'OTAN (1) dimanche (1)

(b) de l'Australie/c'est un avion australien (1)

(c) Il va laisser tomber en parachute (1) 15 tonnes de riz (1) parce
qu'il y a des milliers de réfugiés qui souffrent de faim (1).

(d) une semaine

4   Listening

(a) convertie au catholicisme

(b) conteste cette décision

(c) elle fait valoir

(d) (ne) récupère en quelque sorte

6   Writing (possible answer)

Cher Paul

Je suis arrivée ici en Afrique il y a deux jours. Après m'être installée
dans le camp je suis allée avec mes collègues voir les familles qui
souffraient à cause des inondations.

Tu ne croirais pas combien la situation est difficile pour elles. Les
inondations ont détruit les récoltes, donc il n'y a rien à manger.
L'eau même est contaminée, donc beaucoup de gens souffrent du
choléra. Heureusement nous pouvons les aider un peu: nous avons
apporté des médicaments afin que les malades puissent être guéris
aussi vite que possible. Mais en me promenant parmi les logements
misérables je me suis rendu compte de l'écart qui existe entre les
pays riches de l'Ouest et les pays en voie de développement qui ne
disposent pas encore des moyens de se débrouiller dans une
situation pareille.

Espérons qu'on pourra améliorer leur niveau de vie à l'avenir.

Amitiés

Anne

Chapter 1

1 Des soupçons de plus en plus lourds pèsent sur Yves Godard, ce médecin du Calvados qui a disparu depuis le début du mois avec sa famille à bord d'un voilier. Hier, les analyses des traces de sang trouvées à son domicile et dans sa voiture ont établi que le sang en question était bien celui de son épouse. Á Saint-Malo, Y.C.

– C'est une partie du mystère qui vient de se lever dans cette affaire de disparition et les soupçons qui pèsent sur le Docteur Godard se précisent un peu plus. Les premiers résultats des analyses sont formels; ils ont été communiqués hier par le procureur de Saint-Malo, R.E.

– Les premiers résultats des analyses génétiques effectuées dans le cadre de la mission d'expertise ordonnée par le magistrat instructeur, font apparaître: que le sang prélevé au domicile de Tilly-sur-Seulles ainsi que dans le véhicule découvert sur le parking du port provient de Madame Godard.

L'information judiciaire pour homicide volontaire ouverte la semaine dernière par le parquet de Saint-Malo trouve là une première justification. Pour O.Q., le maire de la commune de Tilly-sur-Seulles dans le Calvados, où résidait la famille Godard, l'évidence est devenue une partie de la vérité.

– Je suis très soulagé de savoir qu'il y a un seul sang – en tout cas, d'après ce qu'on a entendu – comme ça, ça laisse supposer que les enfants sont toujours vivants et je pense qu'à partir du moment où on a retrouvé le sang dans le véhicule et la maison dans l'état où elle était, qu'il est difficile de concevoir qu'elle soit vivante. Derrière ça, ça fait bientôt quinze jours, elle aurait paru quelque part, si ce n'avait pas été elle. Elle n'aimait pas le bateau, on ne passe pas quinze jours en mer quand on ne supporte pas le bateau, hein?

Mais il reste beaucoup de zones d'ombre dans cette affaire. A la question, où et quand Madame Godard a-t-elle été vue pour la dernière fois, il n'y a toujours pas de réponse. Impossible de savoir également ce qu'a pu faire Yves Godard depuis son départ de Saint-Malo. Les communications de son téléphone portable sont à l'étude, ainsi que les mouvements de ses comptes bancaires, sans résultat pour l'instant. L'enquête s'annonce difficile, d'autant plus qu'on n'a toujours aucune trace du voilier, loué à Saint-Malo.

2 Contre la montée de la délinquance les élus et des habitants de Givors et de Grigny près de Lyon ont manifesté hier soir devant la préfecture du Rhône. Ces deux communes sont pourtant les premières à avoir signé un contrat local de sécurité, mais aujourd'hui ils dressent un constat d'échec. Á Lyon, le reportage de L.C.

– Le maire communiste de cette ville du sud de l'agglomération lyonnaise vient d'être reçu par le directeur de cabinet du préfet, une rencontre pour dénoncer l'insécurité mais surtout pour être enfin entendu. Le weekend dernier la terreur a encore régné: les vitres de l'hôtel de ville ont volé en éclats, les façades de verre de la médiathèque ont aussi fait les frais de cet acharnement. Pourtant Givors est la première ville française à avoir signé un contrat local de sécurité; c'était en janvier 98. Aujourd'hui M.P. admire l'efficacité du CLS mais comprend surtout le désarroi des Givordins.

Quand quelqu'un détruit des vitrines, casse les vitres de la mairie et que deux heures après il est dehors, ça a un effet déplorable, un effet déplorable sur la population qui pense qu'il y a une réelle impunité pour les délinquants. Je pense sincèrement que sur cette question les différents institutions doivent parler plus fort et y réagir plus fermement.

Les gens n'osent plus sortir le soir, dans la mesure où il y a des bandes qui traînent. Les gens sont complètement stressés. Il y a une coupure totale de la population.

Chapter 2

2 Le SMIC – salaire minimum interprofessionnel de croissance – est une rémunération qui varie en fonction de l'inflation, c'est-à-dire des prix à la consommation. Où trouve-t-on les Smicards? Comme toujours dans les entreprises de moins de dix salariés. Les femmes sont aussi les premières concernées, mais égalité des sexes oblige, l'écart avec les hommes tend à se réduire d'année en année, signe que le sexe féminin accepte de plus en plus souvent des postes de responsabilité. Il y a aussi de moins en moins de jeunes au SMIC: 31% des Smicards ont moins de 25 ans, contre 43% en 1997. Les jeunes poursuivent plus longtemps leurs études et ils entrent donc plus tard sur le marché du travail. Et puis de nombreux Smicards restent Smicards en vieillissant.

Chapter 3

3 Un médicament contre la grippe sera commercialisé en Europe au mois d'octobre. Élaboré par les laboratoires britanniques Glaxo-Wellcome, le Relenza – c'est son nom – a demandé dix ans de recherches. Son efficacité ne semble pas contestée, en revanche certains chercheurs redoutent une utilisation excessive de ce nouveau médicament. P.R.

Testé sur plus de 6000 patients, le Relenza est le premier médicament réellement efficace contre le virus de la grippe. Jusqu'à présent il n'y avait aucun remède pour soigner cette maladie; les antibiotiques n'avaient pour effet que de calmer les douleurs et de baisser la fièvre. Le Relenza, lui, stoppe le virus et donc l'infection. Chaque année en France plus de trois millions de personnes en moyenne sont atteintes du virus de la grippe. Mais toutes ne pourront pas se soigner au Relenza: pour l'instant le médicament est réservé aux plus de 12 ans et aux moins de 65 ans.

Par ailleurs certains chercheurs comme A.G., spécialiste des virus, redoutent une utilisation excessive de ce nouveau produit.

– La production mondiale du Relenza sera assurée par le site normand des laboratoires G-W implanté à Évreux. Disponible sur ordonnance dès le mois d'octobre, le médicament devra être prescrit dans les 48 heures après l'apparition des symptômes de la grippe. Il ne sera pas remboursé par la sécurité sociale, il faudra attendre l'hiver 2000/2001.

4 Le virus informatique I Love You se répand à la vitesse grand V en Europe et dans le monde. Il a déjà contaminé des millions d'ordinateurs et il est particulièrement dévastateur. Á Washington, P.R.

– Le directeur d'une télévision de Minnéapolis a regardé sa messagerie électronique lui répéter quatre cent fois 'I love you. Lisez la lettre d'amour attachée'. Il n'a pas craqué, et il a sauvé son ordinateur et son carnet d'adresses. Le dernier virus informatique aurait sa source aux Philippines, et déjà il y a d'autres variantes au message.

Beaucoup de compagnies comme Microsoft, vecteur du virus, ont coupé le courrier. Les diplomates du département d'Etat ont fait pareil. Certains médias ont perdu leurs archives sonores ou en images. La principale messagerie n'est pas touchée. Elle avertit: N'ouvrez pas la lettre d'amour, même signée de votre fiancée.

Chapter 4

Politique matin

4 L'euro a perdu près de 15% de sa valeur par rapport au dollar depuis le début de l'année. Et rien n'indique que cette spirale infernale doive s'arrêter. Depuis sa création l'euro a ainsi perdu 23% par rapport à la monnaie américaine. Laissons aux économistes et aux financiers le soin d'expliquer cette dégringolade. Si tant est qu'il existe une explication rationnelle. Un euro faible n'est pas inquiétant, soit il aide plutôt nos exportations, et ne pénalise finalement que ceux qui ont décidé de passer leurs vacances aux États-Unis. Mais ce qui est en revanche plus inquiétant, c'est le silence assourdissant des politiques. Mis à part les contempteurs de l'Europe, comme Charles Pasqua qui voit là une nouvelle raison de partir en guerre contre le traité de Maastricht, rien – ou presque. Ceux qui ont fait de la construction de l'union européenne leur fond de commerce, tel Valéry Giscard d'Estaing, Jacques Delors ou François Bayrou, sont aujourd'hui aux abonnés absents. Or, la question posée par la baisse de l'euro est bel et bien une question politique posée à l'Europe. La monnaie unique n'a pas suscité, il est vrai, le choc fédérateur que prévoyait Hubert Védrine. Et mise à part l'Allemagne, toujours très attachée symboliquement à sa monnaie, la dépréciation de l'euro se déroule dans la plus grande indifférence.

Hier Lionel Jospin n'a pas caché que cette baisse ne le satisfaisait en rien, même s'il s'agit pour le premier ministre d'un phénomène purement conjoncturel. La force d'une monnaie s'apprécie sur la durée et non sur le court terme, a plaidé de son côté Jacques Chirac hier, lors de sa visite en Savoie. Pour le chef de l'état l'euro repose sur un socle solide, mais il reconnaît aussi que la force de l'euro repose sur une entente politique toujours plus étroite.

Chapter 5

2 Les Bretons ont toutes les raisons d'être découragés. De nouvelles nappes de fioul ont souillé hier les côtes du Morbihan. La pollution a touché les plages de Belle-Ile, de l'Ile d'Houat et de l'Ile de Hoedic. Ces nappes sont équivalentes aux premières arrivées en décembre; ce sont parfois des semaines d'efforts réduites à néant. Une bonne partie du travail de nettoyage est à refaire.

Nouvelle alerte à la pollution dioxyde d'azote à Paris; c'est la deuxième en deux jours. Comme hier, le manque de vent empêche la dispersion des polluants qui stagnent sur la capitale. Les automobilistes sont invités à laisser leur voiture au garage, et à utiliser en priorité les transports en commun. Le stationnement résidentiel est encore gratuit aujourd'hui. Pour les adeptes de la voiture, rappelons que la vitesse est réduite de 20 km à l'heure. Les contrôles anti-pollution ont été renforcés toute la journée.

Chapter 6

2 Après une série de tentatives infructueuses, mission de la dernière chance pour l'émissaire américain. R.R. est retourné à Belgrade ce matin pour s'efforcer d'obtenir un retrait des troupes serbes du Kosovo. Bien que la Russie y soit opposée, les grandes puissances dont les États-Unis, la France et la Grande-Bretagne ont affirmé hier qu'elles étaient prêtes à intervenir militairement en Serbie.

3 Les premiers Casques Bleus doivent arriver dimanche au Timor Oriental. En attendant, un avion australien va parachuter aujourd'hui 15 tonnes de riz aux milliers de réfugiés menacés par la famine. L'Indonésie a donné son feu vert après toute une semaine de négociations.

4 Pour la première fois une juive convertie au catholicisme va être canonisée par l'église catholique. Édith Stein est morte en 1942 dans le camp d'Auschwitz. Jean-Paul II va donc la proclamer sainte aujourd'hui à Rome, mais la communauté juive conteste cette décision. Elle fait valoir qu'Édith Stein est morte parce qu'elle était juive et non chrétienne; et elle craint que l'église catholique ne récupère en quelque sorte le martyre des six millions de Juifs pendant la guerre.

Index

accuracy 113, 148–9
acronyms 43, 56
adjectives 113, 116
adverbs 57, 104–5
Africa 39, 72, 102
aid 102–4
air pollution 85–6
Airbus 54
Airparif 86
Alcatel 54
alcohol 22
Algeria 72, 101
alternative energy 88, 89
anglicisation 72
answers 30
army 100–2
art vocabulary 126–7
balancers 117
ballots 68
Basque separatists 101
belief 98–100
benefit system 36–8, 43
bibliography 138–9
books – vocabulary 114–15
border conflicts 101
Buddhism 98, 99
campaigns 83–4
car pollution 85–6, 87
Catholics 98, 99
Christians 98, 99
cinema 128–9
commands 92
common agricultural policy
    70, 71
commune 67
compound tenses 114
comprehension exercises 29–30
computer vocabulary 54–5
conclusion 111
conditional perfect verbs 26–7,
    44, 113
conditional verbs 44, 74–6, 90
conflict 73, 100–2
conservation 84–5
consonants 147
conversation 140–5
Corsica 101
Council of Europe 71
countryside 35, 125
coursework 136
court cases 20–1

court structure 19–21
crime 22–4
Dassault 54
defence policy 100–1
definitions 61–2
demonstrations 23
départements 67
developed countries 102
developing countries 73, 102–3
dialogue 93–4
disability 42
disasters 73, 103–4
dissidents 101
domestic waste 87–8
drugs 22
EEC 70
elections 69
electronic tagging 24
employment 37–8
energy 88–9
environment 83–9
equality 41–3
equivalents 61–2
essays 93, 111–17, 136–9
ethical issues 55–6
ethnic conflict 101
euro 70
European Court of Justice 19
European parliament 70, 71
European Union 70–2
exclusion 38–9
explanation 92–3
faith 98–100
false friends 77
feast days 99
filming 128–9
fluency 145–6
fossil fuel 88, 89
francophone countries 72–3
French administration 66
French colonies 40, 72
French regions 125–6
Friends of the Earth 83
future passive verbs 44
future perfect verbs 25–6, 27, 44,
    74–6, 90
gap-fill 46–7
geography 125
government 66–8
grammar 148–9
Greenpeace 83

grid-completion 29–30
health 36
history of France 72
history vocabulary 124
hobbies 126–7
homeless 38–9
housing 35–6
human rights 73
idioms 58–9, 77, 114
illustrations 139
immigration 39–41, 72
imperfect subjunctive 45
imperfect verbs 44, 58–9,
    74–6, 90
impersonal verbs 91
indefinite adverbs 104–5
indefinite pronouns 104–5
infinitive 74–6, 92, 113, 114
instructions 29
interaction 146
interests 126–7
international aid 102
internet 54
interpreting 144–5
intonation 148
introduction 111, 144
Islam 98, 99
Jews 98, 99
job creation 39
juvenile crime 22
legal system 19–21
letters 94
linking words 117
listening passages 106–7
literary vocabulary 114–17
literature 110–11
living conditions 34–6
Maastricht Treaty 70
marriage 67, 99
matching 61
mayor 67–8
medical advances 52
MEPs 71
military 100–2
morality 56, 99
multiple choice 61
music vocabulary 127–8
national assembly 66
national parks 84–5
National Service 100
NATO 73, 101

nature 84–5
noise pollution 86
non-verbal exercises 60–2
nouns 114
nuclear power stations 88–9
nuclear tests 100
oil spillages 86, 87
opinion 93, 116
oral examination 140–9
packaging 87, 88
paraphrase 92–3
passive verbs 44, 114
past historic verbs 45, 74–6
past participle 25, 27–8, 44, 114
pensions 36
perfect verbs 44, 58, 74–6, 90
phrases 117
pluperfect verbs 44, 90
police 21–2, 24
politics 66–9
pollution 85–7
power 88–9
preceding direct object 27–8
prepositions 113
present participle 57, 74–6, 114
present subjunctive 74–6
presentation 144
presidency 66
pressure groups 83–4
preventative medicine 36
Prime Minister 66
prison 24
pronouns 47, 58, 104–5, 113, 114
pronunciation 147

Protestants 98, 99
public transport 86
punishment 23–4
Quebec 72
question and answer 29–30
racism 39–41
rail transport 54
recycling 87–8
referendum 68
reflexive verbs 26, 27, 58
régions 67
religion 98–100
rented housing 36
Resistance 100
responses 145
Roman Catholics 98, 99
rural living 34–5
SAMU social 38
satellites 53
science 51–3, 55–6
science heritage 51
Second World War 100
sects 98, 99
sentence completion 46
sentence structure 149
Single European Currency 70–1
smart card 54
social outcast 38–9
social security 36–7, 43
soil pollution 86
space travel 53
speech 94
standard of living 34, 36, 103
starters 117
state 66–7

stimulus passage 143–5
Strategic Arms Reduction Talks 100
subjunctive 113, 114
technology 54–6
telecommunications 54
terrorism 101
theft 22
tick-box questions 61
topic areas 123–9, 136–7, 141–2
towns 34–6
transfer of meaning 77–8
translation 77–8
transport 54, 85–6
true/false questions 60
understanding 30
unemployment 37–9, 40
United Nations 73
Upper House 67
urban living 34–6
verbs 25–8, 44–5, 58–9, 74–6, 90–2, 113, 115
voting 68–9
vowels 147
war 73, 100–2
water pollution 86
wealth distribution 102–4
women 41–2
word count 138
word processing 138
work 37–8
writing tasks 92–4
youth crime 22